From the producer of the documentary
'Antifa: Rise of the Black Flags'

THE

ANTIFA

STORIES FROM
INSIDE THE BLACK BLOC

From the producer of the documentary
'Antifa: Rise of the Black Flags'

THE

ANTIFA

STORIES FROM
INSIDE THE BLACK BLOC

JACK POSOBIEC

Published by

The Calamo Press
Washington D.C.

calamopress.com
Currente-Calamo LLC
2425 17th St NW, Washington D.C. 20009
© Copyright by Jack Posobiec
All rights reserved

ISBN: 978-0-9997059-6-4

This book is dedicated to the victims of communism

TABLE OF CONTENTS

INTRODUCTION
THE TRUMP-WRAY CONVERSATIONS

P resident Trump had had it. The Director of the FBI, Chris Wray, was sitting across from him as the president leaned forward on the Resolute Desk of the Oval Office, arms-crossed. Director Wray shrugged and put his hands in the air like all middle managers do when they don't have a good response to the boss. He then proceeded to get chewed out because President Trump, or "the Boss" as staff called him, hates when people shrug in response to his questions.

"Antifa, they're a non-factor," pleaded Wray, citing the extremism/domestic terrorism database compiled by FBI analysts working in the cubicle farms of the J. Edgar Hoover Building.

"That's a damn lie, Chris, and you know it," shot back the president. "I see this stuff night after night on Twitter. We've got Homeland Security up in Portland getting attacked by gangs of these thugs and you're going to sit there and tell me it's not happening?"

Wray paused, looking out the window, searching for something to say. "Sir, we're working on it" he ended up going with.

"We'll see," responded the President with his characteristic New York sarcasm.

It was the morning after the October 28, 2020 rallies in Arizona, and the President was putting Wray on notice, as he had many times

1

before, according to interviews I had conducted with multiple administration officials with Oval Office access.

According to a senior White House official of the Trump administration, this was the latest in a series of three occasions that the President and Wray had butted heads over the subject of Antifa. The first time was at the height of the Floyd riots around the country, and the second was during the height of the federal courthouse attacks in Portland. The official told me, "It mostly consisted of Wray playing them down as a minor inconvenience with no real training, even though we know about People's Protection Units (YPG), or saying the FBI can't got after a political ideology, or playing them off like a bunch of anarchist LARPers. Wray would say Fox and OAN were exaggerating. He got tag-teamed by the Boss and O'Brien every time, and always promised to come down harder after every scrap but obviously never did."

The fact that the director of the FBI would push back against a direct request from the president, as well as his national security advisor is disconcerting, to say the least. This factor becomes even more troubling in light of the fact that during Wray's tenure in January 2021 he mobilized the full force of the FBI to track down non-violent MAGA protesters nationwide.

I have received dozens of reports of peaceful MAGA-supporting families and individuals who received knocks on their door from their local FBI field office simply for attending a rally for President Trump in Washington, D.C. These supporters participated in first-amendment protected activity exercising their civil rights in the nation's capital, and ended up under the aegis of federal law enforcement. Why would Chris Wray balk at investigating violent anarchists while sending teams of FBI field agents after peaceful MAGA supporters? Why is the FBI crowdsourcing the ID of peaceful MAGA teenagers but disinterested in investigating and prosecuting the perpetrators of the 2020 riots? What it comes down to is the prioritization of resources within the bureau, the same way every department of the federal government is run. Simply, the federal government is biased towards targeting right-wing groups rather than left-wing groups. This derives from a number of factors, but a strong component of it is single-source media consumption by those who live in the Beltway and truly run the government of the United States: the interagency bureaucracy.

Throughout President Trump's first term in office, he had often highlighted the dangers of Antifa's form of domestic terrorism, a phenomenon which first appeared on the 2016 campaign trail at Hillary's DNC in Philadelphia, and eventually culminated in the attack on Trump's inauguration in Washington D.C. in January 2017.

Beginning in Trump's second year in office, he began focusing on Antifa as a potent force for destabilization of the country, and also one that was directly attacking his supporters in the streets and in their homes.

However, what has never-before been reported are the conversations between President Trump and Chris Wray in which the FBI director balked at designating Antifa a domestic terror threat and frequently undermined this initiative of the 45th president. For this chapter, I interviewed current and former officials of the United States government, from the White House, the National Security Council, the Department of Homeland Security, the Federal Bureau of Investigations, and US SOCOM (Special Operations Command).

The picture that emerged as to why the U.S. government was reluctant to take action against the Antifa movement, despite their repeated acts of fatal violence, was the result of confirmation bias and bureaucratic mismanagement. That is a fancy way of saying the feds refused to take Antifa reporting seriously and refused the order of the president of the United States. For anyone who has followed national politics in recent years, this should come as no surprise. The intelligence community lied to President Obama and Congress for years about the extent of their domestic surveillance programs, only to be exposed by the leaks of Edward Snowden. The same intelligence community then spent the first two years lying to the world about President Trump to falsely accuse him as a Russian asset, only to be exposed by independent investigations.

The intelligence community is run by rent-seeking bureaucrats all vying to lie, cheat, and fail their way into making the next rank and one day winning the ultimate prize of attaining entry into the highest caste, the Special Executive Service (SES). There is no real oversight of the intelligence community, as they long ago learned how to selectively leak to their media allies in order to secure ever-increasing budgets from congress and compliance from whoever is elected president. Recently, this dynamic has evolved into former leaders of the intelligence community actually becoming so-called expert contributors themselves on establishment outlets such as CNN and MSNBC. Using these outlets as mouthpieces, the intelligence community is able to exploit their information-warfare expertise to shape domestic narratives among U.S. citizens and drive government action favoring their interests.

During the Trump era, the American left embraced these information narratives peddled by the intelligence community, making strange bedfellows for a political movement that had recently stood against endless overseas wars and domestic surveillance operations.

What the intelligence community understood was that many in Washington D.C. on both sides of the aisle had begun to outsource their personal responsibility to the assessments and reporting of so-called experts. Rather than taking the time to dig in and understand an issue, a report is placed on a congressman's desk, or a briefing is conducted, generally with staff, and their decisions are essentially made for them. Since nearly the entire D.C. bureaucracy, which includes the intelligence community, is made up of liberal Democrats, this becomes an issue. Much of this comes from firsthand knowledge from my years serving in the intelligence community in Washington DC, as well as interviews I conducted with current and former members for this book.

One active member of U.S. SOCOM told me "the Beltway intel community is one big circle [expletive]. They read the *Washington Post* every morning, watch CNN all day, and consider themselves informed. They never consider the fact that they might be getting information from bad sources." He continued, "Look at 2020. You had looters and Antifa tearing up American cities every night of the summer, biggest riots since LA, but FBI barely even mentioned them. All these kids come in with criminal justice or poli sci degrees and think that counts as real-world experience, but they wouldn't even know how to clear a corner."

I asked what sorts of reports were coming in during 2020. He said, "Well all the analysts were working from home because of COVID so they really only had access to unclassified. So they're sitting home using Google and CNN to write OSINT (open source intelligence) and everyone wants to write about the same Q Anon or white supremacist nut so we end up with 15 reports about one event and the SES thinks it's some kind of crisis. Then they brief the director about it, and then he goes to congress and tells them it's the biggest threat in the country."

The intelligence community has fallen for the trap of circular reporting in the past, when the CIA falsely reported to the Bush Administration that Iraq had active weapons of mass destruction program. This led to a chain reaction of ruining the credibility of the institution, as well as thousands upon thousands of avoidable deaths. Following this disaster, the intelligence community was supposed to put in safeguards to protect it from every happening again. No such safeguards were ever put in place, and instead the intelligence community grew at an even faster pace, so that now multiple agencies may be producing overlapping reports and analysis based on the same thinly-sourced raw intelligence. It is this same circular reporting that intelligence leaders exploit to shape narratives by selectively leaking to media, and then using the media reports as further confirmation of their preferred conclusions. This is the exact same dynamic that led to the Iraq War.

It is due to this same dynamic that President Trump's request for security on January 6th, 2021 was denied. As reported by both Acting Secretary of Defense Chris Miller in *Vanity Fair* and White House Chief of Staff Mark Meadows in an interview, President Trump ordered 10,000 troops from the National Guard to be activated to defend Washington D.C. on the date in question when he held a rally on the Ellipse outside the White House. Instead of deploying the soldiers, the Pentagon balked, in the same way that Wray balked at the president's order to deploy assets against Antifa as domestic terrorists. The Pentagon reportedly was worried about the "optics" of deploying the National Guard on January 6th, as they had been criticized by establishment media and Democrats for deploying the National Guard during the Floyd riots over the summer of 2020 in Washington D.C. The fact that the leadership of the United States military is terrified of criticism from media and politicians not in the chain of command should be a wakeup call to the nation about the current state of the brass within the Pentagon following eight years of liberal Democrat governance and a corporate management-style embrace of woke ideology over the basic tenets of war-fighting and national security.

In fact, this dynamic has become such a threat to national security that officials in the all-powerful bureaucracy known as the "interagency" will refuse to act on their intelligence if it conflicts with the prevailing view. I will show later in the book how it was a Department of Homeland Security memo that reported they had obtained "overwhelming evidence" of "Violent Antifa Anarchist Inspired" involvement in the Floyd riots in Portland, specifically the nightly attacks on the courthouse. Yet at the same time, the FBI director was denying it to President Trump.

From the July 25th DHS memo: "We have overwhelming intelligence regarding the ideologies driving individuals towards violence and why the violence has continued. A core set of threat actors are organized, show up night after night, share common TTPs and drawing on like-minded individuals to their cause."

As the Floyd riots began, the New Jersey Department of Homeland Security and Preparedness produced the following assessment of Antifa extremists. On June 1st, 2020 they published:

"The nationwide protests resulting from the death of George Floyd have given Antifa-affiliated anarchist extremists the opportunity to infiltrate protests in order to further their violent ideology."

"On May 31, President Donald Trump announced that the US government would designate Antifa as a terrorist organization, although there currently is no domestic terrorism statute that could label it as such. Attorney General William Barr stated violent incidents in Minneapolis were driven by groups using "Antifa-like tactics." Barr vowed that prosecutors across the country would use federal riot statutes to charge protesters who cross state lines to participate in violent rioting. Federal law defines terrorism as a criminal attack intended to intimidate and coerce civilians in order to influence government policy or otherwise affect government conduct."

"According to open source media, an initial New York Police Department (NYPD) analysis indicated that of those arrested in the New York City protests, one in seven people were from outside areas, including from the states of Massachusetts, Connecticut, Pennsylvania, New Jersey, Iowa, Nevada, Maryland, Virginia, Texas, and Minnesota. The NYPD stated "agitators" had planned violent interactions and vandalism ahead of the weekend rallies demanding justice over Floyd's death, which occurred in Minnesota on May 25."

Yet, despite state and federal agencies collecting the intelligence, in the end, President Trump's efforts on Antifa anarchists were delayed and blocked by the same interagency bureaucrats that stymied much of his agenda during his first term in office. This dynamic was exacerbated by the biased leadership of the interagency and their tunnel vision-like worldview derived from CNN and the *Washington Post* rather than following the evidence where it lies. To the interagency bureaucrat that runs our government, stepping out of line beyond the realm of what is the accepted and preferred narrative is like trying to breathe without air. Despite the interests of the victims of Antifa violence, the interagency cares little for them, as long as it does nothing to challenge their grasp on power. And, because the interagency has significant overlap with academia who, frankly, are pro-Antifa, this creates and echo chamber which permeates our government.

There is a reason you rarely see Antifa challenge the actual power structure in the United States.

Those in power use Antifa as their shock troops to go after anyone who challenges them.

ONE

THE RISE

T he riots began at the end of May, and by the end of August nearly every state in the country had been hit. The pandemic lockdowns had everyone on edge, and then a viral video of a suspect dying in police custody was the spark that lit the fuse. It was the summer of 2020. Riots raged in Minneapolis, from there, spreading to the West Coast, and flaring to the East. Cities like Portland and Seattle saw protests, then mobs of violent activists appear overnight. In Chicago, New York, St. Louis and Philadelphia, looters took to the streets, smashing storefronts and stealing their pick of what was inside. Cable networks and smartphone screens alike filled with scenes of violence and carnage across American streets. Statues of America's founders and religious figures were toppled. Lafayette Park outside the White House filled with occupiers who set fire to a historic church.

Amidst the mayhem, a singular force emerged; black-clad militants joined in the fray from city to city, urging protesters to go further, to cross the line. In some cases, armed militia wearing patches and flying flags of red and black appeared, chanting that they now controlled the streets. The coronavirus pandemic had forced mask-wearing in many American cities, and so the militants easily weaved in and out of the larger crowds that summer. Pallets of bricks and construction materials sitting out on city streets became caches of weapons. By the end of the summer, over 30 people had been killed in the riots. Nearly 700 police officers had been injured nationwide. Damages were estimated in the billions across the country, the highest in American history.

Most people who participated in the summer riots of 2020 were supporting the Black Lives Matter (BLM) movement, who for the most part peacefully exercised their First Amendment right. But another force attempted to infiltrate BLM, a force dedicated to overturning the establishment through a violent insurrectionist revolution.

This was the Antifa.

An internal memo released from the Department of Homeland Security dated July 25, 2020 explained the situation as it related to the city of Portland, which weathered some of the most violent riots:

"Starting now for Portland, replace the V.O. definition accompanying our FIRS (field intel reports) and OSIRS (open source intel reports) to VIOLENT ANTIFA ANARCHISTS INSPIRED (VAAI). Why? Myself and I&A leaders have been reviewing the Portland, FIRS, OSIRS, baseball cards of the arrested and FINTEL as well as the Ops info. The individuals are violently attacking the federal facilities based on these ideologies.

We can't say any longer that this violent situation is opportunistic. Additionally, we have overwhelming intelligence regarding the ideologies driving individuals towards violence and why the violence has continued. A core set of threat actors are organized, show up night after night, share common TTPs, and draw on likeminded individuals to their cause."

The memo went on to state:

"Here is the VAAI definition which will be applied from now forward: Threat actors who are motivated by Anarchist or ANTIFA (or a combination of both) ideologies to carry out acts of violence against state, local, and Federal authorities and infrastructure they believe represent political and social ideas they reject."

- Acting Undersecretary for Intelligence,
Department of Homeland Security

America had seen this movement's violence the previous summer. On August 4, 2019, 24-year-old Connor Betts, dressed in black and clad in body armor, walked into Ned Peppers Grill in Dayton, Ohio, and opened fire with a semi-automatic .223 caliber long gun. Before police killed him, he had murdered nine people, including his own sister, and injured 27 others.

As in many such cases, Betts had been troubled for years. A bully in high school, he spent his aimless twenties living with his parents and devoted to what *Vice* termed the "extreme metal music scene." He performed in purportedly antiracist metal bands such as the Menstrual Munchies and Putrid Liquid. A ex-girlfriend reported he'd confided to her his bipolar disorder and he suffered from obsessive-compulsive disorder.

In the wake of his horrific attack, the mainstream media struck familiar notes: mournful reflection – and anger. Pundits pontificated on the sickness in America's soul, editorialists blasted the NRA and the (overwhelmingly Republican) politicians who support it. But, what for so many made the Dayton tragedy especially heart-rending was that it closely followed two other mass shootings in the summer of 2019; one in Gilroy, California and one in El Paso, Texas, that were also perpetrated by young, single white men.

Social media sleuths began tracking the shooter as soon as he was identified, and quickly found numerous references to his extreme leftwing politics. He viewed conservatives, especially Trump supporters, as enemies, and he supported a movement known as "Antifa."

Indeed, one of Betts' last acts before launching into his killing spree was to support a Twitter post calling for my own death.

A *New York Post* headline blared just two days later: *DAYTON SHOOTER CONNOR BETTS MAY BE ANTIFA'S FIRST MASS KILLER.* It noted that, "Betts had long expressed support for Antifa accounts, causes and individuals. That would be the loose network of militant leftist activists who physically attack anyone to the right of Mao in the name of 'antifascism.' In particular, Betts promoted extreme hatred of American border enforcement."

In the aftermath of the Dayton tragedy, the connection was impossible to miss. "Kill every fascist," the shooter proclaimed on Twitter, echoing Antifa militants everywhere. Over time, his Tweets dramatically increased in violence: "Nazis deserve death and nothing else," he tweeted in October 2018. Betts labeled those with whom he disagreed as "Nazis" online.

The Post continued: "By December, he reached out on Twitter to the Socialist Rifle Association, an Antifa gun group, to comment about bump stocks, and the SRA responded to him (A bump stock is an attachment for semiautomatic rifles that allows them to fire much faster.) In the months leading to his rampage, Betts expressed a longing for climactic confrontation. In response to an essay by *Intercept* writer Mehdi Hassan titled, 'Yes, Let's Defeat or Impeach Trump—but What If He Doesn't Leave the White House?' Betts wrote: 'Arm, train, prepare.' By June he tweeted: "I want socialism, and I'll not wait for the idiots to finally come round understanding." Moreover, in the days leading up to the shooting, he made posts that demonized Senators Ted Cruz and Bill Cassidy for their resolutions against Antifa extremism.

Betts's Twitter account also contained statements directly supporting Antifa's call for "revolution" against the rich, posting rhetoric in favor of beheading corporate leaders. Videos showed Betts among the Antifa counter-protestors at a failed KKK rally in Dayton two months before the shooting.

Betts was a member of the Antifa movement.

Betts's shooting rampage is the most chilling early evidence of Antifa's penchant for ruthless brutality. Violence perpetrated by leftist anti-government extremists had been sharply mounting in frequency and severity for years, and especially since the election of President Donald Trump.

Starting with the attack on Trump's inauguration, antiracist violence has become omnipresent in the Trump era. Though only a handful of its actions drew more than passing notice from the largely sympathetic press – those in Portland, Berkeley and Charlottesville – a partial list of the cities where Antifa thugs have assaulted peaceful marchers and otherwise inflicted mayhem include Kansas City, Saint

Paul, Minneapolis, New Orleans, Washington, Berkeley, Laguna Beach, Sacramento, Tucson, Portland, Milwaukee, Richmond, Atlanta, Asheville, Lexington, Phoenix, Chicago, Boston, New York, Philadelphia, Seattle, Vancouver (Washington), Tacoma and Cambridge, Massachusetts. Many "actions" on college campuses are excluded from this count.

Why has establishment media remained indifferent? The answer lies in the personal politics of many reporters, who consider themselves to be champions of ideals espoused by Antifa's militants. In short, they see themselves as fellow travelers for the Antifa movement, rather than critical observers or journalists.

Yet Antifa remains hard to define by traditional terminology. It is not a gang, a political party, or even a national collective. Rather than a readily identifiable organization with a distinct purpose, vision, and leadership, it is a loose confederation of far-left, semi-autonomous cells and individuals in an open source movement. In a Fifth Generation Warfare environment, these entities unite for specific actions, and disband, often connecting only over social media. This phenomenon not only spans the United States, but also extends to like-minded groups abroad. Antifa originated in Europe, and is united by vaguely articulated but passionately held core beliefs – a commitment to "social justice" in its fluid varieties and an equally intense hatred of capitalism and its practitioners. Its activity ebbs and flows, but its goals remain the same.

Joe Biden infamously claimed that "Antifa is just an idea." Is that true? Antifascism is an ideology espoused by numerous groups, cells, and individuals, harnessing unique entities into a united movement. Throughout this book, I refer to Antifa as a movement, and I will demonstrate that this term is appropriate for the observed phenomenon. So - what are the goals of the Antifa movement?

The ultimate goal is revolutionary change. Antifa is an anti-government insurrectionist movement, guided by a belief in anarcho-communism, which combines critical ideas of anarchism and communism. Antifa's emblem melds the black flag of anarchism paired with the red flag of communism. While various Antifa cells may ascribe more closely to one ideology over the other, they share a common belief in the destruction of the Western system of democracy, freedom of speech, freedom of press, free market competition, freedom of religion, and rule of law. The Antifa movement is outside the realm of the traditional mainstream of politics, and both Democrats and Republicans have found themselves in their crosshairs; however, since 2016, its target has become President Donald Trump and his supporters. Key to understanding Antifa is their lack of discrimination based on establishment party affiliation.

In the anarcho-communist doctrine, the larger systems and institutions of the United States, Canada, and Europe constitute "fascism" and must be overthrown. Indeed, Antifa predates MAGA by nearly 80 years, a fact unacknowledged by the mainstream media.

Thanks to a sympathetic press, the Left has largely succeeded in redefining the terms "white nationalist," "far-right," and "extremist," to reflect their use in the Antifa and far-Leftist lexicon. Once, such extreme terms were reserved for swastika-carrying Neo-Nazis and white-hooded Klansmen, but today they include mainstream conservatives, all Trump voters, members of law enforcement and the military, traditional Christians, and anyone who disagrees with the progressive Left.

Establishment media outlets, many corporate leaders and extreme-left Think Tanks employ similar tactics to use such labels to falsely smear their political opponents, rather than exchange in honest debate over policy or issues. Indeed, the ruling class frequently uses the antifascist movement to target their populist opponents.

Despite its symbiotic relationship with the media, Antifa never hesitates to intimidate journalists. Prior to one action in Washington, D.C., its local political arm, AllOutDC, distributed a handout warning reporters to "avoid publishing any potentially incriminating photographs or video footage…" and to "ensure that you have explicit consent before capturing auto recordings or directly quoting interviewees… Members of the media who refuse to comply with these reasonable guidelines will be removed." Shortly after this warning, *Washington Examiner* reporter Julio Rosas, doing his job in a public space, was assaulted for defying the order.

The Antifa movement's clandestine operation has been critical to its growth. Like all fanatical organizations, it is a beacon for angry, lost souls. It is understandable that many Millennials would be attracted to this movement. Millennials experienced 9/11 and the subsequent war in Iraq during their formative years, and graduated from college as America was in the throws of the Great Recession. Wealth and family formation for Millennials has stagnated, been delayed, or obliterated for many. Antifa offers an outlet for rage against the system.

Betts' Dayton attack took place just two weeks after a firebombing incident in Tacoma, Washington. Antifa member Willem van Spronsen, identified as a 69-year old "carpenter and musician," attempted to firebomb an ICE immigrant detention center. He arrived at the facility with a rifle and incendiary devices at 4 a.m. on Saturday, July 13, 2019, following an Antifa protest there the previous day. He attempted to burn buildings, vehicles, and ignite a propane tank when he was shot by Tacoma police.

Reportedly, Spronsen had participated in a previous Antifa assault on the same center months earlier. When he was arrested, he was carrying a blackjack and a knife; and yet, the judge hearing the case released him without so much as a day of jail time.

Democrat mayors have long given Antifa virtually free rein. In places like Tacoma, Seattle, Portland, Charlottesville, and, later, Minneapolis, the behavior of local authorities (including orders to police to "stand down") clearly enabled greater violence. Quite simply, Antifa's militants were seen not as violent insurrectionists, but as deeply committed Leftist warriors who had the guts to stand up to America's true enemies -- Donald Trump and his evil white nationalist supporters. This of course, is the preferred narrative pushed by media elites and politicians.

The Trump years were a godsend for Antifa, promoting favorable press coverage, and engendering a swell of support, especially on college campuses. By early 2020, the Twitter account of NYC Antifa alone had expanded by more than ten-fold from 2017. Its Twitter account had more than 41,000 followers, while that of the Antifa-related Democrat Socialists of America had more than 210,000.

The Press Freedom Tracker, which publicizes attacks on reporters, details on its website many, many incidents of Antifa assaulting journalists between 2017 and 2019. In Charlottesville, Antifa activists punched *The Hill* correspondent Taylor Lorenz in the head; in Berkeley, they beat reporter Dave Minsky with a pipe; in Richmond, they trounced a CBS cameraman; in Chicago, they punched *Sun-Times* writer Sam Charles. And these were journalists presumably sympathetic to Antifa – at least at the beginning.

Even more menacing is their attitude toward top targets. The home security system of Fox star Tucker Carlson picked up audio of activists discussing a pipe bomb and saying, "We know where you sleep at night." They proceeded to smash his door and threaten his family as his wife hid in the pantry. The Antifa group, Smash Racism DC, had earlier posted on their Twitter account, "We remind you that you are not safe."

After Trump's inauguration, and while reporting for Rebel Media, I was attacked by an Antifa militant myself. It was in April 2017, and I was covering a rally of the D.C. Anti-Fascist Coalition at George Washington University. I showed up with a camera and a case of Pepsi to distribute to potential interviewees. What did they want? Were they willing to disavow violence? Alas, I didn't get very far before a militant sped up on his bike and started screaming at me. When I responded, he punched me in the head. Campus police rushed over, and he tried to flee, but when he was stopped, my attacker – identified as Sydney Ramsey-LaRee – and his friends claimed the violence was in response to "ethnic slurs" I'd directed at him. Unfortunately for him, I had taped the altercation, and he was cuffed and arrested. He was jailed after I testified at his trial.

One of the biggest differences between the new Right and the old Right? We don't just complain about things. We take action.

I've always been drawn to media. In high school, I hosted the morning TV news. In college, I studied media production and performance, as well as political science and international relations, while interning with talk radio and with campaigns. After college, I moved to China for two years to work for US businesses and learned fluent Mandarin (more on that in my next book). In China, I learned about Communism. Upon my return home, I joined the U.S. Navy to work in intelligence. That work sent me to the Guantanamo Bay Naval Base in Cuba, where I served in detainee operations as an interrogator-analyst. During my deployment, the detention center held high-level members of Al Qaeda and the Taliban – this was pre-

Bergdahl. Through my training and this HUMINT (human intelligence) experience, I became more familiar with the ways of thinking and patterns of behavior common to radical movements. Years later, when I began to seriously investigate Antifa, the parallels in decision-making, rationalizing, cognitive dissonance, and thrill-seeking were interesting to note. The distinct psychological causes are there.

Antifa preaches international revolution. Like their comrades elsewhere, the Americans in its ranks have no regard for national sovereignty. Their loyalty is to the religions of anti-capitalism, "social justice," and, now, fiercely "woke" identity victimology. *Crimethinc*, one of Antifa's most popular websites, promotes violence worldwide and has posted videos celebrating the burning of Chilean churches.

I've reported both online and on the One America News Network (OANN) on the connections between Antifa and the Kurdistan Worker's Party (PKK-YPG), designated a terrorist group by the U.S. government in the 1970s, and responsible for hundreds of bombings, and between 30,000 and 40,000 deaths. PKK has drawn as many as five hundred Antifa fighters to Syria from Western nations, including America. One was arrested after coming home and participating in CHAZ, and later planning to attack the Florida capital on inauguration day 2021.

For years I infiltrated Antifa meetings. Through this, I came to understand Antifa's structure, organization and strategic intent. Like the Taliban, Antifa operates through localized cells, and both employ an organizing principle intelligence professionals referred to as TTP – Tactics, Techniques and Procedures – which allows for procedures in one place to be followed in another with a minimum of direct coordination. They are comprised of innumerable individual groups, and operate under a variety of names. Most comparatively small, yet Antifa's reach is vast, extending to cities and towns across the country.

When I began sounding the alarm about what I'd discovered, my cover, of course, was blown. Ever since, as one of a handful who have worked tirelessly to expose Antifa, I've been the target of vicious attacks from Antifa supporters on the streets and in the media – including more than a few who have revealed themselves on social media to have been devoted "friends" of the murderer I mentioned, Connor Betts. Indeed, just four hours before the shooting, Betts himself retweeted a not-so-subtle threat aimed my way. I was responding to the El Paso shooting and wrote "Raise your hand if you agree it's time to put parties aside and rebuild America's mental health system," in what I took to be a fairly innocuous message. In response Betts' Antifa comrade exploded: "Raise your hand if you agree it's time to crush these vile little worms into dust once and for all."

Antifa's ultimate goal is the destabilizing of our nation and the undermining of our democracy, leading to a revolution on an updated version of the Maoist model that I learned about while living in China. The violence they advocate and nurture is a means to that end, intended to sow chaos and raise suspicion of traditional institutions of order.

Perhaps most chilling, up close, is its adherents' absolute confidence in the righteousness of their cause and their certainty about its eventual triumph. Like the Taliban – and those behind The Terror in revolutionary France, or the Bolsheviks in Russia – it is a belief system that allows not the slightest reflection or hesitation. The most extreme measures and heinous acts are acceptable when done in its behalf.

In fact, they are so secure in their beliefs (and so confident of not being fully exposed in today's media and civic environment) that they rarely bother to hide them. A year before the summer 2020 riots, a New York Antifa member identifying herself as Maura blithely explained to a CNN reporter why she and her comrades felt no hesitation to wreak havoc on private property – and those with whom they disagree. "Violence against windows," she scoffed, "there's no such thing as violence against windows. Windows don't have – they're not persons. And even when they are persons, the people we fight back against, they are evil. They are the living embodiment, they are the second coming of Hitler."

Antifa's leading academic apologist Mark Bray, assistant philosophy professor and author of *Antifa: The Anti-Fascist Handbook*, the widely-cited true-believing authority on Antifa's beliefs and tactics, once noted that Antifa adherents "have no allegiance to liberal democracy… They're anarchists and communists who are way outside the traditional conservative-liberal spectrum."

That view is evident in Antifa's online TTP guide, Black Bloc Tactics Communique, which mocks pacifism and sets out Antifa's immediate goals:

1. Increased organization of street fighting force.

2. Regular physical training in between actions.

3. Facilitation of pre-emptive strikes.

4. Preparation for eventuality of intensified state oppression and the shifting of the movement of social protest into that of direct social revolution.

In short, what we've seen to date is only a prelude.

Former Australian Antifa leader Shayne Hunter once said of his former comrades, "The radical left of Antifa presents itself as being about compassion and empathy; it's a Trojan horse."

Antifa, he added, "is more dangerous than ISIS."

death – of van Spronsen in Tacoma. What did he think, he asked Betts, was van Spronsen a "villain or martyr?"

Betts didn't hesitate: "Martyr."

TWO

THE TRUE BELIEVERS

Who, exactly, are the individuals behind the black masks, Antifa's foot soldiers, those now seen in countless videos assaulting cops, tearing down statues, burning local businesses, assaulting ordinary citizens? What is it that draws them to this insurrectionist movement so ready – *eager* – to turn the nation's streets into war zones? What is it in their background, or psychology, that drives them to anti-social behavior and extremism?

Vital as such questions are, they almost never get asked – certainly not by the mainstream press. They are as uninterested in the Antifa movement's nature as they are in the enormity of the threat it poses.

Antifa is a left-wing, leaderless "horizontal" movement found across America and Europe. Its followers adhere to a supposed ideology of "anti-fascism," one that is based on a strange mix of seemingly incompatible philosophies of anarchism, communism, and far-left extremism.

The stated goal of "antifascism" is to oppose the rise of fascism through any means necessary, an essentially rhetorical sleight of hand that enables and justifies what they call "grassroots direct action" – violence against persons and institutions deemed fascist. Who does the defining? They do. In this way, antifascists parallel the anarchist opposition to the state. If the state is fascism, and the state is thought of as the embodiment of violence through its use of police, military, and border enforcement, then violence against institutions and individuals that enable the state is justified because these organs of the state are the root cause of fascism – or so they argue.

As has become clear to all but the willfully blind – including the Democrat Party and almost the entirety of the mainstream media – the goal of Antifa is nothing less than the wholesale destabilization and destruction of the state itself. All organs of the state are therefore targeted by antifascists in their direct actions, from commercial and financial institutions, to border and border enforcement agencies, transportation infrastructure, organized religion, and the justice system – especially the police, but also the army, courts and prisons.

It has also become clear that a specific type of individual is drawn to Antifa and its methods.

Although there are obviously exceptions – 69-year-old Willem van Spronsen being one – both in America and abroad, Antifa members tend to be young. Too, most fit the same basic profile: unmarried and unemployed. Its ranks increasingly number women, but it still remains predominantly male. While there have been no in-depth studies in this country, the German news magazine, *Bild*, looked specifically at those identifying as Antifa supporters who admitted to acts of violence. Of the 873 antifascists surveyed, 72% were aged 18 to 29; 84% were male; 92% lived with their parents. Of those surveyed, 34% were unemployed and 90% were unmarried.

The typical age of offenders was 21 to 24, and four of 10 had prior criminal records. Among the most common offenses admitted to were fire-starting and assaults of police officers. Arson is one of the most common forms of modern Antifa violence.

As much as anything, attachment to Antifa implies a certain lifestyle. Comrades often take on new names or monikers used within the movement. Like other extremist groups, they use encrypted apps and private groups or channels to avoid tracking and to plan direct action. It is partly fun and games, a way to play both James Bond and Che Guevara. But at deeper levels it feeds the potential for extreme violence. So too, Antifa's clandestine meetings and furtive training sessions establish a lifestyle and behavior and fill a psychological desire to be working toward something greater than oneself.

Though he died nearly 40 years ago, no one wrote more persuasively about mass movements than the Longshoreman Philosopher Eric Hoffer. During the Roaring 20s, Hoffer lived a life of desperation on LA's skid row, and during the distress of the Great Depression he worked as a fruit picker, miner and longshoreman. Along the way, he learned an invaluable lesson: that even the most demeaning and low-paying job was more satisfying than unemployment – what was vital was leading a "purposeful" life. It is the search for purpose, the sense that one's life has hit a dead-end, that moves so many to give themselves over to larger movements that profess great, even historic ends. And always, such movements need – and are dedicated to fighting – a great, all-consuming enemy.

"Hatred is the most accessible and comprehensive of all the unifying agents," Hoffer wrote in his classic *The True Believer*. "Mass movements can rise and spread without belief in a god, but never without a belief in a devil." He also poignantly noted that while the fascists and antifascists in 1930s Germany were ostensibly enemies with views that could not be further removed from one another, they occasionally drew upon one another's ranks and competed for the same pool of angry, marginalized, frustrated people – usually youth. The irony of the "true believer" is that the beliefs themselves are not what is important, what is important is the escape from the burden of the autonomous self. Hoffer rightly cited the "new poor" as the group most likely for converts due to their remembrance of recently-lost wealth, and when it comes to Antifa, it is usually the children of privileged, wealthy, upper-middle class families and the "chronically bored" that join the ranks of the movement. True working-class people, according to Hoffer, rarely join mass protest movements or subcultures because they have entry to meaningful labor as a rite of passage from adolescence into adulthood. Hoffer understood meaningful work as not only essential for livelihood, but also to fully develop as an individual, and that lack of meaningful work would relegate an individual to a perpetual state of adolescence. It is this psychological need that allows mass movements to grow, even in times of relative wealth and stability, for in times of abundance more and more individuals enter into meaningful work. When it comes to Antifa, Hoffer was exactly right – the vast majority of them have no working-class background or real jobs. Hoffer's diagnosis of the perpetual adolescence and search for rite of passage is key to understanding the motivations of those attracted by the antifascist movement.

For all their professed concern for minorities and dedication to the underprivileged, Antifa members are overwhelmingly white and are themselves far more likely to have come from the middle or upper class than from genuine working-class origins. Why? Because they also tend to carry a fair amount of bitterness, either toward those in their past (very often their families) or about their own aimlessness and poor life prospects.

If nothing else, Antifa activism holds the illusion of being an antidote to that frustration. It promises meaningful action in today's greatest combat theater, the fight for social justice; and without the risk of having to be an actual soldier.

For such young men, the violence is not a bug; it's a feature. When a comrade posts a video on an Antifa site like *ItsGoingDown* of an assault on a "fascist," there follows an explosion of favorable comments, many of them tinged with envy.

As noted, the most widely-read book-length promotion of Antifa is *Antifa: The Anti-Fascist Handbook* by Dartmouth's hard-left Mark Bray, who also – no surprise – doubles as the media's go-to source on all things Antifa-related. But rather than a source manual on Antifa beliefs or procedures, it is primarily a series of celebratory accounts of violent Antifa actions, with the good guys beating the heck out of their adversaries in various locales. The stories differ in detail, but all make the same point: Those doing the bludgeoning are heroic. The second point is implicit: no matter how peaceable their behavior, their victims deserved what they got.

THREE

THE MANIFESTO

"to my comrades: i regret that i will miss the rest of the revolution."

Soon after Willem van Spronsen was shot dead by Tacoma police while trying to firebomb an ICE detention center, Seattle TV station KIRO published on its website a three-page "manifesto" he left behind. Openly declaring, "I am Antifa," in attempting to justify the extreme violence its author was about to commit, it offers insight into the "thinking" of Antifa's most dangerous militants. It is reproduced here in its entirety, faulty punctuation included. It should convey something of what and who Antifa represents:

> "there's wrong and there's right. it's time to take action against the forces of evil. evil says one life is worth less than another. evil says the flow of commerce is our purpose here. evil says concentration camps for folks deemed lesser are necessary. the handmaid of evil says the concentra-

tion camps should be more humane. beware the centrist. i have a father's broken heart i have a broken down body and i have an unshakable abhorrence of injustice. that is what brings me here. this is my clear opportunity to try to make a difference, i'd be an ingrate to be waiting for a more obvious invitation. i follow three teachers: don pritts, my spiritual guide, 'love without action is just a word.' john brown, my moral guide, 'what is needed is action!' emma goldman, my political guide, 'if i can't dance, i don't want to be in your revolution.' i'm a head in the clouds dreamer, i believe in love and redemption. i believe we're going to win i'm joyfully revolutionary. (we all should have been reading emma goldman in school instead of the jingo drivel we were fed. but i digress.) (we should all be looking at the photos of the YJP heroes should we falter and think our dreams are impossible, but i double digress. fight me.) in these days of fascist hooligans preying on vulnerable people on our streets, in the name of the state or supported and defended by the state, in these days of highly profit- able detention/concentration camps and a battle over the semantics, in these days of hopelessness, empty pursuit and endless yearning, we are living in visible fascism ascendant. (i say visible, because those paying attention watched it survive and thrive under the protection of the state for decades [see howard zinn, 'a people's history of the united states.') now it unabashedly follows its agenda with open and full cooperation from the government. from governments around the world. fascism serves the needs of the state serves the needs of business and at your expense. who benefits? jeff bezos, warren buffet, elon musk, tim cook, bill gates, betsy de vos, george soros, and need i go on? let me say it again: rich guys, (who think you're not really all that good,) really dig government, (every government everywhere, including "communist" governments,) because they make rules that make rich guys richer. simple. don't overthink it. (are you patriots in the back paying attention?) when i was a boy, in post war holland, later france, my head was filled with stories of the rise of fascism in the 30's. i promised myself that i would not be one of those who stands by as neighbors are torn from their homes and imprisoned for somehow being perceived as lesser. you don't have to burn the motherfucker down, but are you just going to stand by? this is the test of our fundamental belief in real freedom and our responsibility to each other. this is a call to patriots, too, to stand against this travesty against everything that you hold sacred. i know you. i know that in your hearts, you see the dishonor in these camps. it's time for you, too, to stand up to the money pulling the strings of every goddamn puppet pretending to represent us. i'm a man who loves you all and this spinning ball so much that i'm going to fulfill my childhood promise to myself to be noble. here it is, in these corporate for profit concentration camps. here it is, in brown and non conforming folks afraid to show their faces for fear of the police/migra/proud boys/the boss/beckies... here it is, a planet almost used up by the market's greed. i'm a black and white thinker. detention camps are an abomination. i'm not standing by. i really shouldn't have to say any more than this. i set aside my broken heart and i heal the only way i know how - by being useful. i efficiently compartmentalize my pain... and i joyfully go about this work. (to those burdened with the wreckage from my actions, i hope that you will make the best use of that burden.) to my comrades: i regret that i will miss the rest of the revolution. thank you for the honor of having me in your midst. giving me space to be useful, to feel that i was fulfilling my ideals, has been the spiritual pinnacle of my life. doing what i can to help defend my precious and wondrous people is an experience too rich to describe. my trans comrades have transformed me, solidifying my conviction that we will be guided to a dreamed of future by those most marginalized among us today. i have dreamed it so clearly that i have no regret for not seeing how it turns out. thank you for bringing me so far along. i am antifa, i stand with comrades around the world who act from the love of life in every permutation. comrades who understand that freedom means real freedom for all and a life worth living. keep the faith! all power to the people! bella ciao don't let your silly government agencies spend money 'investigating' this one. i was radicalized in civics class at 13 when we were taught about the electoral college. it was at that point that i decided that the status quo might be a house of cards. further reading confirmed in the positive. i highly recommend reading! i am not affiliated with any organization, i have disaffiliated from any organizations who disagree with my choice of tactics. the semi automatic weapon i used was a cheap, home built unregistered 'ghost' ar15, had six magazines. i strongly encourage comrades and incoming comrades to arm themselves. we are now responsible for defending people from the predatory state. ignore the laws of arming yourself if you have the luxury, i did."

FOUR

WHITEWASHING ANTIFA

B efore August 2017, most Americans had never heard of Antifa. Then came Charlottesville.

First, a bit of essential background.

In Charlottesville, home to the University of Virginia, tensions had been building for weeks around the issue of the removal of a Robert E. Lee statue. A rally was planned to defend the statue on Aug. 12, 2017. The organizers of the rally were white supremacists. Given the passions surrounding the issue, there should have been ample time for police and local authorities to prepare for the possibility of violence. Protesters and Antifa quickly arrived to condemn the rally. Yet by every account, as violence broke out between white supremacists and opposing anarchists, the police stood by as it escalated into a deadly brawl.

In the tidal wave of media coverage that followed, millions took – and were encouraged to take – the wrong message. Based on the reporting in the mainstream press, and echoed by progressives ever since, the lesson of Charlottesville was simple: Trump and his supporters = racists and white supremacists, Antifa = warriors against racism and injustice.

Charlottesville was an unmitigated disaster, resulting in the tragic deaths of three people – including the murder of demonstrator Heather Heyer, horrifically mowed down by a neo-Nazi. The left continued to bring up this event almost daily for years throughout the Trump presidency, and Joe Biden made it central to his election campaign in 2020. Through endlessly repeated lies and misrepresentations, in the minds of millions, Donald Trump remains branded as a racist, while Antifa was all but absolved of its role in the violence.

The list of news organizations that either blamed the president directly or tacitly for the tragedy is a roll call of the American mainstream media: ABC, CBS, NBC, CNN, MSNBC, NPR, *The New York Times*, *The Los Angeles Times* and *The Washington Post*. Hollywood also got in its heavy-handed shots, most notably in the Spike Lee film *BlacKKKlansman*.

In short, Charlottesville was among the first of the great false narratives of Trump's aptly named "fake news" era. By "whitewashing" the role played by Antifa's thugs in the violence – and also keeping the klieg lights far from the local Democrat officials who conspicuously failed in their sworn duty to uphold order – the national media more dramatically than ever before exposed itself as terminally corrupt.

President Trump did not speak at the event, nor endorse or promote it. The brawl took place while he was playing golf in North Jersey. In order to make him culpable, the media's indictment was made on the basis of his reaction to it after the fact. This is where the media's infamous "fine people" hoax arose, which, on the left became instant shorthand for the appalling president's inability to acknowledge even *Nazism* as an obvious evil.

What did Donald Trump really say about the violence in Charlottesville?

It's worth going back to the timeline.

– At 12:19 p.m. upon learning of the violence, he tweeted: "We ALL must be united and condemn all that hate stands for. There is no place for this kind of violence in America. Let's come together as one!"

– 15 minutes later Vice President Mike Pence retweeted this message and added his support. An hour earlier, First Lady Melania Trump had tweeted out her own message: "Our country encourages freedom of speech, but let's communicate w/o hate in our hearts. No good comes from violence. #Charlottesville."

– Less than an hour after his first message, the president tweeted another: "Am in Bedminster for meetings & press conference on V.A. & all that we have done, and are doing, to make it better-but Charlottesville sad!"

– In the immediate aftermath of the riots, the President again condemned "in the strongest possible terms this egregious display of hatred, violence and bigotry on many sides," adding, "This has no place in America."

Trump: "What do you think of Thomas Jefferson? You like him?"

Reporter: "I do love Thomas Jefferson."

Trump: "Okay, good. Are we going to take down the statue? Because he was a major slave owner. Now, are we going to take down his statue? So you know what, it's fine. You're changing history. You're changing culture. And you had people – and I'm not talking about the neo-Nazis and the white nationalists – because they should be condemned totally. But you had many people in that group other than neo-Nazis and white nationalists. Okay? And the press has treated them absolutely unfairly."

What is usually missed from this exchange was the president's comments about Antifa.

President Trump: "Okay, what about the alt-left that came charging at – excuse me, what about the alt-left that came charging at the, as you say, the alt-right? Do they have any semblance of guilt? Let me ask you this: What about the fact that they came charging with clubs in their hands, swinging clubs? Do they have any problem? I think they do."

The president condemned the white supremacists, and also condemned the black-clad anarchists who arrived to the event armed. Indeed, also present at the event were Antifa militants who had come to rumble. They were seen burning flags, forming battle phalanxes, and wielding metal shields, bats and sticks.

Yet to most effectively sell their narrative, the media also had to peddle another one: They went to great lengths to legitimize Antifa's role in the mayhem. CNN host Chris Cuomo infamously compared their actions in Charlottesville to those of the soldiers who landed on the Normandy beaches in 1944.

Thus began the legitimization of Antifa in the eyes of the media.

When Cuomo was mildly criticized for condoning violence, he doubled down, insisting, on camera, that "I have watched them (Antifa) in the streets protesting in different situations. There's certainly aspects of them that are true to a cause. That's a good cause."

"No organization is perfect," his CNN colleague Don Lemon readily agreed.

CNN personality Michael Eric Dyson informed viewers that Antifa is "preserving the fabric" of America, while CNN host W. Kamau Bell actually suggested his followers contribute money to an Antifa gun club. MSNBC's Nicolle Wallace, for her part, declared that Antifa is "on the side of the angels," while on flagship NBC Chuck Todd turned Meet The Press into a sympathetic forum for one of Antifa's most rabid advocates. CBS, meanwhile, devoted an entire episode of its show "The Good Fight" to a justification of Antifa violence.

This book could be entirely comprised of nothing but major media praise for Antifa in the wake of Charlottesville.

Interestingly, Antifa tactics were well known to Charlottesville area law enforcement. Included in an After Action Report (AAR) on the event is the following note, detailing observations made in July:

"Law enforcement personnel immediately noticed Antifa's sophisticated level of organization. Lieutenant Hatter observed that Antifa coordinated with local activists, had logistics and medical support, and figured out the Klan's entrance location to the park. Lieutenant O'Donnell characterized Antifa as 'very organized' and 'totally coordinated.' He spoke with a 'street medic' who revealed that she had protested at Standing Rock, South Dakota for eight months before arriving in Charlottesville. At 2:15 p.m., Antifa was spotted wearing gas masks, padded clothing and body armor. Captain Shifflett recalled being surprised at the planning by some counter-protesters who brought organized medics, used walkie-talkies to share information, and wore helmets, full body pads, gas masks, and shields. CPD Lieutenant Dwayne Jones observed counter-protesters actively monitoring scanners and other devices to track the movements and communications of the police."

This detailed report regarding the relative sophistication of Antifa militants was not featured prominently in media coverage of Charlottesville; instead they opted to lionize Antifa, while twisting the words of the president.

FIVE

DEPLORABALL

For the left, Trump's election was a nightmare. As reality began to sink in on election night, Rachel Maddow quite literally said as much. "You're not having a terrible, terrible dream," she grimly intoned. "Also you're not dead and you haven't gone to hell. This is your life now, this is the election now, this is us, this is our country. It's real."

By the end of that night, the left was already moving into a sort of revenge mode. Their rallying cry became to stop Trump by any means necessary.

"To call Trumpism fascist," as radical journalist Natasha Lennard wrote in the far-left *Nation*, "is to suggest that it demands from us a unique response. We *can* deploy the 'fascism' moniker to Trump's ascendance by recognizing features like selective populism, nationalism, racism, traditionalism, the deployment of newspeak and disregard for reasoned debate. The reason we *should* use the term is because, taken together, these aspects of Trumpism are not well combated or contained by standard liberal appeals to reason. It is constitutive of its fascism that it demands a different sort of opposition."

"A different sort of opposition."

As the organizer of the Deploraball, I had an early preview of exactly what that would mean.

Though it vastly outgrew that original concept, at its inception the Deploraball was just a group of friends holding a party in our nation's capital to celebrate Trump's win. At the start, all we wanted to do was get together with like-minded people, tell stories from the campaign trail, and raise a glass to a hard-fought victory. The number of public Trump supporters in 2016 was small, and people forget that even most Fox News hosts and contributors did not support Trump in the election.

Little did we know it would turn into one of the most controversial events of that entire tumultuous year.

I live in the Washington, D.C. area. Throughout the campaign, there had been lots of opportunities for me to travel across the country to swing states, debate locations, and generally anywhere where we could find Trump or Hillary Clinton events, to let people know what was going on in the race, and try to tell the true story from the ground level. I also got the chance to meet thousands of amazing people through social media, and would sometimes later speak with them in person at rallies or events. Sometimes we labeled our events Citizens for Trump, other times we used the term MAGA3X, but mostly it was simply a grassroots effort of thousands of people to motivate millions, and eventually win the election.

After Nov. 8, 2016, lots of our followers started talking about coming to Washington for the inauguration. *'Great,'* I thought, *'finally, everyone is coming to visit me, and I don't have to sit in the car or on a flight for hours!'*

As inauguration-week plans began coming together, I started talking to a close group of friends about holding a meet-up for social media friends – Mike Cernovich and Jeff Giesea, among others. I came up with the name, "Deploraball." Many Trump supporters were coming to Washington for the inauguration, but were unable to obtain tickets for the official inaugural ball. So, I figured we should hold our own. Our concept was a "ball for us all" – a play on the fact that normally the many inauguration balls are exclusive, invite-only affairs.

Early on, the first drama erupted when we released a statement that no alt-right slogans or symbols would be allowed at the event, and formally banned white nationalist Richard Spencer from the Deploraball. We were not interested in holding an event that was open to Nazi kids like him. However, activist Baked Alaska took issue with our statement, and began blasting us online as well as making a series of anti-Semitic remarks. We gave him an opportunity to apologize and retract, but he refused. In the end, he was also removed from the event. This drama was written up in TMZ and various other outlets, which we welcomed, as we wished to show a clear split between the Trump-supporting new right, and the white nationalists who had attempted to infiltrate the MAGA movement. We later held an anti-hate event in June 2017 at the White House on the same day they held a white nationalist rally at the Lincoln Memorial.

The next turn in the Deploraball saga came when we were finalizing a contract with Clarendon Ballroom for about 500 people. At that point Dan Lamothe, a reporter for the *Washington Post*, tweeted out the Evite for Deploraball: "Trump fans to hold 'Deploraball' at Clarendon Ballroom around inauguration," it noted. "Various Breitbart/Infowars folks going."

Immediately, the Clarendon Ballroom was inundated with hate comments from the left, attacking us as Nazis, homophobes, and every other name under the sun, and the business then shifted into damage-control mode, tweeting to media outlets a denial that any events were "contracted" for Jan. 19, 2017.

Behind-the-scenes, I was contacted by reporters looking for a comment on the fact that we did not have an official inauguration event contracted, and they were asking if I had misrepresented the nature of the party at the Clarendon. I went back and looked at my emails, and every single one was signed with Citizens for Trump. I had represented the event as an "inauguration celebration of the victory of Donald Trump."

Clearly they were looking to discredit us, and were trying to make our audience think we were engaged in some kind of money grab without offering any actual event, which could not be further from the truth. We countered this by releasing the original paperwork from Clarendon, saying, "Here is the proposal to Clarendon Ballroom for Deploraball. They are refusing to honor the proposal, won't host event." The proposal had been sent to us. We simply hadn't yet finalized the contract.

No-platforming is a common tactic of the far-left, but this was the first time I had been no-platformed myself. I quickly learned that the radical left would say or do anything to come after their political opponents. No lie was too big, no falsehood was too egregious. As Lennard wrote, this was a different kind of opposition.

Ever hear of Hillary or Biden voters getting no-platformed, as Trump supporters routinely have been? Ever hear of harassment campaigns from businesses, governments, and social media companies? Heck, ever once hear of discrimination against a leftist for refusing to violate his personal beliefs, as are religious conservatives for refusing to bake a cake?

Fortunately, once the story got out, many other venues and event centers who wanted our business reached out to us. We had hundreds of guests coming, including some who'd asked to take part in what promised to be the best inauguration party. In fact, the media blitz was actually giving us a lot of buzz, and we realized that even more people now wanted to come to the Deploraball.

We decided to double the size of the event to 1,000 people.

I now took the opportunity to ruffle the feathers of low-info trolls and fake news operatives alike by tweeting, "LOL no, guys, we are not going to have Deploraball at the Russian Embassy."

Deploraball then released the following official statement:

"After selling 500 tickets in just over 24 hours, the Deploraball learned that the venue hosting the event would not honor its proposal after they were harassed by Hillary supporters. The good news is that demand is far greater than expected, and the fecklessness of the venue means we can now have a larger party in a bigger venue. The Deploraball is still on. Details coming soon!"

Failing-forward, we settled on our new venue, the media's own hallowed ground of the National Press Club. Needless to say, when it was announced many in the mainstream media had a conniption fit. It was delightful. To their credit, the Press Club remained totally accommodating, and they'd prove incredible to work with throughout the process. I've since held several more events there and cannot speak more highly of their professionalism (But their goodwill would later be put to even harsher tests as the event date drew closer).

Once we released new tickets, it was less than 24 hours before the entire event sold out. It was the hottest party of Inauguration 2016.

Eager to put on a great event, we'd kept ticket costs down – after all, this was the people's party – but it also meant we had to keep the budget within bounds. We ended up securing a ton of great entertainment – folk singer Tatiana Moroz, viral superstar Scott Isbell, epic American flag live-painter Scott LoBaido, and Sheriff David Clarke agreed to stop by to greet the crowd. We even had a great photo booth with lots of costume props to take pictures with everyone. It seemed like everything was going well.

And it was too good to be true.

As preparations continued apace, we got word that a group of radical leftists, calling themselves DisruptJ20 (in reference to the inauguration date), was planning to provoke chaos in D.C. that week.

Learning they were holding planning meetings in the D.C. area, I decided to head down myself to get a firsthand look at what they were up to, and find out what they had in store for our guests coming into town, – among them, my parents. Having witnessed first-hand violence against Trump supporters along the campaign trail, I was extremely wary of what they might try at the inauguration.

I went to my first DisruptJ20 meeting in early January, in the basement of an old church in D.C. This was the first time I had ever infiltrated an Antifa meeting. The stench was so unbearable, at first I thought a sewer main had burst and was seeping into the room. But soon I realized it wasn't the sewer, it was the indifference to basic hygiene of many at the impromptu – literally underground – meet-up. There were about 150 present, in all shapes and sizes; it was like a cross between a Grateful Dead tailgate and a Weather Undergroundrejects society, with 70s-era anarcho-socialists mingling with their modern SJW descendants, sitting around in circles discussing how to best prevent Donald Trump from being inaugurated president, and how to prevent anyone from celebrating it.

It took me about a half hour to break down their organizational hierarchy. "Leadership," such as it was, ran the gamut from trained organizers to rank and file college dropouts and vagrants.

I left at the end of the meeting, taking with me a stack of documents, a map, and notes outlining some of their intended crimes for the week. They were planning to attack inauguration visitors at subway station entrances; use roller derby skaters to harass guests; throw smoke bombs into crowds; even rig up quadcopter drones with bottle rockets and dive bomb the assembled masses.

They also intended to specifically target the "Nazi Ball."

In other words, the Deploraball – our own event.

I turned the information over to the security director of the Press Club, who handed it to the D.C. Police Department.

As I was getting ready for the next planning meeting, DisruptJ20 threw me another curve. They publicly released a list and photos of individuals they were targeting for attack at the Deploraball. It included: "MIKE CERNOVICH, JACK POSOBIEC, LAUREN SOUTHERN, CASSANDRA FAIRBANKS, BILL MITCHELL, STEPHEN LIMBAUGH, ROGER STONE, JIM HOFT, and SCOTT ISBELL."

On the list, I was quoted as saying that Star Wars *Rogue One* was an anti-Trump film. They were completely correct. As an aside, I started the #DumpStarWars campaign all the way back in 2016, a full year before the debacle of *The Last Jedi* was released.

Still, I'd been burned by the group. Now I would be instantly recognized if I attended another meet-up.

Fortunately, James O'Keefe and the awesome people at Project Veritas stepped into the fray. They conducted an undercover investigation of DisruptJ20, and using their famously-effective hidden camera interview technique, were able to get several leaders of the plotters on tape, divulging some of their plans for attacking the Deploraball.

"I was thinking of things that would ruin their evening, ruin their outfits and otherwise make it impossible to continue with their plans. So they get nothing accomplished," Scott Green, leader of the D.C. Anti-Fascist Coalition, said in one undercover video.

Another activist, identified as Luke Kuhn, said during a sit-down at a restaurant in Northwest Washington, "If you had a pint of butyric acid, I don't care how big the building is, it is closing." Green added: "And this stuff is very efficient, it's very, very smelly, and it lasts a long time. And you add the benefit, everybody is going to walk outside in the freezing cold."

These people were talking about throwing butyric acid at my mother.

Veritas also caught on camera DisruptJ20 organizer Legba Carrefour directing his troops to, as he put it, create a "series of clusterf**k blockades, where we are going to blockade all the major ingress points to the city." Carrefour outlined a plot to sabotage the city's metro lines by inserting metal chains into the gears of transit system machinery, his foot soldiers to act in concert with those of the self-proclaimed Industrial Workers of The World (IWW). The intent was to shut down "every line in the city." Meanwhile, organizer Dylan Petrohilos was orchestrating a parallel "clusterf**k," aimed at "jamming" up the capital's streets.

That plan was literally mapped out by his J20 co-conspirators. Through my infiltration of that group, I obtained a map showing precisely how they planned to shut the city down. The plan had two parts: first, to disrupt the inauguration itself; then, to instigate a riot on inauguration night. J20's maps were to be used to guide Antifa members and their associates to spots along the inauguration parade route where the group aimed to strike.

The plans for the night of the inauguration were under the direction of Mike Isaacson of Smash Racism DC, Project Veritas captured him on camera instructing his lieutenants to attack the city's partygoers, pointing out that "throat-punching is probably a good thing."

In all, J20 organizers had been at it for months, coordinating with so-called affinity groups around the country, who would arrive well in advance. They knew whom to contact when they arrived, where to stay, the locations of the city's police stations, how to strike at the police directly and whom to contact if arrested.

On our end, we had already planned for a heightened internal security presence from the Press Club, as well as for additional security personnel. But with the additional weight of the Veritas videos, the FBI and D.C. police were alerted, which added layers of additional external security for the building and surrounding area.

We also released another statement: "With all the high-testosterone veterans and alphas attending, a protester would be foolish to try to infiltrate the party — but we are still taking every possibility seriously.

"We are more likely to encounter protesters when getting into and out of the Press Club Building and at the check points for the security perimeter. If you encounter protesters, our strong recommendation is to not engage with them in any way. Take the high road. Do what you need to keep you and yours safe, but otherwise ignore them."

Make no mistake, what DisruptJ20 was planning was terrorism against our event – achieving political ends through violent means.

Once the videos were released, we found three of them on our guest list and revoked their tickets. The D.C. police actually arrested the three, who later pled guilty.

We naturally remained wary about how our event would be covered in the press, so did what we could in that regard. While we granted press access to a number of publications, including the *Washington Post, Politico, The New Yorker, New York Magazine,* FOX, Rebel Media, Breitbart, and RSBN, we declined access to CNN. In response to their request for credentials, we sent the following: "Dear CNN, We're hosting the Deploraball at the Press Club because we support quality journalism. Unfortunately, we feel your coverage during the election was biased to the point of being irresponsible. We question your integrity as an institution of journalism. Therefore we will not be issuing you press passes."

In a nutshell: Their reporting just wasn't up to our standards. Sometimes tough love is what it takes.

Then, came Jan. 19, 2017, the night of the Deploraball.

While inaugural balls are traditionally held the night of the inauguration itself, I had pushed for the 19th, inauguration eve, to avoid competing for bandwidth with everything else going on that day. Besides, it also gave us the opportunity to celebrate the end of the Obama era, which many of our guests appreciated.

Before heading to the event, I stopped by a few of DisruptJ20's known staging areas around D.C. to get an idea of their numbers. Not wanting to stand out, I'd delayed putting on my tuxedo. It didn't look like many people had shown up so far, and I hoped it might be a quiet night.

Still, better safe than sorry. When I got to the Press Club, I entered through the main door, and made sure it was verified I really was Jack Posobiec. Photo ID required. This was real security, not like voting in Philadelphia. They wanded me, checked my ID, and escorted me inside. Even now, hours before our scheduled start, police officers surrounded the building and stood ready to protect the attendees from the violent leftists. I thanked as many of them as I possibly could.

I changed in the bathroom, and left my bags and jacket downstairs, as was required by security, then headed up to the 13th floor for a pre-event dinner. I greeted many of the event organizers and was glad to see so many familiar faces. Everyone looked tremendous in their evening best: people I had spent countless days with on the road, at flash mobs, in the middle of protests and riots, and everything in between. We went around the table and introduced ourselves. Everyone applauded when James O'Keefe entered.

Just as dinner was being served and I had taken a few bites of steak, my phone started blowing up.

It was my parents downstairs, and they were having a problem getting inside – trying to pull up e-tickets from their smartphones. I called my mother, usually the most sensible one in a crisis, and in the background I could hear some kind of noise. I asked her what it was, and she shouted, "They're rioting! Firecrackers are being thrown at us!"

I bolted out of my seat and ran down the hallway to the elevator, frantically jabbing my finger at the button for the lobby floor. After what felt like an eternity, it finally deposited me on ground level. I burst through the doors and bounded up the stairs three-at-a-time to the main entrance, just as my family was making its way through. My parents and my aunt were there with my fiancée (now wife) Tanya, and my brother Kevin who was ushering them forward. I showed my organizer pass to our security, who waved them inside. I made sure they were okay, and then looked past them to the chaos beyond.

What only an hour before had been an ordinary city street was now a war zone.

A sea of disheveled rioters teemed outside the National Press Club, menacing partygoers, setting random fires and vandalizing storefronts. "Racists," they screamed at those attending our party. "Neo Nazis!" "Fascists!" "Get off our streets, Nazi scum!"

Some threw eggs, while others threw bottles or swung sticks at the heads of partygoers as they tried to get by. Others used their fists.

Police fired pepper spray into the crowd, trying to disburse the anarchists. Others, in full riot gear, clashed with the activists.

I opened my iPhone and started Periscoping the event, trying to show the world what was going on, although the signal strength was low. In front of me was a sea of rioters; the street had completely disappeared. Lacy MacAuley, lead organizer of anarchist group DisruptJ20, had lit American flags on fire and was chanting "And, we are dancing!"

Suddenly, I heard a whizzing past my ear. Reminded what it sounded like to be shot at, my training kicked in. Dropping to the ground, I found the ammo – it wasn't a bullet, but a large D-cell battery. It was quickly followed by others.

"They're throwing D-cells!" I narrated on the Periscope feed.

Security now came up – "Sir, you can't be here" – and, with a hand on my shoulder, tried to usher me inside.

"What do you mean I can't be here? This is my event."

"Sir, no, you're in danger!"

I protested. I didn't want to stop Periscoping, but the security situation was definitely deteriorating, and I knew I was a target on their list. It was becoming even more dangerous for the security personnel.

As I stepped back into the lobby, behind the glass doors, I could hear more batteries clanging against the windows.

Suddenly the door opened, and 6-foot-5 of tuxedo and quaffed silver hair strode inside – talk show host Bill Mitchell, here for the party.

"Bill!" I yelled. Though we had talked over Twitter, and he'd had me on his show as a co-host many times over the campaign, we'd never actually met in real life before, "Quick, take my Periscope!"

I threw him my phone over the security guard standing between us. Bill caught the phone and held it up high above the fracas.

"It's special guest cameraman Bill Mitchell!"

He panned the phone across the crowd of Antifa rioters as they rippled and surged, smoke bombs casting billowing gray plumes in the darkness, while fires burned behind.

It was vital that everyone see what we were seeing, and what the violent left was doing to the streets of our capital city.

After a few minutes, security pulled Bill in, too. The mob roared outside, deprived of their target.

I discussed the situation with the security people as attendees continued arriving. Wanded, IDs checked, they continued up to the 13th-floor elevators.

The problem was that the process was slow, and there were still hundreds of ticketholders outside in the cold January air, needing to get past the rioters. The D.C. police came up with an idea that reminded me of the ancient Roman phalanx. They held the partygoers down the street and around the corner from the violence, out of harm's way. Then, they formed a human barrier of police in riot shields, body armor, and helmets around groups of 10 or so. Decked out in fancy dresses and tuxedoes, the groups slowly made their way to the entrance, one at a time. The process was slow, and it necessitated pushing back our program for two hours from 8 p.m. until 10 p.m. But it was essential.

Despite the mayhem outside, the atmosphere inside was euphoric. The Deploraball was an intimate affair, because we were a family. There were hundreds of people I'd never met before, yet every one of them felt like a relative.

The hours simply flew by. It seemed like it was over as soon as it began. The Press Club put together a great spread, and there were multiple open bars. We had reserved the entire Press Club, so there were many different rooms, each proving a unique experience. One was like a large bar, another like a cocktail reception. Some were smaller, comfortable sitting areas with light music – I took the chance to stop by the piano at one point to tickle the ivories. The main room at Deploraball started out as a dance floor complete with a DJ and amazing live performances by Tatiana Moroz and Scott Isbell.

Then, the main hall turned into an impromptu Trump rally, with numerous people taking to the stage to speak of what it meant to them to be in D.C. at the impending inauguration of Donald Trump.

In my own speech, I observed how remarkable it was that, even with everything going out outside, we in this room were so warm and filled with exhilaration. It was fitting, because we'd had to fight hard to get here. Every day of the campaign had been a street fight against the left, the media, the establishment – sometimes a physical one, but we'd won. It's not hard to win the argument when you have truth on your side.

I closed by referring to a letter John Adams wrote in 1818, explaining the American Revolution to a friend:

"The American Revolution was not a common event. Its effects and consequences have already been awful over a great part of the globe. And when and where are they to cease? But what do we mean by the American Revolution? Do we mean the American war? The Revolution was effected before the war commenced. The Revolution was in the minds and hearts of the people; a change in their religious sentiments of their duties and obligations."

What they called the American Revolution in 1776 had now been followed by what might be called the Populist Revolution in 2016. It was 240 years after the original revolution that Americans had once again decided they were fed up with how their government was treating them and had fought back against forces of globalization and corporate conformity.

Hillary Clinton called us "deplorables," and in defiance, we embraced it. We wore it as a badge of honor. Our celebration was the Deploraball, for the regular, ordinary Americans who gave their energy, time and voice to the cause.

But though we had begun to take the country back, for now, it was clear that this was just the beginning of the fight. All it took was our seeing what was going on outside with the rise of Antifa.

SIX

THE BLACK BLOC

What we saw on the streets of Washington, D.C. on inauguration night was Antifa employing a tactic that has since become familiar to millions, watching on their computer screens as militants mindlessly wreak havoc on America's cities. This tactic, the black bloc, has become Antifa's brand.

In the most basic sense, the black bloc is a mode of presentation and mutual identification – black clothing, masks, helmets, melee weapons. Even as it serves to both protect and arm the wearers, crucially it also serves the purposes of intimidation and obstruction of justice. By facilitating mass action, it enables mutual protection, and it's otherwise effective in frustrating law enforcement as it creates a multiplication effect of violence and property damage. And it makes it difficult, if not impossible, to identify the faces of the perpetrators.

Quite simply, Antifa "fighters" aim to terrorize opponents, and they don't want to face the consequences for doing it.

From media reports, it would almost seem that black blocs arose spontaneously with the election of Donald Trump in 2016. In fact, black blocs predate the Trump era by decades. The first major black bloc activity in the United States to achieve nationwide attention was the Battle of Seattle in 1999, a protest of the WTO and globalization. Black blocs were also seen at the 2009 NATO Summit in Strasbourg, France. Two years later in 2011, black blocs accompanied much of the Occupy movement that broke out starting on Wall Street in New York City, but appearing in many cities across North America and Europe.

The term itself appears to have been coined in West Germany in the late 1970s and early 1980s during clashes between police and left-wing Bohemian youth squatters known as the Autonomen. There is dispute over which side used the term first, either the police or the Autonomen. In German, the phrase is *der schwarze block*. When the West German police carried out eviction actions against Autonomen, the activists defended their squats by wearing heavy black clothing, helmets, ski masks, boots, and carrying melee weapons such as clubs, projectiles, and shields. The Autonomen would then respond to police officers by constructing barriers and throwing Molotov cocktails. Indeed, right from the start, in 1980, the black blocs of West Germany were as militant and violent as those that would become commonplace in the United States over 40 years later.

The West German police eventually defeated the Autonomen when new laws were passed that banned the carrying of weapons by protesters and the wearing of helmets and padding. These laws would likely have trouble getting passed in most Democratic jurisdictions in America today.

Though predating the rise of the internet, the black bloc tactic moved rapidly throughout Europe and eventually to North America, and has been key to the spread of the international anarcho-communist movement. It was helped by the punk scene of the 1980s, which was closely aligned with the far left. Many bands were openly political, and spread the word in fan magazines and tours, across Western Europe and the U.S. A black bloc was used in at least one protest against the Gulf War in Washington, D.C. in 1991, probably the earliest use of a black bloc in the United States.

The tactics of a black bloc are more complex than they may appear at first glance, and they have been refined since the days of West Germany in the 1970s. The Antifa blog *Crimethinc* states, "The Bloc tactic is best for conditions in which the action called for occupies the grey area between overt and covert, and as such it must be applied carefully."

Crimethinc lays out three types of black blocs.

The first is an Open Bloc. "In an Open Bloc, a general call goes out to all interested to gather and act in a Bloc; open meetings are held to discuss goals, strategies, and so on. The benefits of such an approach are that more people can be involved; the obvious drawback is that security is so compromised that the possibilities for action are severely limited."

The second type is the Semi-Open Bloc. "In a Semi-Open Bloc, the organizing takes place in secret, between people who know and trust each other, but when the Bloc itself comes together, others in Bloc attire are welcomed to it; in the past few years of Black Bloc activities, this has been the most frequent format. In such Blocs, it is still necessary that the participants be prepared to deal with infiltration, but they at least have the benefit of secure planning and internal structures."

The third and final type is the Closed Bloc. "In an entirely Closed Bloc, the participants prepare in secret and do not welcome the participation or company of any outsiders during the action. Even when such a Bloc is called for, it can still be valuable to act openly, as a Bloc, rather than covertly: the public nature of the action may send an important message, others outside the Bloc may be inspired to engage in similar actions of their own, the crowd cover itself might enable an escape that would be more difficult for those opting for a clandestine approach."

Black bloc planning is extremely advanced and methodical. Organizers will bring together so-called affinity groups, or cells of supporters. These will then be organized into various units that cluster together: medics, scouts, internet fusion cells – watching for police activity and monitoring scanners, security, legal, communications, flag-bearers, and musicians/music players. The last is key for morale.

In general, and unlike most paramilitary units, black blocs are not hierarchical; they pride themselves on their decentralized structures. Mapping is integral to the black bloc planning cycle, as they will lay down staging areas, main routes, escape routes, locations where the police will mass, targets for violence and spots where resources can be had.

Black bloc participants are encouraged to write the phone number of legal contacts on their bodies in permanent marker before an action. They are then told to remove identifying piercings, cover up tattoos, not carry identification, anarchist literature, and in some cases are told cell phones must be left at the staging area. All of this is done to prepare for illegal activity, and to prevent identifying individual members of the bloc.

According to Occupy.org, there are three zones of a black bloc: green, yellow, and red. "The green zone was a sanctuary where demonstrators were, theoretically, in no danger of being arrested. The yellow zone was for those undertaking nonviolent civil disobedience and involved a minor risk of being arrested. The red zone was for protesters who were ready for more aggressive tactics, including skirmishes with the police."

There's an element within Antifa that's just looking to pick a fight. And there are organizers within Antifa that are utilizing it as a tool. And then there are people like Bray and sympathetic journalists and bloggers who go out into the maelstrom in order to provide air cover for it and try to justify it. To take but one example, CNN said they were seeking peace through violence. This is straight out of George Orwell: "peace through violence."

This sort of psychological tactic is not meant exclusively for people outside the "in-group." It's meant for those inside the group, galvanizing them into continuing action – a justification to continue their violence.

Progressivism is structured with the belief that the highest principle of progressivism is victimhood and victim status. Yet victim status is an inverted pyramid by which an individual is defined not by his accomplishments or his merits but by past oppressions or past victimization. And so that's what they rack and stack – who's the most victimized. Even if it's not you personally, maybe it's your family or your identity. That's not to say that oppression or victimization hasn't happened, but to the left, victimization is sacrosanct. Ironically, this leads to a group of people who have become victims of the left: victims of violence, victims of assaults, victims of doxxing.

But those aren't the victims the media focuses upon. They are more interested in someone like Thomas DiMassimo. In 2016, he rushed the stage at a Trump rally in Ohio screaming that he was going to get Trump, and CNN gave him an interview. By platforming violent extremism, CNN sent the message that if you commit violence, but are anti-Trump and hostile to Trump's supporters, the in-group will elevate you and give you a platform, support and praise you. However, anything that happens to the "out-group" is OK. That doesn't matter.

The following is a list of black bloc events starting with the Battle of Seattle, according to the *Journal for the Study of Radicalism*:

• Seattle, 30 November 1999, Summit of the WTO — Far from the demonstrations, a black bloc targets capitalist symbols in the city's shopping district.

• Washington, D.C., 16 April 2000, Meeting of the IMF and the World Bank — The black bloc directs its efforts toward protecting nonviolent demonstrations against police assaults.

• Prague, September 2000, Meeting of the IMF and the World Bank — A black bloc armed with clubs, rocks, and Molotov cocktails confronts a police barrage in a vain attempt to force its way through to the convention center.

• Quebec City, Canada, April 2001, Summit of the Americas — Several small black blocs harass the security perimeter and the police officers assigned to it, while at the same time protecting other demonstrators against police attacks.

• Gothenburg, Sweden, May 2001, Summit of the

European Union — A black bloc confronts the police, who fire real bullets at the crowd.

• Genoa, Italy, June 2001, G8 Summit — The black blocs and their allies strike symbols of capitalism, attack a prison, and retaliate against police officers who assaulted them. A police agent kills a demonstrator with two gunshots to the head.

• Prague, Czech Republic, 21 November 2002, NATO Summit — Sensing a provocation, a black bloc maneuvers to escort a police vehicle slowly making its way through a rally of some 3,000 anarcho-communists.

• Geneva, Switzerland, May 2003, G8 Summit (in Évian) — A black bloc of about 100 takes independent action in Geneva, suddenly appearing late in the evening in Geneva's downtown shopping area when everything is quiet, hurling stones and Molotov cocktails at the shop windows, only to vanish a few minutes later. Over the following days, black blocs together with other groups of demonstrators engage in street-blocking actions, preventing access to Summit meeting places.

• Thessaloniki, Greece, June 2003, Summit of the European Union — Black blocs participate in street-blocking actions and battle police officers defending the Summit. The next day they demonstrate in the city along with tens of thousands of people, and attack capitalist symbols. They set fire to a McDonald's and Vodafone store and wreck some 30 other establishments, including three banks.

• Miami, November 2003, Summit of the Americas — The black bloc takes part in the rally, endeavoring to protect some giant puppets from the police, who spend about thirty minutes destroying the puppets abandoned by the routed demonstrators on Seaside Plaza.

• New York, August–September 2004, Republican Party Convention — Members of a black bloc march without masks among the crowd until they arrive at the convention site. There they don their masks and a giant puppet representing a green dragon is set alight, signaling the start of a confrontation with the police.

• Scotland, June 2005, G8 Summit (in Auchterarder) — A black bloc undertakes a Suicide March, leaving the temporary autonomous and self-governed camp before dawn to draw the attention of the police away from the many affinity groups who have independently spread out in the countryside to block the highways at sunrise. The Suicide March finally reaches a highway and blocks it after repeatedly confronting a police barrage with clubs and stones.

• Hillemm-Rostock, Germany, June 2005, G8 Summit — A huge black bloc participates in the rallies against the Summit, and the next day attempts to spark a riot in a gentrified neighborhood of East Berlin, an action called "Plan B."

• Strasbourg, France, April 2003, NATO Summit — A black bloc skirmishes with police.

• Vancouver, Canada, February 2010 — A small black bloc targets corporations sponsoring the Olympic Games.

• Toronto, Canada, June 2010, G8 Summit — A black bloc targets dozens of capitalist symbols (banks, McDonald's, American Apparel, etc.), a strip club, and vehicles belonging to the media and the police.

All these episodes preceded the Occupy Movement. They were dry runs. In the years that followed, the movement expanded. Then, finally, in the summer of 2020 it exploded all across America.

But where had the philosophy come from? Was it something new – or of considerable vintage?

SEVEN

ANARCHIST ASSASSIN

I t was a hot day in September, and Leon Czolgosz had decided to kill the president. The 1901 Pan-American Exposition had been going on that year in Buffalo, New York, and even though summer had nearly ended, the heat was topping 80 degrees. Czolgosz was a gaunt man of 28, looking every bit the profile of a turn-of-the-century factory worker, though wearing a dark suit that day. He wrapped a handkerchief around his hand, concealing a .32 caliber Iver Johnson revolver.

Czolgosz had waited over two hours in the crowd of 50,000 for the chance to meet President William McKinley, a Republican from Ohio, who had just been re-elected the year before along with his running mate Theodore Roosevelt. As it turned out, Czolgosz was also living in Ohio.

Born in Michigan, he had spent his life working in various factories and mills as a laborer throughout the Midwest. During a strike after the economic crash of 1893, he joined a socialist group called the Knights of the Golden Eagle, and later, another more extreme organization known as the Sila Club. Around this time, he reportedly began to show an interest in anarchism. This was a new movement arriving from Europe. Czolgosz had never been much interested in his family's Catholicism.

For a time, Czolgosz attempted to work his way into a connection with anarchist firebrand Emma Goldman. He had been stirred after attending a speech of hers in May of 1901 in Cleveland, and he had spent the next few weeks traveling to wherever Goldman would be speaking or staying. Yet he was unable to gain acceptance into her circle, and many regarded him as a spy.

It's likely he knew about the assassinations of numerous European leaders that had taken place across the continent over the past few years. King Umberto I of Italy was killed in 1900 with the same type of weapon that he used. In fact, because of anarchist assassinations at the turn of the century, many world leaders began to create strict security apparatuses, like the United States Secret Service, and took to limiting public engagements.

Here is how the *New York Times* reported the assassination:

"It was shortly after 4 o'clock when one of the throng which surrounded the Presidential party, a medium-sized man of ordinary appearance and plainly dressed in black, approached as if to greet the President. Both Secretary Cortelyou and President Milburn noticed that the man's hand was swathed in a bandage or handkerchief. Reports of bystanders differ as to which hand. He worked his way with the stream of people up to the edge of the dais, until he was within two feet of the President."

"President McKinley smiled, bowed, and extended his hand in that spirit of geniality the American people so well know, when suddenly [Leon] raised his hand and two sharp reports of a revolver rang out loud and clear above the hum of voices and the shuffling of myriad feet. The assassin had fired through the handkerchief which concealed the revolver."

McKinley would die from his wounds eight days later on Sept. 14, 1901.

Immediately after the shooting, a former slave named James Benjamin Parker intervened. He had been standing behind Czolgosz in the queue. Parker punched him in the neck and tackled him to the ground.

Following the crime, Czolgosz was arrested and eventually confessed. In his confession, he confirmed that he was an anarchist, and that he had been inspired by the rhetoric of Emma Goldman, although he claimed he undertook the killing by himself. Anarchists of the late 19th century embraced a concept called "propaganda of the deed" in order to justify the use of violence and assassination.

Leon Czolgosz was tried, found guilty, and executed by electric chair on Oct. 29, 1901. His last words were, "I killed the President because he was the enemy of the good people – the good working people. I am not sorry for my crime. I am sorry I could not see my father."

Following McKinley's assassination, President Roosevelt urged the passage of the Anarchist Exclusion Act.

In 1903 the bill was signed into law, and it was later expanded in 1918. Under the new act, Emma Goldman and other anarchist agitators from abroad were deported.

The following is a short list of anarchist and revolutionary acts and assassinations:

1881: The assassination of Russian Tsar Alexander II, by the anarcho-socialist group Narodnaya Volya.

1886: Haymarket Riot, Chicago bomb kills seven police officers and four civilians. Four anarchists hung after sentenced to death.

1894: The assassination of the French president Sadi Carnot by Italian anarchist Sante Geronimo Caserio.

1897: The assassination of Spanish Prime Minister Antonio Cánovas by Italian anarchist Michele Angiolillo.

1898: The assassination of Empress Elisabeth of Austria by Italian anarchist Luigi Lucheni.

1900: The assassination of Italian King Umberto by Italian anarchist Gaetano Bresci.

1901: The assassination of United States President William McKinley by Leon Czolgosz.

1908: The assassination of King Carlos of Portugal by Manuel Buíça and Alfredo Costa.

1911: The assassination of Russian Prime Minister Pyotr Stolypin by Dmitry Bogrov.

1912: The assassination of Spanish Prime Minister José Canalejas by Manuel Pardiñas.

1913: The assassination of King George I of Greece by anarchist Alexandros Schinas.

1920: Wall Street bombing kills 38 people and wounded 300, unsolved but suspected to be Italian anarchists.

The anarchist movement is not new. It is simply a dead phenomenon that has been resurrected.

EIGHT

WEIMAR ANTIFA

The seeds of what would become the present version of the worldwide Antifa movement were planted in 1930s Germany, and the group likes to present itself as the inheritor of a tradition of fighting fascism. But was this true? And, even if so, what does it tell us about the current followers of that Antifa faction? To understand that question we have to step back in time and examine the group's history.

The first eponymous Antifa group was *Antifaschistische Aktion*. It was founded by a Soviet agent and committed Stalinist named Ernst Thälmann in 1932 in Weimar Germany.

Like many of the critical figures in Germany during the 1930s, he was a product of the events of the World War I. That conflict led to the rise of communism and fascism in Germany, as the defeat of the Kaiser led to a weakening of the country's spiritual foundations, a deterioration that the Weimar Republic was never able to correct.

The rhetoric popular nowadays within the radical movement is that Antifa was born out of a small core of iron-willed resisters to the rise of German fascism. But this view does not match with the historical record. In fact, the extreme left often worked glove-in-glove and hand-in-hand with the extreme right in Germany to bring about the collapse of the Weimar government following the onset of the Great Depression. This directly aided in the rise of Hitler and the triumph of fascism.

Hitler's popular appeal was principally based in a widespread belief that German communists would use the economic chaos of the Depression as a vehicle for taking power and installing a regime like the Bolshevik dictatorship that had been established in the Soviet Union. Hitler was seen by many Germans as a more rational and less terrifying alternative to communism. That fear was magnified by the fact that a Soviet agent had come to lead the Communist Party of Germany: Ernst Thälmann. Born on April 16, 1886, in Hamburg, he was three years and four days older than Hitler, his eventual rival. His working-class upbringing and values were unparalleled and comported with rarely encountered socialist standards: his father was a coachman turned dock bartender, and Thälmann grew up rubbing shoulders with the sort of rough types to be expected in both locales, especially in pre-war Germany. His family was genuinely poor, and at one point his parents turned to petty crime and were apprehended, causing them briefly to break up.

Despite this turbulent home life, Thälmann excelled at academics. Yet he was held back by his parent's refusal to pay for his schooling. Instead of pursuing higher education, they made him work at their Hamburg coal, vegetable and wagon shop, and this left him angry and miserable. Thälmann did not fail to note the rigid social stratification around him. As he put it, "When I was shopping for customers in the store, I noticed the social differences in people's lives. For the workers and women misery, and sometimes hunger for their children and small purchases, for the middle-class customers' larger purchases." By 1903, at just 16, Thälmann was already registered as a Social Democrat. He excelled at the position, just a year later becoming chairman of the wagons department in a socialist trade union.

A string of menial jobs and more low-level political activity in his native Hamburg followed until he was drafted in 1915. An artilleryman in a conflict heavily dependent upon it, he claimed to have fought in major battles like the Somme and Cambrai. The latter was the first large, organized tank offensive in history. But, alongside a handful of comrades, he deserted his unit in 1917.

After he fled his unit, Thälmann joined the socialist German Revolution against the imperial regime as chief of a short-lived offshoot party of the Social Democrats. This party then splintered further into a pro-Communist wing that joined with the existing Communist Party of Germany.

Thälmann soon became prominent in several left-wing organizations, both those based in Hamburg and nationwide: he was chairman of the *Unabhängige Sozialdemokratische Partei Deutschlands* (USPS), a socialist party, the Workers' and Soldiers' Council, and the Hamburg citizenry group. During this time in Thälmann's life, the relatively quiet interwar years, he toiled at several jobs for the city of Hamburg: first as an emergency worker in a city park and then at an employment office.

A few days before his 1915 enlistment Thälmann married Rosa Thälmann, née Koch, the eighth daughter of a cobbler. In 1919 they welcomed daughter Irma, who would grow up to be a prominent politician in East Germany. Through these developments, both personal and professional, his socialist credentials became ironclad.

In 1920, the most radical and leftist wing of the USPS decided to join the Communist International (Comintern), merging with the existing Communist Party of Germany. Thälmann became the most prominent Hamburger in the movement, taking nearly 100% of the USPS with him when he joined the Communist Party.

In 1921, Thälmann rose to the Central Committee of the Communist Party of Germany, and shortly afterwards he was sent to represent the Party at the 3rd Congress of Communist International. There he met Lenin.

Soon, Ernst Thälmann was the most important communist in Hamburg, working so hard at his political activities that he was terminated from his employment due to absences. He was deemed so important, in fact, that at one point a rival extremist threw a grenade into his apartment while his wife and daughter were home. Neither was seriously injured, and Thälmann was not present at the time. But being the target of an assassination attempt was another rite of passage for the revolutionary.

Another hallmark was passed in October of 1923 during the Communist Party's Hamburg uprising, that northern German city's attempt to overthrow the government in a kind of homage to Russia's October revolution. They were not successful, and Thälmann was forced underground for a time.

The Communist Party acted alongside the Comintern, a body that facilitated operations, exchanged messages and generally unified communists internationally under the control of the USSR. Following the failure of popular communist uprisings in Germany, the 2nd World Congress of Communist international in 1920 had decided that a "united front" of activists would be needed to foment the revolution.

In January of 1924, no less communist personages than Leon Trotsky and Karl Radek decreed that this "united front," including paramilitary groups, would be the instrument of the global revolution. Another Bolshevik luminary, Grigory Zinoviev, put it succinctly, if ominously:

"The Communist Party of Germany must, under no circumstances, remove the question of the armed insurrection and the conquest of power from the agenda. The arming of the workers and the technical preparation of the decisive struggles must be continued with all tenacity. Red hundreds cannot be found on paper, but in reality, only if the whole working class sympathizes with them and supports them. To achieve this support and sympathy, it is essential to develop it in the closest context to the partial struggles of the proletariat."

Just as he suffered defeats, arrests, and exile, he was like any other truly effective revolutionary in that Thälmann was a mixture of equal parts politician and thug.

From February 1924 on, Thälmann was the leader of the Communist Party of Germany in the Reichstag, the leading German communist, both at home and abroad, and he saw his first order of business as cleaning out and strengthening of the Communist Party, which was about to enjoy its apogee of prestige and power in Germany. Going forward, the KPD was to embrace Soviet-style Bolshevism and especially Stalinism with full effect. Genuine anarchist beliefs were rejected. Anti-fascism and communist totalitarianism were to be one and the same. With these pronouncements and developments, the foundation for what would become Antifa was laid, though at the time it was not particularly noted. But, the ramifications of it are still with us today.

Soon after, the first Marxist street brigade in Germany was organized with the Red Front as its name. In this way, Thälmann began to put Trotsky's wishes into action, creating a communist paramilitary organization to coincide with his rise and the official nod from the Bolshevik guard in the Soviet Union. This group was called the *Roter Frontkämpferbund* (Rotfront) The term is variously translated into English as Red Front Fighters Association or Alliance of Red-Front Fighters. While these are grandiose names, they were not without cause, since the Rotfront had an agenda of worldwide revolution via armed, violent agitation. And just like any other paramilitary organization in Germany at the time, the Rotfront recruited its members from the almost five million demobilized soldiers from the First World War. Subject to scaling down by the Treaty of Versailles, the former military man who still craved excitement or who held political ideals could find a measure of manly employment and fulfillment in the *Freikorps* if he so chose, the Iron Front of the Socialist Party or the *Roter Frontkämpferbund* of the communists.

The Rotfront used military terms for arranging and training its recruits, as befitted an organization consisting of former army veterans. At its most basic level, this consisted of what would be called today in military organization a squad: a team of eight men with a party leader in charge. Four of these squads constituted a platoon. Three platoons formed a unit unique to the *Roter Frontkämpferbund*, a "camaraderie." Larger organizational units consisted of groups, departments, and finally districts. This is not unlike a military table of organization such as companies, battalions, and regiments.

Unique among paramilitary political forces at the time was the naval forces of the Rotfront, dubbed the Red Navy. Naval tradition and discipline sets itself apart from land or air-based forces in militaries then as well as now. The Red Navy was considered an elite unit in the Rotfront. It was made up of sailors from various civilian maritime organizations and formed a bulwark on Germany's coastal cities.

The Rotfront was not merely a paramilitary antifascist fight club. It was an ingrained way of life with duties and benefits that went far beyond demonstrating or direct action.

Alongside this was a youth wing. Many political organizations have youth wings, of course, and the Hitler Youth may have been the most infamous political organization for young people in history. What the Hitler Youth had in common with the Communist Youth groups was that in them, impressionable young people were indoctrinated and introduced to martial concepts. The Rotfront's youth wing was originally called the *Roter Jungsturm*, or Red Youth. Two "summer camps" were set up for the communist youth for the purposes of training and indoctrination. Also included were courses on military drill, ceremony, and fitness.

The Antifa of today is largely a clandestine organization, but the Rotfront was a full-fledged political tool. Just as Antifa does for affinity groups today, the Rotfront escorted proletarian demonstrators at protests to work as security. Pageantry at rallies and parades was also valued as a means to stir up communist sentiment. But the primary role of the Rotfront, like some of Antifa's more hardline cells, was direct action.

In keeping with the military motif of the Rotfront and its successor organizations, "direct action" in this context was agitation, destruction of property and violence. In an early campaign of what would today be called "doxxing," the Rotfront exposed the plans of its counterparts in rival political parties. Should there be legal consequences, the Rotfront members imprisoned could depend upon *Rote*

Hilfe, or Red Help, an international communist social aid and justice organization.

Every Rotfront member swore the following oath:

"I vow to never forget that world imperialism is preparing the war against the Soviet Union.

It should never be forgotten that the fate of the working class around the world is inextricably linked to the Soviet Union.

Not to forget the experiences and sufferings of the working class in the imperialist world war, August 4, 1914 and the betrayal of reformism. Always and always to fulfill my revolutionary duty towards the working class and socialism;

I vow always and always to be a soldier of the revolution.

Always and always in all mass organizations, in trade unions and companies to be a pioneer of the irreconcilable class struggle.

To work for the revolution on the front and in the army of imperialism; to lead the revolutionary struggle to overthrow the class rule of the German bourgeoisie.

To defend the Russian and Chinese revolution by all means;

I vow always and always - to fight for the Soviet Union and the victorious world revolution."

A conflict was inevitable.

The Rotfront communist militants clashed with Berlin police all throughout May 1929, a month so fraught with destruction that is now known in German as *Blutmai,* or "Bloody May." The police's response to what the volunteers and Rotfront irregulars could muster was characteristically sharp and escalated. Gunfire was exchanged and barricades against police were erected with the Berlin districts of Wedding and Neukölln becoming particularly dangerous.

The Rotfront also featured a women's organization, again like the Nazi Women's League. Women were originally allowed to also be "front line fighters" – at least until the men complained. Ironically, when the *Roter Frontkämpferbund* as a whole was banned in May 1929, the men demonstrated side by side with the women's branch, which hadn't been noticed by the government and was not banned yet.

That banning came swiftly, however. For despite a swell of support for the Nazi Party, the Social Democratic Party (SDP) of Germany was still very much in control in 1929, and the Rotfront was outlawed by its order. The movement then split up into several organizations, some namesake, others impromptu, all of them illegal.

The Communist Party then brought their fight to the ballot box as the Weimar Republic teetered on the brink.

With hindsight, it may seem to a modern reader that the KPD and Thälmann's primary adversary should have been Hitler's fledgling National Socialist German Workers' Party (Nazi Party), rather than the Social Democratic Party of Germany (SPD). But, before the final multi-party election was held in Germany in March of 1933, the SPD was the largest, most vociferous party in German government, and even today it remains the second most represented party in the Federal Republic's Bundestag. The Communists and their party army resented this. What's more, Comintern policy stated that parties like the SPD were just as offensive and detrimental to the worldwide revolution as fascism, and that where socialism was entrenched, it should be removed by any means in order to pave the way for communism.

Thus, the Rotfront and the Communist Party initially focused directly on the establishment of their day, the Social Democratic Party of Germany, as they viewed them as "social fascists." So though Hitler was already gaining in power in the Reichstag, Thälmann adopted the Stalinist view that the Communist Party's main enemy was the Social Democratic ruling party.

In fact, in 1931, Thälmann and Hitler joined forces in an unsuccessful attempt to dissolve the parliament of Prussia. Moscow ordered Thälmann to oppose the Social Democrats, even in the face of Hitler's rise. In the 1932 presidential election in Germany, Thälmann ran as the communist candidate, coming in third against incumbent Hindenburg and Adolf Hitler. Communists and Red Front groups were not permitted to ally with Socialists against Hitler and the Nazis.

This was when Antifa was formally created. In July of 1932, Thälmann inaugurated *Antifaschistische Aktion*. While the Rotfront has been formally banned and existed in only splinter cells, now Thälmann sought to use the Antifa banner to rally followers to the cause. However, due to Stalinist policy, Thälmann continued to mock the Social Democrats. Instead, Antifa and the Communist Party saw the Nazis – the true fascists – not only as rivals but also as potentially useful allies in the cause of bringing German democracy to an end.

In other words, today's Antifa propaganda misleads us about the true origins of Antifa. The reality is that in November 1931, the Communist Party newspaper printed an open address to the Nazi Party, calling them "the United Front of the proletariat" who "carried out their revolutionary duty." (*Rote Fahne*, 1 November 1931). Moreover, just before Antifa was founded, the Communist Party held a large meeting in May 1932 with the Nazi Party that included a Nazi speaker and hundreds of Nazi participants. (*Rote Fahne*, 20 May 1932). Then, later, in November 1932, the Nazis and communists jointly took part in a transportation strike in Berlin. Indeed, at the street level, many of the communists and Nazis viewed themselves as common enemies of the system: the sickly Weimar Republic. Consequently, while they often disrupted each other's party meetings, there were significant overlaps between the organizations.

For this reason the term "Beefsteak Nazi" was coined in 1936 to illustrate the concept – brown on the outside, red on the inside – as a term to describe former members of the Brownshirts who once had been communists. Though no one is sure of their precise numbers, it has been suggested that as many as 70% of the Brownshirts may have been Beefsteak Nazis. This reflected both the practical desire of former communists for offices and positions and the common beliefs held by the two groups.

Many of the anti-fascists soon became Nazis themselves, as many of the Nazis, including Hitler's early comrade, S.A. leader Ernst Rohm, had started as communists. Indeed, as early as 1925, Nazi Propaganda Minister Joseph Goebbels acknowledged in a speech that the difference between the two groups was "very slight." At base, both promoted a new religion, replacing traditional belief systems with the worship of the state and its leaders.

Communists and *Antifaschistische Aktion* are like Antifa today in that they applied the term "fascism" whenever it suited them and to anyone who opposed them, and not merely the Nazi Party itself. Similarly, the concept and term of "anti-fascist" was always linked with revolutionary communism, and it was drawn into official Communist International jargon. Because the term was (and is) so loose, it was not hard for former Antifa members to then swing over to the Nazis when Hitler came to power. After all, their motives had been as much a desire to engage in hooliganism and a hatred of democracy as any systematic set of beliefs.

Nonetheless, its double flag symbol was originally two red flags, and elements of it are still used by antifascists today. Even so, at the original Antifa unity rally of 1932, there were banners mocking the Social Democrats and attacking capitalism. But, as Moscow had given them orders to focus on these targets rather than Hitler, the original

Antifa rally is not known to have featured banners denouncing Hilter and the Nazis. Simply put, from its very first days, Antifa was only play-acting at antifascism. Its real battle was with democracy and freedom.

And Antifa has always stood for the overthrow of social order. Writing in 1932, Thälmann explained, "Industrial mass movements, struggle and strikes, against wage robbery and fascism up to the higher task, the application of the political mass strike and the general strike against the ruling system of the bourgeoisie - these are some of the main factors of anti-fascist action!

"It is a non-partisan collecting tank for all workers willing to ruthlessly fight against fascism. It is not an organization, but a mass movement. It is the stream into which all the militant forces flow, who really want to carry out the struggle, the mass attack against the current government."

Ironically, Thälmann's fight against democracy and his devotion to Stalin would be betrayed. Despite being a dedicated Stalinist, when the USSR bellied up to the table for the Molotov–Ribbentrop Pact in 1939, his release from Nazi imprisonment was not requested by the Soviets, nor was it granted when prominent, exiled German communist Wilhelm Pieck pleaded for it from afar. Thälmann wrote numerous letters to his great leader Stalin requesting his release during this period, but he received no response. During his imprisonment, his wife Rosa and daughter Irma visited him many times, and smuggled letters in and out for him so that he could maintain his correspondence.

One anecdote, recounted in the book *Hitler's Rival* by Russel Lemmons, is particularly revealing. In 1937, Thälmann's wife Rosa wrote a letter to Nazi official Hermann Goering, and tried to force her way into the Hotel Atlantic in Berlin to deliver it to him. While she did not succeed, Goering did accept her letter, and made an allowance for Rosa to spend Christmas 1937 alone with Thälmann for two hours. Reportedly, she became pregnant after the evening, despite being 51 years old. Goering's kindness is consistent with statements that the Nazi Party leader made during the 1920s that the difference between the Communists and the Nazis were relatively minor.

Nonetheless, throughout this period, Thälmann remained a steadfast revolutionary, even to the point of seeming cold and aloof in his letters to his own daughter, discussing politics and revolution. This was even as World War II began, and then raged on. His imprisonment became a *cause celebre* to the international left, with rallies held for him around the world by socialists and communists. During the Spanish Civil War, international communist brigades were even named after Thälmann.

On Hitler's orders, Thälmann was summarily executed at Buchenwald concentration on Aug. 18, 1944. The leader of the largest and most frightening communist party in Western Europe left a legacy of agitation and violence and Antifa, the namesake organization, would gleefully continue it afterwards.

In East Germany, Thälmann became a communist legend. Many films, novels, and even a TV series were made about him, though highly fictionalizing the events of his life. Today, there are still statues and public memorials to Ernst Thälmann, though debate continues in modern Germany about whether he should be memorialized, pointing to his anti-democracy stance, Stalinist loyalty, and policies which enabled the rise of Nazi power in the Weimar Republic.

After World War II, those *Antifaschistische Aktion* members who had not joined the Nazi party found themselves in former concentration camps, now prisoner of war camps, and side by side with many of their former enemies. The Soviet secret police, the NKVD, immediately saw the usefulness of Antifa, and absorbed its members. Then, for decades after, Antifa lost its individual identity and became only another communist citizens group.

The modern Antifa movement has grown out of various counter-cultural elements in Europe in the 1960s and has spread around the globe. Antifa membership in America has skyrocketed with the beginning of the Trump era. While initially Antifa was directly organized by the Communist Party, modern Antifa has infused many aspects of the anarchist movement, becoming decentralized and harder to effectively track or pin down. Yet it can still execute direct action, destroying private property and engaging in violence against individuals and attacks on government facilities. This potential has multiplied exponentially in the era of social media, encrypted communications, and open source movements.

The Antifa movement may have had street-level beginnings and ambitions, but its actions now play out across the whole of the world stage. From the smallest American towns to the G20 summit in Hamburg, Antifa's birthplace, the reactionary and violent leftist group is determined to make its voice heard. Much as the specter of communism still hangs over Western civilization, the actions and philosophies of violent reactionaries may likewise loom over America for years to come.

NINE

THE STATE RELIGION

The Second World War ravaged Europe and large swaths of the globe. There has not been a conflict like it since, and hopefully, there never will be another on its scale. The Axis was defeated by a military machine with more resources and manpower than the world has ever seen. One by one, fascists fell and their war crimes were exposed.

Though World War II had burnt itself out by the 1960s, West Germany was still smoldering with the embers of fascism and the expansion of communism. The swastika and many other National Socialist symbols had been banned. Disappearing, too, was homegrown German communism. Stalinization had absorbed all native communist bodies and activists into direct communion with the Motherland. Ernst Thälmann would have been pleased to see the expansion of the so-called World Party of the Communist International that he had worked so hard to achieve.

In East Germany all political parties, including the SPD and its Social Democrats, who had enjoyed a great deal of prestige and governance in Germany, were oppressed. The Communists and the Social Democrats again squared off and renewed hostilities. "Fascist" became a term applied so indiscriminately that it referred to everything from West Germany to the United States to the system of capitalism itself.

Conversely, "antifascism" became a noble concept, symbolizing communism's struggle against the tyranny of NATO, capitalism, and the West. In East Germany the phrase "antifascism" became almost synonymous with revolutionary communism, and the two were used freely and interchangeably. Any foreign influence or ideology or religion was to be regarded with a modicum of distrust and a healthy repugnance. America and Israel were particularly suspect – even West Germany didn't escape this heightened ideological scrutiny.

Antifascism was the state religion that embodied the spirit of the revolution and was contained within every good communist man, woman and child. In fact, for the majority of its existence the Berlin Wall was officially called the "Antifascist Rampart."

East Germany was by far the largest, most industrialized and most important Soviet satellite state. No dissent was tolerated, all while flying the banner of antifascism. Dissidents were labeled "fascists," and the party commissars dealt with them as enemies of the state. State organizations like the secret police, the infamous Stasi, made sure to monitor and stamp out troublemakers with methods that ranged from the merely nefarious to the downright lethal.

Modern Antifa was founded by a West German communist.

In the last chapter, we looked at how Antifa helped destabilize the Weimar Republic and how the failure to stop Hitler led to the rise of the Third Reich and the outbreak of the war. After the war,

West and East Germany became very different nations from each other and from the one that plunged the entire world into war. One became a communist dictatorship, the other a fledgling democracy. Even so, some of Nazism's twisted ideals were still alive in the form of the party's former officials. When the Spiegel Affair broke in 1962, many thought that the censoring of the numbers of the West German military in its biggest newspaper, *Der Spiegel*, was a return to authoritarianism. In addition, Kurt Georg Kiesinger, a sometime-member of the Nazi Party, was elected chancellor of West Germany in 1966. Many at home and abroad saw this as a quiet admission that the National Socialist era was going to return.

Further compounding matters was divisive politics, a hallmark of German democracy then as it had been in the Weimar years. One part of the Social Democratic Party split from the main body of the organization in 1968 to form the *Außerparlamentarische Opposition*, or APO. The APO was a united wing of students who were considered extreme by more traditional, older groups. The APO was initially nonviolent, and one prominent member was the dedicated German Marxist, Rudi Dutschke. Dutschke was a youth of his time, and he embraced many of the new values and spirit of the 1960s. In this he was quite unlike the 1930s revolutionaries.

When fellow Marxist and activist Benno Ohnesorg was shot by West German police in 1967, and the rest of the APO rioted or further splintered into the terrorist Red Army Faction, Dutschke preached nonviolence. He stated that meaningful change could only be realized through creating a utopian society and abandoning the fragments of the old.

But revolutions are not for the gentle, and if history has taught us anything, it is that direct action and a hard heart usually lead to violence. So, on April 11, 1968, Rudi Dutschke was shot in the head by an anti-communist activist, Josef Erwin Bachmann. Incredibly, Dutchke survived the assassination attempt, and even more incredibly but characteristically Christian, he forgave and corresponded with Bachmann for the rest of his life. Dutschke suffered complications from the shooting and eventually passed away due to a seizure in the bathtub, drowning in 1979. His shooting would serve as a great catalyst for change in Germany, but not the kind Dutschke wanted. When the attempt was made on Dutschke's life, the APO leaders intent on violence rejected his ideas and began to turn to violence.

It is from the *Außerparlamentarische Opposition* that the modern, global Antifa movement takes its methods and direct lineage. Parts of APO became radicalized in the late 1960s and 1970s, and resurrected the Antifa name, slogan and symbol. Interestingly, this is the point that the new Antifa changed the double-red flag symbol to the new one black, one red flag, symbolizing both anarchy and communism. The elite cadre of the APO linked up with the terror groups of the Red Army Faction, the 2nd of June Movement or Revolutionary Cells. It should be noted that the Red Army Faction was directly trained and financed by the East German and Soviet governments.

Antifa in Germany is now a decentralized and leaderless leftwing reactionary group. It considers Thälmann's Antifaschistische Aktion to be a noble ancestor and not the anti-democratic group that made common cause with the Nazis, which it actually was. Along with this inspiration from the past, APO is Antifa's direct forebear, imbuing it with its ideology, methodology and tactics.

Antifa used the counterculture to expand the movement worldwide.

As has been described, modern Antifa is not one organization, ideology or movement. It is a gradual coalescing of feelings and organizations with one shared goal: anti-democratic action by any means necessary.

In 1974, a group known as the Communist League, originally Maoist in orientation, founded a national "Antifa commission" for the fight against fascism, which focused on local groups in Germany that it claimed were attempting to revive the legacy of Hitler.

All wars are information wars. In an early example of what would now be called doxxing, Antifa in Germany in the form of the Communist League released private information about a fascist group. In 1983 that organization was banned and its leader arrested.

In a nod to changing times, the Communist League antifascists also organized *Rock gegen Rechts*, or rock against right-wing violence. It was the motto of several different rock concerts, festivals, and block parties in an effort to spread awareness against what it saw as a new rise of German fascism. This was the first attempt by Antifa to capture the spirit of youth via counterculture, one that continues even today.

In November of 1981, the first regional gathering of Antifa cells in Europe took place in Hanover with the North German Antifa Meeting, orchestrated by the Communist League. This cell of Antifa in Germany was particularly active in counter-protesting, doxxing, and direct action.

In May 1983, an Antifa group in northern Germany disrupted a veterans' meeting of SS concentration camp guards. That led to rioting and clashes with police and the powerful national trade union organization. As a result of the violence, the Communist League attempted to distance itself from Antifa.

With reunification of Germany in 1990, there came the open return of the far right and a growth in the far left. Nationalism grew. It was not considered taboo to be proud to be a German anymore. In the burgeoning punk rock scene, both left and right-wing extremists found a toehold. So-called "Nazi punks" were so rife in the punk rock scene that a profane and famous song was written about them. In this, the left and right extreme activists are more alike than they think. Both employ infiltration tactics of more mainstream groups to exploit their legitimacy.

In the early 1990s, the violence of the German left was loosely gathered together under the umbrella group *Antifaschistische Aktion/ Bundesweite Organisation* (AA/BO), which began to again fight against what they considered to be fascist undercurrents in the new Germany. The cells then became more decentralized throughout Germany, and even reached out from large cities into small towns. Often Antifa was the only political activity in rural areas. Gradually, Antifa became more and more extreme, and lines between its working class origins and terrorism faded.

Antifa in Germany is now splintered into three general groups. Anti-Imperialist Antifa is the largest group and considers itself the most "traditional" in terms of its ideology, including its anti-Semitic crusade against global Zionism. The second group is the Anti-Germans, who do not think their country should exist and stand in solidarity with Israel. Finally, there are leaderless bands of Antifa in Germany who do not adhere to either of these sects.

In 2017, Antifa in Germany pulled off its most ambitious and eye-catching direct action in modern years, protesting the G20 Hamburg summit. The Group of 20 summit is a periodic meeting of the world's 19 largest individual economies, and the European Union. It controls 90% of the world's gross domestic product. To some, it is a luxurious retreat for the wealthy and important, but for others, like Antifa, it is the pinnacle of what they consider capitalist fascism.

During the week of July 2nd thru the 9th, 2017, formerly quiet areas of Hamburg were rocked by outbreaks of arson, railway attacks, and full-blown bombings. Protests and marches soon followed, along with peaceful demonstrations and even a festive dance march from non-violent protesters. The whimsical spirit did not linger for long, however. Protestors soon clashed with police, leading to injuries on both sides as well as arrests. Stores were looted, and vandalized, and stacks of building blocks were collected to use as ammunition against riot shields. The fracas was so chaotic that the American First Lady Melania Trump, attending the summit, was unable to leave her hotel room.

TEN

RED ULRIKE

She was 41 years old, a mother of twin girls, and the West German guards had just found her hanging from the window of her prison cell. The 1976 death of one of the most notorious leftist agitators and terrorists in Germany was officially deemed a suicide. Some called the group she ran the Baader-Meinhof Gang, though she preferred the name Red Army Faction.

Ulrike Meinhof looked the part of an anarcho-communist gangster. In the pictures that survive today, she has an open, honest, plain face, staring directly and immodestly at the camera. She often smokes a cigarette, wearing stylish, if simple, clothing. Her hair is usually unapologetically short, and she's typically in men's trousers, flouting what was still a strong social convention in Germany during the sixties and seventies. Her expression is also strong, a fierce, unapologetic bearing, as if she was still expressing defiance on the way to the gallows.

In her mind, she had a great deal to be proud of. Before or after the war, things hadn't ever been easy for Meinhof, despite her bourgeois credentials, a family history of academics, opposition to Nazism, and strong Protestant faith. Both of her parents had died of cancer-related causes, her father, educator Werner Meinhof in 1940, when she was only six years old. That same year, her mother Ingeborg took in a housemate to help pay the bills, a woman barely a decade older than her daughters, an activist and art history student named Renate Riemeck.

Ulrike attended the prestigious *Philippinum* in Weiburg. She was a gifted student, considered popular and charismatic by her classmates, but her rebellious side was already rearing its head. She was nearly expelled for speaking out against school policies by day, and by night she danced to rock and roll and smoked tobacco, a very unladylike habit for one so young growing up in the '50s.

Ulrike matriculated to the University of Marburg in 1954, with a focus on psychology and, like her parents, education. She was active in Protestant youth groups on campus, another vestige carried over from her upbringing. It wasn't unusual at the time for religious ideology, especially Christianity, to be wrapped up in revolutionary or socialist rhetoric. Meinhof's own caregiver Renate Riemeck left a lasting legacy of Christian social justice, as did her socialist contemporary, Rudi Dutschke.

At the University of Muenster in 1957, Meinhof joined a socialist students' organization, the Socialist German Students Union (SDS). Nuclear weapons, then ubiquitously called "atomic," were a hot button issue among liberal university students of the day. Meinhof was involved with a student body that opposed then-Chancellor Konrad Adenauer's nuclear rearmament program. The organization went by the name of *Anti-Atomtod-Ausschuss*, which in English means

"Anti-Atomic Death Committee." In 1958, she gave an impassioned speech to 5,000 students, a move that many consider to be her entry into public life and the political arena.

The Communist Party had been banned in Germany, but by 1959, Meinhof was a member. In 1960, Ulrike underwent surgery for a brain tumor, receiving a silver clamp in her skull. She worked for the leftist newspaper *konkret,* and in 1961 married its co-founder and editor Klaus Rohl. Their marriage resulted in twin girls, Regine and Bettina. Bettina is today a passionate journalist and researcher on anarchist terrorism and violence, at times being unabashedly critical of her own mother Ulrike's agenda and methods. Meinhof divorced Klaus in 1968. Also in 1968, the wave of revolutionary activism sweeping Western Europe and America reached home. That was when her colleague Rudi Dutschke survived an assassination attempt.

In 1970 the other half of the now notorious Baader-Meinhof gang, Andreas Baader, was imprisoned, along with his girlfriend Gudrun Ensslin, for arson after torching two department stores. While incarcerated he was permitted to conduct an interview with a young, up-and-coming journalist, none other than Ulrike Meinhof. Instead of an interview Baader was sprung from jail in one of the most daring and dramatic episodes in the new Baader-Meinhof Gang's history. In the jailbreak, a librarian was shot by one member of the Red Army Faction, and in the chaos that followed, Ulrike made the split-second decision to join the group and go underground with them. Originally, she had merely planned to exist outside the group and help them as an advocate through her writings.

Just as they still do today, the anarchists traveled to the Middle East to receive training in guerilla insurgency and terrorism, including explosives, tradecraft, and firearms from jihadists like infamous Palestinian Liberation Organization Chief Abu Hassan.

Tensions within the group already began to rise during their training. The three Europeans clashed with their Jordanian handlers over their food, living quarters and creature comforts, much like Millennial teenagers who left their Western homes to fight for PKK and found their accommodations lacking. Baader was of the opinion that the hardships they were enduring while training would not prepare them for their fight across Europe. He also surmised that Meinhof was "useless" – a comment that she did contradict.

Gradually Meinhof became estranged from her children, who were raised by their father. In one incident, Gang members and Meinhof attempted to kidnap the twins to send them to be educated and trained in the Middle East by terrorists, to indoctrinate them into the revolution, but the attempt was thwarted in Sicily and the girls were returned to their father.

In Germany, Meinhof found herself a wanted woman, with a reward on her head of no less than 850,000 Deutschmarks. She used this to elicit sympathy from her contacts as a journalist, attempting to build a network in Berlin.

The group never referred to themselves as anything but the Red Army Faction. The nicknames of the Baader-Meinhof Group or Baader-Meinhof Gang equated them with criminals in their eyes. But, like many revolutionaries, they needed capital, most if not all of it stolen, to begin operating. They robbed banks, stole cars, and rented apartments across the city of Berlin as flop and stash houses. Police officers were slain and the West German police, still sensitive to their role during the National Socialist period, were slow to respond.

Meinhof, despite her fervor, charisma and undoubted inner strength, did not have a revolutionary temperament. She was fidgety, with nervous tics, and one of them led to her capture. Apparently, Meinhof would cope with tension by tearing paper and rolling it into tiny balls, leaving it in apartments the group frequented. The police added this tidbit to their investigation dossier. She was animated, impassioned politically, but her discussions with other members of the group devolved into petty bickering, so much so that political discussions with her were forbidden. Delegated to finding apartments for the group to stay in, Meinhof was limited to political discussions with the group's hosts.

Originally, the Red Army Faction (RAF) consisted of 25 members. More people had been arrested than could be summoned for a Christmas 1970 meeting in Stuttgart. The dynamics of the group's leadership, which was composed of Baader, his girlfriend Ensslin, and Meinhof, began finally to fray for good. Meinhof argued that they were not prepared enough. Baader blamed the group's failings on her and her alone. This fundamental change in the trio's working and personal relationship signaled the beginning of the end for the original generation of the RAF.

In early 1972, the RAF began a bombing campaign against U.S. military forces in West Germany, which was to include headquarter facilities, public areas of Hamburg, and eventually the Campbell Barracks of the U.S. Army. In total, these bombings killed four American officers, and wounded over four dozen others. During this period, the RAF received funding from the Soviet Union.

Following the bombings, the authorities cracked down. During a roundup of anarchists in June of 1972 Meinhof was arrested and detained. At first, the police were not aware of the high profile fugitive they had caught. Meinhof looked ill and thinner than their most recent pictures. Resisting to the end, she was finally and forcibly put under anesthesia so that an X-ray could be taken, confirming her identity due to the silver clamp inserted into her head a decade prior during her brain surgery.

What followed was perhaps the most bizarre episode in the story of Ulrike Meinhof, one so temptingly mysterious and unresolved that it is debated vigorously to this day. Traditionally, gang members, anarchists and the like end their days imprisoned or killed in action, but this was not the case for Ulrike Meinhof. From her arrest in 1972 to her death four years later she was incarcerated at a variety of institutions across Germany. Ultimately she severed all contact with her family, including her 10-year-old twins, refusing all correspondence and returning their gifts. It is debated whether her brain surgery in 1960 had some effect on her mental state.

The RAF trial took place at Stammheim prison in May 1975. Five members of the group were identified as its ringleaders and most dangerous: Andreas Baader, Gudrun Ensslin, Ulrike Meinhof, Hoger Meins and Jan-Carl Raspe. The courtroom was quite rowdy, more akin to a '90s American circus than a European courtroom trial. Attorneys were expelled. Ever the passionate revolutionaries, the five defendants often had to be removed from the proceedings. They admitted that they had conducted bombings and killings as part of a political campaign, but refused to admit they had committed any criminal acts. To the revolutionaries, it was all a justified means to an end. But there, the camaraderie and unity ended.

The infighting that the group had experienced at the time of their arrest intensified while they were in prison, particularly between the two women, Ensslin and Meinhof. The pair was cruel and petty with one another, even playing harsh tricks. Ensslin distanced herself from a particular attack; Meinhof was excluded from the trial for a short while. Cracks began to appear. Charges came against the group for the murders and attempted murders.

Then Ulrike Meinhof was found hanged dead in her cell.

The German government's actions were swift and resolute. A state autopsy was carried out. The official cause of death was suicide by hanging, a line that was also toed by German newspapers, many of which spoke of Meinhof's fractured state of mind at the time of her death.

Questions were raised regarding the circumstances. Though she was dispirited about the turns her trial was taking, and her rancor at her former RAF members, she did not appear to be suicidal, her prison captors noted. She reportedly told her older sister Weinke on her last visit, "You can stand up and fight only while you are alive. If they say I committed suicide, be sure that it was a murder."

Still, even after the mysterious death of Ulike Meinhof, the RAF continued its reign of terrorism across West Germany for more than a decade. This continued up until the fall of communism and reunification. With the defeat of the USSR, their major patron disappeared. Numerous films and TV shows were created about the RAF – even the American film *Die Hard*, with its main antagonist Hans Gruber, was inspired by the RAF.

Years later, in 2020, Ulrike's daughter Bettina Rohl wrote that the Red Army Faction did have a successor in modern society, and that spiritual heir is now called Antifa.

ELEVEN

CHILDREN OF MAO

While Germany was Antifa's cradle, its guiding philosophy and tactics were nursed in a very different place and culture, a half a world away; Communist China.

Mao Zedong's Cultural Revolution in the late sixties was determined to destroy every vestige of humanity's oldest cultures – and, to a remarkable degree, it succeeded.

America's social justice revolution shares features of the Chinese Cultural Revolution.

In the late 2010s, a soft Cultural Revolution began in the United States. The goal of the revolutionaries was insurrection, overthrow of the republic from within, and replacing it with a new order. In many ways, their tactics and concepts are similar to the Chinese Cultural Revolution under Chairman Mao Zedong. Chairman Mao destroyed traditional Chinese culture. He tore down statues; he tortured dissidents, priests, and intellectuals, anyone who stood in his way, anyone who stood against what was ordered by the communist dictatorship.

The Chinese Cultural Revolution lasted for a period of about 10 years from 1966 to 1976. The most turbulent years were roughly 1966 to 1968. The Holocaust Memorial Museum estimates the death toll of that period as between five and ten million. During that time, communist revolutionaries shut down nearly every school and institution of higher learning in the country. They destroyed Chinese culture, specifically ancient Chinese culture. Chairman Mao saw the destruction of the past as the only way forward for his progressive revolutionary movement. His destruction of Chinese culture is akin to what the far-left sought in the late 2010s – the destruction of American history and American culture.

The Cultural Revolution was an act of pure evil, and it happened to one of the largest groups of people in the world. Its victims were the Chinese people, the Laobaixing, the Old Hundred Names. Although the Cultural Revolution did not take place all that long ago, there are no movies about it, there are hardly any popular history books about it, and no one on the History Channel is talking about it. This is because Chinese money is everywhere in the media. As a result, no mainstream media outlets or Hollywood studios ever touch the Maoist Cultural Revolution.

Ancient Chinese history was attacked, destroyed, and systematically erased from modern China. Relics, paintings, statues, and old books were smashed and burned to ashes. This was not simply a by-product of the communist revolution; it was their specific and stated purpose. Not a flaw, but by design, statues were destroyed, temples burned, gravesites smashed, and even parts of the entire language itself transformed.

Mao mobilized militant youth socialists to carry out fanatic acts. The primary group Mao mobilized was known as the Red Guards (Hong Wei Bing). The Red Guards were an organization of Chinese youth that Chairman Mao directly set up to be his unquestioningly loyal soldiers in the streets. He did not trust the police and the military to do exactly what he wanted to the letter, so he bypassed them. Chairman Mao broadcast their extremist manifesto on national radio and had it printed in the official communist propaganda newspapers such as *The People's Daily*, using the slogans "bombard the headquarters" and "it is right to rebel." Mao called it "the great chaos under heaven."

The Cultural Revolution was Mao's way of re-asserting dominance over the regime following his fall from grace due to the disastrous effects of his Great Leap Forward: The famine that ensued in the 1950s resulted in the death of tens of millions of Chinese citizens.

Red Guard factions began to sprout up in every province and region. In May 1966, Mao's wife Jiang Qing and several top officials of the Chinese Communist Party formed the Cultural Revolution Group to start the campaign and mobilize the Red Guards.

The first step was taken on July 16, 1966, Chairman Mao swam in the Yangtze River, using the event to send the signal that the Cultural Revolution was to commence. He appeared in Tiananmen Square multiple times, donning the olive green uniform of the Red Guards and their signature armband. It is estimated that at his final rally on Nov. 25, 1966, he spoke to 2.5 million Red Guards. The mainstream media of the time all broadcast the ideals of the militants, and decried any who stood against them as "anti-socialists." Mao used the campaign to solidify these militant youth socialists against his critics in the party.

But the first aim of the Red Guards was to cleanse China of ancient culture. The Cultural Revolution represented a sort of sanitization process. The so-called Four Olds were specifically targeted: old ideas, old culture, old customs, and old habits.

In Shanghai, tens of thousands were forced from their homes and attacked in the streets, beaten or killed, and the ones who survived were exiled to the countryside. The Forbidden City itself in Beijing was almost destroyed by the militants, but only saved at the last minute by an order from a top party official. The excesses of violence, bloodshed, and murder only ended with the death of Chairman Mao. Some scholars refer to the Chinese Cultural Revolution as state terrorism.

If any monument, fixture, institution or structure was suspected of connection to ancient China, or traditional values, it was targeted for destruction. This targeting especially focused on Western influence. The Red Guards considered both ancient China and Western influence sources of anti-socialism and imperialism that needed to be cleansed from the land so that communism could be achieved. This also included Western religions; Christian churches were burned and Catholic nuns attacked. China's world-famous Peking Opera was banned, along with many classic plays. Homes were ransacked, belongings confiscated, and books designated as counter-revolutionary were piled up and burned in the street. These were not isolated events. This took place in every city, town, and village across China.

Individuals were isolated and put on public trial by the revolutionaries in what became known as struggle sessions.

As the Red Guards continued their destruction of property and history, they then turned to human beings whom they could pillory and destroy for their supposed crimes against the revolution. Public struggle sessions were the main vehicle for this persecution – mock trials where militants would hang a sign around the accused's neck, force him to kneel, and demand confessions, during which people denounced themselves and their past. In many cases, it was their own children and grandchildren who were leading the struggle sessions. These were ritual debasements that increased in violence as the Red Guards became more militant in their revolutionary act and more fervent in their cause.

In an interview with *Foreign Policy* magazine, a reporter asked his uncle about the Cultural Revolution, which started when he was just 18. He did not apologize for any excesses, including targeting his own grandfather for a struggle session. "We were loyal, and we were following Chairman Mao's guidelines," the former Red Guard explained, "and what's more important, we believed we were doing things that were good and meaningful."

During the Cultural Revolution, killings became the new normal. Many intellectuals, professors, factory managers, and teachers were targeted. Some were beaten and killed on their way to their struggle sessions. Many committed suicide before the militant youth could get their hands on them, or while held captive. Some were permitted to return home, some were sent off to labor camps and gulags. Li Zhengtian, a graduate student, was able to get an article printed criticizing the excesses of the revolution, but not Mao himself. Li was subjected to over 100 struggle sessions.

While most information about the Chinese Cultural Revolution is suppressed today by the Chinese Communist Party, one incident has leaked out, despite the party's best efforts. At the peak of the hysteria during the socialist campaign, anti-socialists were killed, their bodies defiled, and then they were eaten in what have become known as "human flesh banquets." This horrific phenomenon reportedly took place in the remote southeastern province of Guangxi.

According to a manuscript obtained by AFP, a retired CCP cadre wrote that during the Cultural Revolution in Guangxi:

"There were beheadings, beatings, live burials, stonings, drownings, boilings, group slaughters, disembowellings, digging out hearts, livers, genitals, slicing off flesh, blowing up with dynamite, and more, with no method unused."

In total, it is estimated that 100,000 to 150,000 people were slaughtered in Guangxi alone; women and teenage girls were subjected to public gang rapes and men were publicly castrated.

The Cultural Revolution was particularly brutal in Guangxi because two rival military and civilian factions emerged in the province, each purporting to be the true revolutionaries fighting to defend Chairman Mao. One faction supported General Wei Guoqing, the chairman of the province, and the other opposed him. The opposition faction was supported by Chinese Premier Zhou Enlai. These two factions then began waging war on one another, each receiving support from a civilian base in various parts of the province. Each accused the other of being counter-revolutionary traitors to Mao's socialist ideals.

According to documents smuggled out of China by Chinese scholar Zheng Yi after the Tiananmen Square Massacre, local government offices had investigated the ritual cannibalism in the 1980s and knew what had happened there.

The New York Times reported in 1993:

"At some high schools, students killed their principals in
the school courtyard and then cooked and ate the bodies
to celebrate a triumph over 'counterrevolutionaries,' the
documents report. Government-run cafeterias are said

to have displayed bodies dangling on meat hooks and to have served human flesh to employees."

"The incidents reported from Guangxi were apparently the most extensive episodes of cannibalism in the world in the last century or more. They were also different from any others in that those who took part were not motivated by hunger or psychopathic illness. Instead, the actions appeared to be ideological: the cannibalism, which the documents say took place in public, was often organized by local Communist Party officials, and people apparently took part together to prove their revolutionary ardor."

In 1993, journalist and scholar John Gittings visited Guangxi and spoke to a local who knew of the killings some 28-years earlier. The local told him, "We ate more people than anywhere else in China." (*The Guardian*, Nov. 27, 1993)

The Chinese military had to be called in to quell the Red Guards.

By 1968, even Chairman Mao had had enough. After his party rivals were purged or killed, Mao began calling for the Chinese military to come in and quell the militant Red Guard factions. It is reported that at one point, even Mao himself had to flee from violence in one city that had erupted without knowledge that the Great Helmsman was present. Mao's useful shock troops had served their purpose and now he wanted to be rid of the worst of them. The army was mobilized to confiscate weapons and ammunition from the Red Guards and to begin rounding up the youth.

But, instead of merely detaining leaders of the Red Guard, Mao ordered that all so-called urban youth were to be sent to the countryside to learn how to be farmers. In total, it is estimated 17 million Chinese youth were exiled from cities into the countryside and sent to work on farms. The cult of Mao, which focused upon his *Little Red Book*, brought its fervor and fanaticism to the communes, where they continued memorization and recitation contests of the chairman's work. The Cultural Revolution did not end with this act, but the frenzy of militarized and chaotic youth socialists were effectively purged from the cities and the revisionist cleansing greatly subsided thereafter.

There are surely many lessons to be learned from the Chinese Cultural Revolution. First and foremost, it is that the ruling class in a society has in the past used militant youth to serve as shock troops to achieve their ends. By militarizing the natural rebelliousness and impiety of teenagers to wage unrestricted war against a designated evil enemy or group of enemies, the powerful are able to risk awakening terrible destructive forces.

The Cultural Revolution was a deliberate act by Mao to cement his grip on power over the country by mobilizing youth radicals against his political enemies at a time when he felt threatened. The irony, of course, is that the Red Guards were fighting a revolution against their own fellow citizens in the service of the autocrat who controlled the regime. Their actions served only the interests of Mao, and when they were no longer useful, he purged them along with the rest of his foes. While the Red Guards were told they were fighting against the forces of capitalism and imperialism, their true victims were their own families, teachers, communities, and cultural history.

Caught up in the fervor of fighting a supposed evil, citizens killed their fellow citizens in peacetime and committed acts of ritualistic ideological cannibalism. As Hoffer wrote, not every movement needs a god, but every movement needs a devil. Politicians, media, activists, and authority figures must never again call upon and rile up these dark, primal forces. As history shows, the results are catastrophic.

The goal of the revolution is the revolution.

TWELVE

THE SIXTIES

If there is a clear and obvious antecedent to the Antifa movement in America, it is of course the extreme radicalism – and glorification of violence – of so many on the left in the sixties.

Those were, by any rational standard, agonizing years for America. Bogged down in an unwinnable war, its young men dying pointlessly in appalling numbers, the nation's social fabric was disintegrating. The bad news was never-ending. Race riots. Campuses under siege. Assassinations.

Yet, it speaks to the mindset of today's progressives – including the dominant voices in mainstream media – that that era is often recalled with great fondness; and to that of their children that they so openly envy their elders for having had the luck to live through it.

Nor are the happy memories focused just on the era's exploding sense of personal liberation or the decade-long bacchanalia of sex, drugs, rock and roll summed up in the word "Woodstock." Perhaps even more so, the aging Boomers speak wistfully of having been so "idealistic" back then, and "committed" to things larger than themselves in ways they've never been since. Even now, in their 60s and 70s, they invoke the buzzwords that set the adolescent mind aflutter – "peace," "social justice," "equality" – still not having learned that they are the same words that have been cynically mouthed by totalitarian leftists from time immemorial.

So a refresher on the radical activism of that time is perhaps in order.

As *The New York Times* wrote in a 2009 retrospective, by the end of the sixties, radical violence aimed at spurring "fear and anxiety" had become a regular feature of American life. "One study found that from January 1969 to October 1970, there were about 370 bombings — most of them minor — in New York, an average of more than one every other day…" Nationally, the numbers were just as staggering, a Senate report at the time having "concluded that from January 1969 to April 1970, the United States sustained 4,330 bombings — 3,355 of them incendiary, 975 explosive — resulting in 43 deaths and $21.8 million in property damage."

And there was more to come in the seventies and early eighties.

So routine was the violence, and so overwhelmed were the forces of order, that a great many remain unsolved to this day.

So let's just hit a few highlights, ones that made headlines at the time, and later even a few history books, before those got rewritten.

- On March 6, 1970, a Greenwich Village townhouse (next to one owned by newly-minted movie star Dustin Hoffman) was blown to smithereens, killing three of the young terrorists who'd been using it as a bomb-making factory.

- On Aug. 24, 1970, a bombing at Sterling Hall at the University of Wisconsin, in protest of the school's research for the military, killed 33-year-old postdoctoral researcher Robert Fassnacht and injured three others.

- On May 17, 1974, a shootout in Compton, California between police and the Symbionese Liberation Army – the radicals who kidnapped Patty Hearst months before – resulted in a fire that left six SLA members dead. The group had earlier murdered Oakland's superintendent of schools.

- On Jan. 29, 1975, a powerful bomb exploded in the headquarters of the United States Department of State in Washington, D.C. Though no one was killed, the damage to the building was great, extending over three floors – and the psychological implications even greater.

- On Oct. 20, 1981, in the bloodiest terrorist episode of the era, seven radicals robbed a Brink's truck in Nanuet, New York, killing a guard and two local policemen.

A fair number of the terrorist acts, including the Nanuet murders, and bombings of the United States Capitol, the Pentagon, and a New York City police station, were committed by the Weather Underground, the most notoriously cold-blooded radical sect of the time.

Yet the group's views on the changes needed in America, and even of the tactics essential to make them reality, were shared widely on the left. Many admired them as idealists, ready to put their lives on the line for the cause; they were the heroes of the much-lauded 1988 film *Running on Empty*, directed by Sidney Lumet and produced by

Naomi Foner, mother of current movie stars Maggie and Jake Gyllenhaal; as well as *The Weather Underground*, nominated in 2004 for an Oscar for best documentary.

Jeremy Varon, a historian at The New School and author of *Bringing the War Home: The Weather Underground, the Red Army Faction, and Revolutionary Violence in the Sixties and Seventies*, spoke of countless academics who came of age in that era, when he told *The Times*, without irony, that young people "will always be inspired by people of intense principles. The bombers represent the extreme edge of the commitment. They will for a long time be regarded for their generational mobilization. It's impressive to most people."

Like so many other violent radicals at the time, the Weathermen – they took their name from the Dylan lyric "It doesn't take a weatherman to know which way the wind blows" – were initially aligned with the Students for a Democratic Society (SDS).

It is hard to overstate the influence of SDS in fostering leftist thought in America. Established in 1960 to promote democratic socialism among American college students, by the late sixties it had chapters on campuses throughout the country; and by the end of the decade, as the war continued and with Richard Nixon in the White House, they had morphed into a virulently anti-democratic organization.

Still, inspired though it was by communist ideologies and dedicated to massive societal transformation, SDS did not move fast enough, or far enough, for many. At its final national convention in 1969, SDS imploded, splitting into rival factions. Theirs was a division of means, not ends; they shared a determination to impose their radical utopianism on an unwilling nation.

The smaller faction, the Revolutionary Youth Movement (RYM), foresaw a future race war, seeing the anarchy it would unleash as the best hope for revolutionary transformation. The larger group, calling themselves Progressive Labor (PL), was comprised of adherents of Chairman Mao and the Cultural Revolution, and favored more direct action. The Weathermen were prominent among these. "Our intention," as they proclaimed in their 1974 manifesto, *Prairie Fire*, "is to disrupt the empire ... to incapacitate it, to put pressure on the cracks."

In the wake of SDS's collapse, those who went underground and turned to outright violence were comparatively few in number. Most militants moved on to more or less normal lives, starting professional lives and families – but with their ideology intact. And in the decades that followed, a great many of them assumed positions of influence in the wider culture – in media and in entertainment on campuses nationwide. To cite a characteristic example, Todd Gitlin, former president of SDS, has taught journalism for nearly 20 years at Columbia University's prestigious journalism school. From this perch he not only teaches new generations of journalists that their job is to promote "social justice," but he also writes regularly for prestigious older publications like *The New York Times*, as well as books like *Occupy Nation: the Roots, the spirit and the Promise of Occupy Wall Street.*

Under the circumstances, it is unsurprising that mainstream reporting on Antifa has been not just dishonest as to its violent nature and horrific intentions, but – as when CNN compared its assaults on American cities to our soldiers fighting at Normandy – celebratory. After all, Gitlin and his like today hold total sway over both journalism instruction and its practice in mainstream newsrooms everywhere. Quite simply, whether they call it that, or even recognize it as such, many of these people are working tirelessly to impose on

America a softer version of the Cultural Revolution Chairman Mao imposed in China.

But for the soft revolutionaries, too, the end is socialism. Nor, in places like Los Angeles, Kansas City, and Charlotte do the Antifa groups with which they are allied even bother to pretend – they *call* themselves Red Guards.

During the Weather Underground's extended bombing campaign, one of its leaders was Bill Ayers. Even more than most radicals, who tended to come from middle and upper middle class backgrounds, Ayers was born to privilege, the son of the chairman and CEO of Chicago's Commonwealth Edison. But radicalized in college, he quickly rose to the top ranks of SDS, before turning to outright terrorism. Following his participation in the 1969 bombing of a monument to the Chicago police, he went underground with his Weathermen comrades. One of the three killed a year later in the explosion of the Greenwich Village bomb-making facility was his girlfriend, Diana Oughton. Incredibly, when he was finally caught three years later, Ayers got off due to FBI malfeasance, never serving a day for his crimes. "Guilty as sin, free as a bird," he later crowed. "America – what a country!"

Ayers and his wife, Bernadine Dohrn, also a former leader in the group, went on to raise the son of fellow terrorists Cathy Boudin and David Gilbert, both imprisoned for the murder of a guard during the Weathermen's robbery of the Brinks truck in Nanuet, New York. That son, Chesa Boudin, is today the San Francisco district attorney, in which role he has been conspicuously friendly toward criminals and fellow leftists.

What's even more incredible is that, working as a professor at the University of Illinois' College of Education, Ayers was able to repackage himself as an educational reformer, and became a leading voice in the leftist drive to remake American education, with an emphasis on the teaching of "social justice." Though as conservative education authority Sol Stern observed in 2008: "Calling Bill Ayers a school reformer is a bit like calling Joseph Stalin an agricultural reformer," his influence is today evident in classrooms around the country.

Like so much of the drastic cultural change of recent decades, this happened under the radar. Parents were startled when their child brought home *Heather Has Two Mommies* or to learn that their children were being taught that the founders were racist.

Only in 2008 did the former Weatherman Ayers once again come to meaningful public notice, and then in a wholly unexpected way. It turned out that he was a friend and neighbor of Barack Obama, then in the midst of his campaign for president. Moreover, there was soon speculation – based on the evidence, quite persuasive speculation – that Ayers had done much of the writing on the Obama's image-making best-seller *Dreams From My Father*.

True to form, as was also the case with Jeremiah Wright, the inflammatory radical who was Obama's longtime pastor, the media went to great lengths to minimize the relationship, and so did Obama himself. But there was no doubt the connection had been both strong and mutually advantageous.

While supposedly a mainstream politician, operating within the traditional rules of the arena, in fact Obama was something entirely new in our national life: a leader determined, as he boasted, to "fundamentally change America."

It is clear now that as a president he was, to put it generously, inept. He achieved almost none of his policy agenda, and since he was unwilling or too lazy to do the hard work of building consensus, what he did was mainly by executive order, which meant it would be readily undone by his successor. His one notable "achievement," Obamacare, passed on a straight party line vote after peddled to the public by lies, and has been a policy disaster and electoral albatross for the Democratic Party ever since.

Yet for all that, to a remarkable degree Obama did succeed in transforming America. By January 2013, at the time he ascended to the presidency, we as a society seemed to have largely moved beyond the most vexing and agonizing issue of all: race. But during the Obama years, Americans were set against one another on the issue to a degree we hadn't been since the sixties, and in new and virulent ways. Before Obama, Americans looked with pride on the reality that the number of actual racists in our midst was vanishingly small, and these had been banished to the extreme margins and darkest corners, despised pariahs afraid to emerge into the light. But under Obama, especially for the young and credulous, the very definition of racism was expanded, so as to encompass the tens of millions who disagreed with any aspect of their radical philosophy. Having arrived as a people at the understanding that race should be irrelevant – that each of us should be seen, and judged, as an individual – those years left millions believing that the very desire for color blindness was *prima facie* evidence of racism.

One after another, racial episodes threw the nation into turmoil – Trayvon Martin, Ferguson, Freddie Gray – with the pro-Obama media every time rushing to endorse the most irresponsible charges, especially against police. Black Lives Matter was born. Anti-white commentators, their bile unchecked, proliferated on CNN and MSNBC. In the schools, America's great historical figures came under systematic assault, condemned as racists by a generation of historical ignoramuses, their monumental achievements overlooked.

On the campuses, where of course such "thinking" thrived, a new terminology had to be created to express the horrors that lay in wait beyond, and even sometimes slipped within, the campus gates: "Micro-aggressions," "Trigger warnings," and "Institutional racism." For many, it became gospel that any speech with which they disagreed in the slightest was "hate speech."

Little wonder that so many of these young people became Antifa's shock troops, its thug enforcers, utterly convinced of the righteousness of the cause.

This last is key. Nurtured in the world of fiction over fact, and feelings over history, Antifa's radicals sincerely believe that anyone who does not support Black Lives Matter in every particular is a fascist. They cannot conceive of Republicans as NOT being a fascist; indeed, a closet supporter of Hitler. Their ideological opponents are not fellow citizens with a different point of view; they are enemies who must, at the very least, be silenced.

The culmination of the effort to revise Americans' understanding of our own past is the so-called 1619 Project, promulgated by "woke" activists/journalists at the vaunted *New York Times*, which asserts that the key moment in the nation's history was not 1776, but 1619, when the first slaves arrived on these shore, and that everything we know about America, its ideals and achievements, must be reevaluated and seen as a product of oppression. While this is so clearly far-fetched that even the nation's leading leftist historians have publicly described it as "a displacement of historical understanding by ideology," nonetheless it immediately became the centerpiece of history curricula in schools throughout the nation.

Meanwhile, the media daily reinforces the indifference to factual evidence essential to such a belief system. In the Ferguson case, for example, it only takes glancing familiarity with the grand jury transcripts to know why Officer Darren Wilson was not indicted for shooting Michael Brown; even African-American eyewitnesses who dislike the police acknowledged in sworn testimony that Officer Wilson was in imminent danger from Brown and that he acted in self-defense. But those crucial facts didn't penetrate the bubble constructed by Antifa and Black Lives Matter, in this and the notable cases that followed – not that it probably would have mattered anyway. "Facts," too, are instruments of the fascist capitalists in power.

THIRTEEN

GUIDING LIGHTS

E ven as Antifa carelessly tosses around the term fascism, the fact is vanishingly few Antifa militants have the slightest idea what fascism really is. But as a political philosophy, it has a clear and distinct meaning and history. First proposed by Benito Mussolini, at the time editor of a Socialist newspaper, the term refers literally to a bundle of sticks bound together, so stronger as a unit than individually. The idea was a nation could likewise be made powerful by surrendering individual autonomy, doing away with elections and giving power to the state. The primary difference between this dictatorial scheme and the Marxist idea resides in the fact that fascists allow for the existence of some private property (though it too is subordinate to the needs of the state) and their emphasis is on national and ethnic identity rather than class division.

That said, fascist and communist regimes tend to have much in common, starting with a totalitarian contempt for individual rights and freedoms, and when their ends were aligned, they have sometimes worked together, as did Nazi Germany and the Soviet Union in their joint invasion of Poland at the outset of World War II.

The truth is in their contempt for democratic norms and the readiness to use extreme violence to impose their will on their fellow citizens, those who now term themselves "Anti-fascists" are today's fascists.

And like the fascists of prior generations, they are easily manipulated and easily led by those casting blame on "the system," and preaching social utopia.

Individuals like Bob Avakian.

A relic of 1960s radicalism, Avakian is among those obscure radical figures who made a comeback in the age of Donald Trump. As chairman of the ultra-left organization Revolutionary Communist Party USA, aka RevCom, for decades he wandered along the furthest fringes of the far-left. Far younger-seeming than his 76 years, eyes alight with the fanaticism of revealed truth, invariably wearing a work shirt that looked like it dated to his student days at Berkeley, Avakian would speak to tiny groups in obscure meeting halls, trying to relight the flame that burned so brightly in his lost youth; preaching that the revolution was not only inevitable, but scientifically ordained.

True, even then he had a handful of fervent acolytes who shared his vision of himself as an epoch-changing figure. He is "the Karl Marx of our time...[offering a] new synthesis of communism," one proclaimed, following the publication of his book *The New Communism*, "a whole different framework, scientifically grounded, for human emancipation..." In a joint review, two others observed that no one had so brilliantly pointed the way to the "Actual Revolution" that would move us "beyond a world of oppression, exploitation, and domination."

Avakian got his start in revolutionary politics in the San Francisco Bay Area in the 1960s. In 1975, he worked with other activists to form the Revolutionary Communist Party (RCP) out of various smaller groups. However, many members left in 1976 following the death of Mao when Avakian opposed Deng Xiaoping for being too moderate and not sufficently loyal to Mao and the values of the Cultural Revolution. Deng later ordered the Tiananmen Square Massacre. Avakian led the RCP through various protests over the years, but it was in 2016 that his organization broke out as a leader in the American antifascist movement.

Soon after President Trump was inaugurated, Avakian seized the opportunity to found Refuse Fascism. With the aid of self-proclaimed antifascists Carl Dix and Sunsara Taylor, it soon emerged as one of Antifa's leading American outfits, and its website today lists active chapters in Atlanta, Austin, Boston, Chicago, Cleveland, Detroit, Honolulu, Houston, Indianapolis, Los Angeles, New York, Philadelphia, San Francisco, Seattle and Tucson.

Refuse Fascism received funds from the Alliance for Global Justice (AFGJ). The AFGJ in turn, according to Influence Watch, is sponsored by the Open Society Foundations, Tides Foundation, Arca Foundation, Surdna Foundation, Public Welfare Foundation, and the Brightwater Fund. AFGJ has been aligned with numerous left-wing authoritarian regimes such as Castro's Cuba, Maduro's Venezuela, the Sandinistas of Nicaragua, North Korea, and has provided financial support for anti-Israel groups.

Today Avakian speaks to crowds of hundreds, often on college campuses, and his audiences are more receptive than ever.

In some respects, Refuse Fascism's thinking was the same as that of every other element of the Resistance: Trump was a monster and (never mind that he was duly elected, largely by the working class they saw as their primary constituency), he had to be removed from office by any means necessary.

From the first, Refuse Fascism made it clear they were not to be outdone in their radicalism. Though they publicly claim to favor "non-violent" action, starting with the mayhem aimed at disrupting Trump's inauguration, they have also somehow been prominent participants in every action involving Antifa violence since. "These fascists are serious," longtime Avakian ally and anti-cop activist Carl Dix proclaimed in 2017. "And we must wake up and confront them with resistance that is just as serious."

Avakian himself, meanwhile, was quite candid about the opportunity Trump offered for the growth of radicalism both in today's America and worldwide. "We need to be on a mission to spread the word, to let people know that we have the leadership, the science, the strategy and program… " he told an enthusiastic crowd (who did not have to be reminded who that "leadership" would be) …."A crucial next step is that thousands need to be organized into the ranks of the revolution now, while millions are being influenced in favor of this revolution."

Of course, Avakian is hardly the only such Antifa leader to emerge in recent years. Among others, there is Shanta Driver, National Chair of By Any Means Necessary (BAMN), also openly communist and eagerly engaged in the recruitment of the impressionable young. Initially formed by former members of the Revolutionary Workers League and the Trotskyite League, BAMN has been especially active on the West Coast, with another leading member, Berkeley Middle School teacher Yvette Felarca, having repeatedly faced charges for acts of violence throughout northern California.

Notably, Felarca has also been suspended for taking her middle school students to Antifa rallies.

Perhaps strangest of all were documents uncovered by the *Daily Caller* in 2017 that connected BAMN's leaders to the pro-pedophilia organization NAMBLA, the North American Man Boy Love Association.

According to internal newsletters, one of the founders of BAMN was also a supporter and lawyer for NAMBLA, a woman who once openly commented: "As an activist in the legal and political struggle for lesbian/gay rights and for freedom of sexual expression, I am here to support NAMBLA and to demand that the witch-hunt against it must be stopped. The media and police are targeting NAMBLA because it stands for the rights of young people to have consensual sex with whomever they want.

"Denying youth their sexuality or driving sexual expression deeper and deeper underground will not stop child molestation. I call on all progressive people in the lesbian/gay community, in the women's movement, and in the community at large to defend NAMBLA and its right to advocate for consensual sex regardless of age, and to unite our forces to make a fight for the real solutions to sexual coercion and abuse." Truly terrifying sentiments.

For even as Antifa continues to draw attention in its ongoing fight against "fascist" America, its larger mission, expanding and growing their militant ranks of those ready to dedicate themselves to revolution, is never out of view.

"Whatever part of the country we are in, and whatever the size of our forces at any given time," Avakian proclaims, "we are doing all this as part of a national movement, together with people in other parts of the country, aiming to impact all of society, and building a revolution to impact the whole system, with the whole world in mind."

Once potential recruits are found, the crucial next step is drawing them further in through "revolutionary clubs," whose purpose is to enhance "commitment to the revolution...under the leadership of the Revolutionary Communist Party."

In short, these are a form of indoctrination session.

Whether under the auspices of Avakian's Revolutionary Communist Party or BAMN or the more palatable sounding Democrat Socialists of America, they are all pretty much the same, which is to say mind-numbingly long, humorless and filled with revolutionary jargon.

Trust me, I've been to a few.

What, precisely, happens? Not much. Speakers drone on about their particular ideological preoccupations, discussing minor matters of doctrine in fine detail. They talk interminably about the horrors inflicted by capitalism, and denounce everyone and everything as racist and sexist. They agree that all divisions of class, race and sex will be gone once the current unjust system is annihilated and replaced by the just one they have in mind.

Disagreement is not expected. After all, many of these "ideas" have already been force-fed to the impressionable young who are present through the American educational system and their years at college. Once they've gotten this far, they pretty much swallow it whole. Certainly few are aware that regimes like the one intended for their homeland have killed tens of millions in the past, and continue to enthusiastically murder today; or if they do know, they readily accept the explanation that those deaths were necessary.

Avakian was asked once whether what he was leading was, in fact, a cult of personality, the unabashed Maoist replied, "I certainly hope so — we've been working very hard to create one."

He wasn't joking – apparently Avakian never jokes.

Yet he also knows that in the age of Antifa, for many attendees, the theoretical stuff is secondary, as it is also for the leadership. For these sessions – and especially the group discussions with which they usually conclude – serve an additional and, for now, even more pressing purpose.

They help sort out the new recruits by their level of commitment.

As Avarkian avers, individuals' "commitment to the revolution" vary from person to person; in most it must be "awakened and brought forward… yes, by struggle, even at times by sharp struggle…" Thus, some "can start with basic tasks, which they can readily carry out, and feel confident, doing…. The important thing is that they are part of the process of building the revolution…. "

Others, however, more advanced in their commitment and less afflicted by hesitation and doubt, are ready for more direct action.

As one who has himself walked the walk – Avarkian was charged with assaulting a cop as far back as 1979 – few are better placed to make such distinctions.

Having closely observed recruits in these sessions, leaders classify them as red, yellow and green.

The Reds, those deemed ready to engage in masked acts of violence, are the sort of young men found outside bars and nightclubs in any city in America spoiling for a fight, or in the early morning hours, brawling.

A chilling undercover video put out by investigative journalist James O'Keefe's Project Veritas, in which a Project Veritas reporter took an Antifa "self-defense" class, revealed their methods; "self-defense" is obviously an Orwellian construction, as the instruction was in how to inflict pain on others. Surrounded by uniformed Antifa members, an instructor showed the undercover reporter how to "get a good kidney or liver shot. It's pretty much crippling them. They're going to be doubled over and in a lot of pain. [Or] if you break one of the floating ribs, which are small and right down here….” at which, the instructor guided all present in the fine points of finding the right ribs to shatter. “Those are also very painful,” he added helpfully. “It's hard to move after that, to catch a breath. Give one good body shot [which] could give you all the time in the world to run away while they're doubled over in pain, or really put a beating on them after that if you really want to make it personal.”

The Yellows are the organizing and recruiting tier. They do not participate in the direct violence, but they are fully aware of it and coordinate it, to enable the Reds to move in on a target and inflict further damage.

Greens, while in sympathy with their bolder comrades, prefer to hold back from direct participation in such activities. They will, however, aid the cause by serving in multiple ways as advocates for the group. Greens often appear on TV and other media as “eyewitnesses,” casting Antifa's behavior in a favorable light. Away from the action, they spread the word through publishing operations and journals; through teaching jobs at high schools and as tenured faculty at universities; or, when called upon, act as legal counsel for arrested members; increasingly, they run for office.

Project Veritas also captured on video a national organizer for Refuse Fascism named Andy Zee discussing a plan to meet with liberal billionaire Tom Steyer. Noting that Steyer was re-tweeting his far left political statements, Zee correctly speculated that Steyer was planning to run for political office, and recognizing that Steyer's political ambitions were subject to manipulation, suggested he might be able to pressure him to fund Antifa front groups.

Perhaps most ominously, the greens doxx – i.e., publish information regarding the whereabouts of patriotic, law-abiding people as a means to place them in danger of physical assault or as psychological intimidation, all perpetrated behind a cloak of anonymity. Nothing more fully puts on display Antifa's mix of cowardice and hate. Horrific examples abound, targeting the well known and obscure alike. During the contentious Kavanaugh hearings, doxxers published the home addresses of Republican Senators Orrin Hatch, Mike Lee and Lindsay Graham online, the information having been stolen by a former Senate aide who broke into a private office to steal it. Other leftists doxxed Senators Ted Cruz and Cory Gardner, and by way of suggesting what might be coming their way, Gardner's wife was sent a video of a beheading.

At the same time, the Kavanaugh hearings prompted an Antifa group at the University of Texas to target incoming freshmen with conservative views before they had even arrived on campus, publishing their names and phone numbers; and to identify and denounce as fascist hatemongers members of the Young Conservatives of Texas (YCT). They further declared they would doxx anyone who joined YCT; tried to get a pro-Kavanaugh student fired from her off-campus job; and encouraged UT coeds to "report" on would-be conservatives. The Antifa group's website includes a section on how to go about doxxing, its enthusiastic title reading, "Research & Destroy."

Similar incidents have taken place at other colleges – far too many to list.

Trust me, speaking from personal experience, to be a victim of doxxing is nothing short of terrifying. In my case, it came via posters with my picture placed by Antifa on D.C. streets. They called for unspecified "action" to be taken against me. Similar posters featured photos of Tucker Carlson and Trump administration staffer Stephen Miller. Antifa members also posted our home addresses and other personal information online, the obvious hope being we would be attacked and, perhaps, killed.

And, too, needless to say, ICE agents have been especially at risk, with an Antifa militant in New York placing the names and large amounts of personal information on 1,595 ICE agents online. Other Antifa members called him a "hero."

Among Antifa's most aggressive doxxers is Jessica Nocero who, before she was identified, went by the pseudonym Fallon. A member of the Great Lakes Antifa chapter, she claimed to have taught more than 300 other Antifa members across the country how to go about finding people's names and hunting down their home addresses, places of work and employers, email addresses and phone numbers. Those, in turn, trained more doxxers.

Antifa leader Daryle Lamont Jenkins is another prominent doxxer, via the One People's Project website. Celebrated on the Left for his efforts, Jenkins appears on MSNBC's Joy Reid and Rachel Maddow shows, treated with respect by the hosts for his efforts exposing "white supremacists"; this despite, by his own admission, the fact that Jenkins used to regularly doxx Right to Life activists. Jenkins claims that he recently took down the profiles of anti-abortion activists. However, questions once arose that one of Jenkins' doxxing targets had committed suicide. Jenkins responded: "If he did commit suicide after being doxxed, my attitude is: Thank you."

In what otherwise might have been taken as a comic twist, at the time of the Charlottesville riots, the Antifa doxxing Twitter account publicly confused a University of Arkansas biomedical engineering professor named Kyle Quinn, who had spent the day gazing at paintings with his wife at the Crystal Bridges Art Museum in Bentonville, Arkansas, with the aforementioned Benton. As a result, he faced multiple threats and he and his wife had to go into hiding.

Perhaps the most notorious of all left-wing doxxers is Shaun King, a social media activist and conspiracy theorist who enjoys such a following among progressives that he was honored by John Legend at a Black Entertainment Television awards ceremony and asked to give the commencement address at New York's City College. King has a particular animus toward police, and has falsely accused a number of them of heinous acts. For instance, he doxxed Texas state trooper Daniel Hubbard, accusing him of having kidnapped and raped a black woman he'd pulled over for drunk driving. Fortunately, the officer was wearing a body cam, proving the charge false – but not before Hubbard received countless death threats.

There are innumerable such cases. Yet, when they are revealed, usually through police proceedings, Antifa militants complain their privacy has been violated. They also routinely stop photojournalists from taking their photos, even to the point of physical violence.

What might be most revealing is that in this they are completely sincere. Victimhood is all they know, it is how they are defined; it is what the Antifa leaders preach, and what has brought them into the movement. It is why the oppressive America where they live must be fought and remade.

And, lest we forget, these are the greens, the least dangerous of the bunch.

FOURTEEN

THE ROJAVA REVOLUTION

In the late 2010s, Antifa actually attempted something new. The movement tried their hand at creating their own state, in the unlikeliest of locales: The Autonomous Administration of North and East Syria, a region about half the size of Belgium, colloquially known as Rojava, in the borderlands of Iraq, Syria, and Turkey.

Antifascists constantly view the Spanish Civil War as a romantic and noble cause. While the world tends to focus more on the events of WWII than the 1936 Spanish Civil War, the latter is seen as something of a prelude – for Antifa it is their lodestar. In their view, the conflict was the just cause of noble antifascists from throughout the West rising up and traveling to Spain to fight the onslaught of the fascist takeover.

While, of course, that is not exactly the true historical record – nor were the Republicans ultimately successful – it is certainly true that many notable figures traveled to participate in that conflict, such as the writers Ernest Hemingway, George Orwell, and anarchist Arthur Lehning. The Spanish Republican foreign allies formed "International Brigades" that held as many as 50,000 members, with over 15,000 dying in the conflict. The International Brigades were strongly supported by the Soviet Union with arms, logistics, intelligence, and officers of the NKVD, the feared internal security force of the USSR. The largest number of communist members came from France, Italy, Germany, and areas of Eastern Europe.

Antifa has always looked for ways to rekindle those glory days of 1930s antifascism on the battlefield, and in the mid 2010s found an unlikely location: the Syrian Civil War.

Interestingly, many media outlets have actually reported on Americans and Europeans who have headed over to Syria to fight in the Civil War. This was the first time since the Spanish Civil War that leftists actually attempted to enact their own nation state. Naturally, the anarchist left who could afford to travel wasn't far behind. In Syria, they formed the "International Freedom Brigades" as an umbrella to encompass the various groups of left-wingers attracted to the borderlands of Iraq, Syria, and Turkey.

But, because those heading over to Rojava were predominantly left-wingers fighting jihadists, outlets like *Rolling Stone* and *Vice* fawned over them.

A 2017 headline in *Rolling Stone* gushed, "The Anarchists vs. the Islamic State. On the front lines of Syria with the young American radicals fighting ISIS." This bit about one of the recruits is particularly poignant: "He lived in San Francisco, where he arranged flowers for a living. Before that, he was a self-described lumpenproletariat, a lowlife punk and petty criminal with a heroin habit who started reading Marx and Lenin seriously in rehab. Once sober, he got involved in leftist causes, marching for tenants' rights, blocking evictions, protesting police brutality."

Vice, of course, also got in on the PR train for the anarchist left on the battlefield, with 2017's "The Most Feminist Revolution the World Has Ever Witnessed - In Rojava, a Kurdish anarchist collective led by women is at the heart of the fight with ISIS, and behind a political upheaval putting equality front and centre."

What was going on was actually more interesting than any of those outlets cared to investigate. While it is true that some veterans, conservatives, and right-wing individuals also traveled to Syria to fight ISIS, it is very interesting to note the motivations behind left-wing activists traveling to the war zone.

Many of these left-wing activists were anarchists, communists, and antifascists. In their view, the jihadist group ISIS constituted a fascist regime, as did the Syrian government.

These anti-fascists and anarchists were not traveling simply to liberate the people of Syria. Their goal was to constitute a new stateless anarchist country in Northern Syria. They called this goal the Rojava Revolution.

While no official figure was ever given for the number of foreign fighters mobilized for this effort, some academic sources have reported that as many as 800 took part in the fighting, mostly within a unit organized by the Kurds called the people protective unit (YPG) International Freedom Battalion, or the female version of the unit, the YPJ or women's protective unit. According to a study by Kings College of London, the majority of foreign fighters were American (173). Next most numerous were British, French, Canadian and

German volunteers; only a miniscule number came from Africa and Asia.

For left-wing foreign fighters, the cause was not religious or ethnic; it was ideological. One of the largest and most infamous Kurdish militia groups is the terrorist-designated PKK (thus labeled by Turkey, the EU, and the United States). Within Syria, their forces took on the name YPG to escape scrutiny; however, the connection between the groups is well known. The founder of the PKK is a communist radical, Abdullah Ocalon, who preaches a new brand of communism known as Democratic Confederalism, based on writings he made in 2011. It's a departure from Marxist-Leninism in that instead of calling for a Stalinist authoritarian national state, Ocalon argues for abolition of the state itself in favor of municipal, community councils on a neighborhood level, which some proponents have likened to the Greek city-states, such as Athens. These ideas were inspired by Murray Bookchin, an American anarchist and professor, and considered one of the founders of "libertarian socialism." Ocalon studied him while in prison.

Kevin Jochim, a German volunteer for YPG who was killed in Syria, gave a belief in democratic confederalism as his motivation when he traveled to Syria and joined the battle. He claimed that the "Rojava Revolution provided a once-in-a-lifetime opportunity to carry out Öcalon's theories."

In 2016, the socialist magazine *Jacobin* wrote: "Rojava hopes to remain an autonomous region in a preserved Syrian state. There, citizens would enjoy equal rights, regardless of ethnicity, gender, or religion. The economy would be organized to serve the whole community with an emphasis on cooperative ventures. An intricate network of elected councils would hold political power." In this way, the movement claims it is building "democracy without the state," since its structure would supposedly eliminate the kind of coercion that gives most states their power. This model, following the party's leader Abdullah Öcalan's ideology, is called a confederal democracy.

For recruiting international foreign fighters, the PKK/YPG are pretty much like everyone else in the world these days. They use social media. Some of their Facebook pages are "YPG International," "Save Kobani," and "The Lions of Rojava." These pages include various examples of classic war propaganda, radicalization videos, and ideological indoctrination, centered around the cult of personality of Abdullah Ocalan.

Some recruits travel to Syria via Turkey – much in the same fashion as ISIS foreign fighters traveling to join the Civil War. However, due to Turkish border enforcement, newer fighters have traveled via Erbil or Sulaymaniyah in Iraq and then overland into Syria. The high cost of a plane ticket from America or Europe to Iraq shows that this is not exactly the working-class rung of society who is getting involved.

According to *Rolling Stone*, "All volunteers arriving in Rojava attend a month-long training course at a place called the Academy, an oil facility with four concrete buildings, running water, intermittent electricity, a laundry line and a potato patch." The training consists of both communist ideological indoctrination and military tactics. Additionally, during training many of the recruits are given Kurdish names and encouraged to learn some of the language. To this day, Antifa militants in the West can be seen wearing Kurdish scarves at events on both coasts.

Foreign antifascist fighters are taught to use rifles, heavy machine guns, and mortars; bomb-making/improvised explosive devices; battlefield maneuver tactics; battlefield communication; and other war skills from PKK/YPG. In some cases, because certain foreign volunteers have received training from American military forces and NATO allies, the training and field operations these antifascist fighters receive will have ultimately come from American and NATO sources, tailored to the specific needs of the PKK/YPG battlefield. This aspect of the situation cannot go overlooked – that American and European antifascists are traveling overseas to attend training camps with a group linked to designated terrorists. The fact that the ideology is communist and not radical Islam should not matter in the eyes of the law – this is training with a foreign terrorist organization. For now, the majority of federal law enforcement has looked the other way as these fighters have traveled to these training camps and then returned home with training and real-world battlefield experience they can pass on to their networks within North America and Europe.

For those who embrace Ocalan's cult of personality, Rojava becomes central to their identity as the new frontier of socialism and revolution in the world. This is why Rojava is so important to the Antifa movement around the world. The Rojava Revolution is seen as their last best chance at creating a society designed around their radical goals and beliefs, and even those who do not actively take part in the conflict regularly post about it and support it, especially when it is threatened from external forces – usually Turkey, the traditional foe of the PKK. Ocalan himself is still imprisoned by Turkey for his terrorist acts.

Here is what the anarcho-communist blog *Internationalist Commune* wrote about the Rojava Revolution:

"Internationalism is an essential dimension in the history of revolutionary movements, and Rojava is today writing an important chapter. From the First International Association of Workers to the Tri-Continental Conference, from the 50,000 of the International

Brigades who travelled to Spain to fight fascism in 1936, to the 500,000 Cuban revolutionaries who travelled to Africa to support decolonisation struggles, from the solidarity with the resistance in Vietnam to the antiglobalisation movements, from the revolutionary inter-communalism of the Black Panthers to the solidarity with Palestinian revolutionary resistance. Rojava is today's heritage of this history of internationalism, and we are called to play our role in it."

As mentioned before, the International Freedom Battalion is the umbrella under which the majority of foreign antifascist fighters in Syria are organized. While the IFB includes Turks, they are joined by several groups from North America and Europe as well. Of course, the IFB's name was inspired by the communists who traveled to fight in the Spanish Civil War.

Organized at some point around 2015, the Bob Crow Brigade is sometimes referred to as the BCB. It is primarily a group of British and Irish antifascists and takes its name from a former British union leader who admired the foreign fighter communists of the Spanish Civil War. The group is best known for its media stunts, and harsh criticism of British politicians and economic systems.

The French version of the BCB is the Henri Krasucki Brigade, also known as the BHK. Henri Krasucki was a union leader as well as a communist. Like the BCB, the group is known for their media stunts and criticism of French politicians and economic systems. The BHK has attempted to raise funds for medical supplies to Rojava, and has launched numerous campaigns targeting French supporters.

Antifascist International Tabur is also known as The International Revolutionary People's Guerilla Forces (IRPGF). Their recruits are avowed Antifa members from the United States and Europe who have traveled to Syria and train with PKK/YPG fighters. While PKK is a terrorist-designated group, these foreign fighters face little legal scrutiny upon returning home. They are adept at social networking and tap into the vast social media web of Antifa and Antifa-supporting groups that are permitted to organize freely on major platforms like Facebook, Twitter, and Instagram.

The Revolutionary Union for Internationalist Solidarity (Επαναστατικός Σύνδεσμος Διεθνιστικής Αλληλεγγύης) is a Greek anarcho-communist group that has also supplied recruits for the revolutionaries in Rojava, receiving training from PKK/YPG.

While noting that the phenomenon has yet to be observed on a large scale, *The Journal for Deradicalization* warned: "There is a risk that post-war anarchists, with experience in the battlefield, might return to their countries and continue their war... In light of the war in Syria and the presence of anarchists on the battlefronts, such as the IRPGF, another challenge is embodied in the potential of post-war anarchists or anti-fascists organizing themselves in paramilitary groups, similar to some anarchists in the United States. With their experience, these veterans can build terrorist networks that one day might participate in riots or even a revolt against the state from within."

The Al-Sarq Forum shares the same concerns, but notes that so far, the observable pattern for Antifa war veterans is usually to take on a symbolic role as an activist abroad for PKK/YPG, spreading the message of terrorist leader Abdullah Ocalan, and also building networks of both financial backers and ideological allies for their revolutionary cause. Additionally, these veterans recruit future members to travel to Rojava, receive training, and take part in the fighting. These activists glorify the cause of Rojava, and especially lionize those who died on the battlefield as martyrs. These activist-recruiters have appeared on major media platforms in their home countries but have not faced serious legal repercussions for taking part in active armed conflict with a terrorist-linked group. Some cases have been sought, only to be later dropped or dismissed; however, some are pending. In fact, their media appearances serve to aid their financial network growth and offer further opportunities for recruiting.

At the time of this writing, there has been a massive development to Northern Syria. This followed the decision of President Trump to pull American forces (who had been defending key locations in and around Rojava following the battlefield defeat of ISIS) out of the area. This effectively ended the Obama-era policy of an unofficial alliance between the United States and the YPG – one that many have noted was destined for friction due to the YPG's close links to the PKK. Following the pullout of American troops, Turkish forces pushed further south than ever before, establishing an exclusion zone on the Syrian side of the border.

This dynamic left the YPG without its major military patron, while facing down their longtime regional adversary of Turkey. In order to deal with this new reality, the YPG's political leaders were forced to make a deal with the government of Syria to allow the region to come under the protection of Syrian patrols, augmented by Russian troops and mercenaries.

This new political situation will undoubtedly require Rojava to fall more and more under Syrian sovereignty, and may well end their experiment at stateless democratic confederalism, though some international forums have attempted to pressure the Syrian government to allow some form of this autonomy to continue.

And naturally, Antifa groups around the world reacted with outrage that President Trump would pull American soldiers from the line of fire at the frontlines of their regional and ideological struggle. American forces were in a desert borderland far removed from the American homeland. Antifa groups denounced the decision, yet few members seemed interested in taking up arms against the Turkish, Syrian, and Russian armed forces now vying for control over the land. It remains to be seen if Antifa will lash out at Turkish or American interests abroad in solidarity with their allies in Syria. However, this threat has the potential for playing out if Western governments continue to ignore the illegal actions of these militant groups. The fact that Antifa members have traveled to the Middle East to train with a terrorist-linked group would easily be grounds for declaring Antifa an international terrorist organization. But to date, no Western governments have shown interest in confronting this real and growing threat.

FIFTEEN

CAMPUS GROUND ZERO

If Antifa can be said to have anything akin to a base of operations, it is on the campuses of Western universities. They are at once a vast network of like-minded true believers and venues where organizing – and sometimes direct action – can occur without excessive scrutiny.

Let's put it this way:

In 2014, the University of Chicago, long a bastion of free thought, issued what soon came to be known as The Chicago Statement.

Responding to the obvious and growing intolerance at America's colleges and universities toward anyone challenging prevailing orthodoxies, especially on the hot button issues of race, gender and sexual orientation, it forthrightly declared: "Because the University is committed to free and open inquiry in all matters, it guarantees all members of the University community the broadest possible latitude to speak, write, listen, challenge, and learn . . . . It is not the proper role of the University to attempt to shield individuals from ideas and opinions they find unwelcome, disagreeable, or even deeply offensive."

This statement embodied classical liberal thought, and many of its creators expected it would be widely embraced as a model by colleges and universities across the country.

Not quite.

Forbes headlined a report three years later: "35 Universities Adopt 'The Chicago Statement' On Free Speech – 1,606 To Go."

What the timid response to the Chicago statement showed was how pervasive and deeply embedded illiberal orthodoxy has become on campuses large and small throughout the West. Many colleges, to a greater or lesser degree, today preach dogma dressed up as learning.

Even those administrators who recognize that their campuses double as training and recruitment centers for far-left extremism seldom do anything about it. To the contrary, many have made it abundantly clear that when it comes to Donald Trump – and the so-labeled "hate speech" he supposedly engenders – they agree with Antifa.

As the Manhattan Institute's Heather Mac Donald points out, college administrators, the vast number of whom were hired on to expand and enforce programs of "diversity" and "multiculturalism," tend to be even further left than faculty. In the open-air indoctrination center that is the modern college campus, administrators are the ones most certain to see people of color as oppressed by definition. The same administrators soon came to see any male student accused of sexual assault as an immediate and obvious offender, and traditional ideals such as due process and evidence gathering were thrown right out the window.

As they said in Soviet Russia, and in Adam Schiff's America, "Show me the man, I'll show you the crime."

It is little wonder that such star chambers turn out many of the eager recruits so readily drawn to Antifa. At the end of four years, the independent-minded have been converted, crushed, or learned to keep their mouths shut. As my friend, author Kurt Schlichter observes, they are "dreary conformity factories," promoting "indoctrination designed to manufacture a generation of goose-stepping creeps who use their bizarre collection of buzzwords and fetishes as weapons to suppress any kind of dissent. And the problem is that this PC Nazism is not just limited to academia...."

What once would have been unthinkable is today's reality: the new moral imperialism of social justice – with its byzantine rules and tortuous belief systems – is no longer limited to admissions offices, faculty lounges and student unions, but has taken firm root everywhere, from media and politics, to Silicon Valley, to the military, to certain religions, and up to and including the boardrooms (and HR departments) of the nation's major corporations. Today's titans of business are cowed by the rampaging forces of illiberal political correctness marketed as social justice, and the shock troops of their movement: Antifa.

As Heather Mac Donald ruefully observes, "Every mainstream institution is either furiously revising its standards or finds itself in the crosshairs for failing to do so."

The fear is everywhere, and growing. Anyone in a position of authority anywhere risks being declared guilty of thoughtcrime or wrong speech.

And there's no end in sight. With every graduating class, newly-minted leftist authoritarians take their places in the world at large; even as, back at their alma maters, they are replaced by fresh undergraduates getting hands-on training in social justice doctrine (in the classroom) and methods of suppression (when dissident voices dare to make themselves heard). However inadvertently, America's campuses are the prime site both for Antifa's recruitment efforts and for many of its most successful actions; successful, at least, in the attention they have generated and the fear they have spread.

By now, the list of colleges where conservative speakers have been deplatformed, or worse, is so mind-numbingly long that it might be easier to name the handful where different perspectives have been welcomed. Nonetheless, a few notable lowlights – just confining ourselves to the early months, when the intolerable reality of Donald Trump's having actually taken office had hard-left activists at the boiling point:

- On Feb. 1, 2017: Violent protests in Berkeley forced the cancellation of a speech by writer and activist Milo Yiannopoulos, causing $100,000 worth of damage. The Oakland-based Antifa group Black Bloc, along with BAMN (the acronym for By Any Means Necessary), masked and uniformed in black, arrived several hundred-strong on the campus, hijacking what had been planned as a peaceful protest, and the school's administrators removed Yiannopoulos from campus "out of concern for public safety." During the hours of violent protests, Antifa threw Molotov cocktails, set fires and threw rocks at police.

- On March 2, 2017 on the other side of the republic, American Enterprise Institute scholar Charles Murray was prevented from speaking at Vermont's Middlebury College when a mob numbering more than 400, mostly students and some in Antifa uniform, shouted him down; the protest reportedly was organized by a local branch called the Green Mountain Anti-Fascist Collective. Murray and a Middlebury professor who was to conduct a Q&A with Murray were forced to relocate to a campus TV studio for their conversation, and when leaving the building were assaulted by infuriated protesters. Grabbing the hair of the professor, a liberal named Alison Stange, they violently jerked back her hair, leaving her seriously injured with a concussion. The alleged "racist," Murray, is the father of two mixed race children.

- On April 6, 2017 the brilliant Manhattan Institute scholar Heather Mac Donald gave a speech at UCLA that "descended into chaos," noted *The College Fix*, "as Black Lives Matter protesters stormed the stage."

Author of the best-selling *The War on Cops*, Mac Donald is utterly fearless. Among her many heresies was her statement that "left-wing activists masquerading as professors are infiltrating traditional academic departments or creating new ones — such as 'Solidarity and Social Justice' — to advance their cause. They are entering the highest circles of college administration. From these perches, they require students to take social justice courses, such as 'Native Sexualities and Queer Discourse' or 'Hip-hop Workshop,' and attend social-justice events in order to graduate. But social justice education is merely a symptom of an even deeper perversion of academic values: the cult of race and gender victimology aka 'diversity.'"

In the question and answer session at UCLA an angry black student demanded to know whether she thought "black victims killed by cops" matter, Mac Donald, typically, held her ground: "Yes. And do black children that are killed by other blacks matter to you?" The audience greeted this, reported *The College Fix*, with "gasps and angry moans and furious snaps." Mac Donald had to be escorted from the hall under guard.

The next evening, at nearby Claremont-McKenna College, would prove far worse, what Mac Donald herself described as an "exercise of brute totalitarian force." Antifa protesters shut down her speech, loudly threatening her as she waited in the auditorium and assaulting those attempting to enter. "This is not just my loss of free speech," she said. "These students are exercising brute force against their fellow students to prevent them from hearing me."

- On May 23, in Olympia, Washington's Evergreen State College, about 50 activist students invaded biology professor Bret Weinstein's class, screaming "You support white supremacy!" and "Stop telling people of color they are f**king useless," and "Get the f**k out!" His crime? Sending out an email opposing the college-sponsored "A Day of Absence," whereby white students and faculty were expected to leave campus for a day so POC (correctese for People of Color) could reflect on their victimhood in isolation. A left/liberal civil libertarian, who a year earlier had supported Bernie Sanders, Weinstein wrote: that "encouraging" whites to stay away was "an act of oppression in and of itself . . . On a college campus, one's right to speak — or to be — must never be based on skin color." As a result, over the following days he was besieged by protesters and demands for his resignation, finally leaving campus for his own safety. In the end, he and his wife, also a professor, left the school entirely.

This is just a handful of such events that occurred in the first months of the Trump presidency. There were many others. In the years since, a range of conservative figures have understood that to accept an invite to appear on a college campus is to risk a confrontation, maybe a violent one.

Undercover video taken by conservative commentator Steven Crowder would subsequently reveal that when *Daily Wire* editor Ben Shapiro, a frequent target of Antifa activists, appeared at the University of Utah in September 2017, local Antifa members, intent on disruption, had prepared themselves with a stash of guns and knives. Happily, the police were tipped off, and they deterred the cell from acting out their wilder schemes. As it was, there was much scuffling and many punches thrown.

Why Antifa's deep hostility toward Shapiro? He refuses to refer to male pre-operative transgenders as women.

Another regular object of their wrath is Toronto Psychology Professor Jordan Peterson, who has labeled Antifa an "evil" group, and in public debate is highly effective at challenging the identity politics in which today's radical leftism is grounded. At Ontario's Queens College, a young female member of an Antifa mob seeking to disrupt a Peterson speech was caught with a garotte – a metal wire used by mobsters for strangulation. According to police, she'd intended it for Peterson.

In an especially bizarre case, when a conservative student group at Columbia University arranged for a public Skype call with British activist Tommy Robinson, campus radicals first formed a blockade outside the building, then banged on the walls, to stop students from hearing someone who was not present – or even in the country. As a reporter noted, "Although Robinson eventually tuned in, protesters continued to shout over him, preventing him from speaking, and later storming the stage, as administrators attempted to dissuade them but to no success. Protesters continued to control the room, shouting at audience members, and chanting 'whose campus? Our campus!' as Robinson was still waiting to speak."

Since security is costly, Antifa is aware that the violence to which they are so readily prone – or even its threat – provides universities with a convenient economic rationale for keeping out controversial speakers. Repeatedly, they have maintained that they would gladly permit more conservatives to appear, but on the condition that they themselves pay for the additional security costs needed to deal with Antifa. At Mohawk College in Hamilton, Ontario, officials at the school insisted that before Canadian conservative leader Maxime Bernier and American talk show host and comedian Dave Rubin be allowed to speak, those who had invited them lay out 10 times the normal sum required for security. The event only went ahead because Rubin agreed to take on the expense out of his own pocket. Meanwhile, at Berkeley, when an undergraduate group invited Steve Bannon and Charles Murray to appear at the school's ironically named Free Speech Week, administrators demanded the group come up with $145,000 to defray costs – knowing full well that was impossible.

Nor, needless to say, in a time when campus conservatives at many schools are an endangered (or at least a very silent) species, they are the only visitors to campus that face Antifa's unhinged wrath. At the University of Missouri-Kansas City, to cite a typical example, a meeting of the conservative Young Americans for Freedom (YAF) was invaded by Antifa, screaming, "Your sh*t is a platform for fascists. We don't give a f*ck what you're fine with... Your sh*tty-*ss meeting is not gonna fly!" Trying to calm them down, YAF members suggested that the two groups have a public debate. Antifa's response: "We don't talk with fascists!" YAF has yet to learn that Antifa is not a group seeking equal debate. They want to destroy the conservative movement, and tear down the American republic. This is a key distinction between Old Right Conservatives and New Right Conservatives.

At the University of Texas' main campus in Austin, the local Antifa affiliate, which calls itself the Revolutionary Student Front, publicly called for "revolutionary violence" against African-American professor Robert Reece – even though Reece himself is an ultra-leftist who writes for radical academic journals and collects Black Panther Party memorabilia. But in the eyes of left "wokesters", he'd sinned, teaching a class entitled Masculinities in America in which he'd challenged the idea that affirmative consent – a woman's public avowal that she wished to have sex – should be required before students engage in intercourse. Reece had suggested there were "gray areas of intimate encounters." Campus radicals were further incensed by word that a former girlfriend had characterized their time together as a "toxic-*ss relationship." The Revolutionary Student Front publicly declared that:

> Reactionary violence, like rape and domestic violence and torture, can only be responded to with revolutionary violence. We are inspired by women across the world from revolutionary movements who have turned on abusive husbands and serial rapists, reclaiming violence and wielding it against their oppressors. Fighting back is the first step... Through his course, he [Reece] is uniquely able to identify potential rapists, yet he does nothing to stop them — and worse, he shows them his sympathy as a fellow misogynist and abuser.

In reaction to the campus radicals' call for violence against their own faculty member, university officials did nothing.

Another UT faculty member who ran afoul of the school's Antifa chapter was Richard Morrisett, a well-regarded, tenured Professor of Pharmacy. A nationally recognized expert on the long-term effects of alcoholism upon the brain, he had taught at the school for 21 years, and had always received excellent write-ups from both his superiors and his students.

Then Antifa learned from an article in the *Austin Statesman-American* that he had pled guilty to domestic violence against his girlfriend, had been placed on probation and was taking classes as required by his plea deal. But it was also clear that the specifics of the case were ambiguous, or at least complicated, as the girlfriend was likewise accused of violence against him.

Nonetheless, Antifa's response was an unchecked campaign of harassment, which included a break-in to his lab. They then provided the local paper with evidence of their work in photos of graffiti sprayed on his equipment. As *The American Thinker* noted:

> "Nearby on the sidewalk, they wrote: 'Watch your back, Richard.' And Morrisett's office door was spray painted: 'Get out Morrisett or else!' The graffiti was signed with hammer and sickle symbols, and later posted on the website of the local Revolutionary Student Front... Left-wing students also blitzed the campus with anti-Morrisett flyers slapped onto light polls, walls, and other high-visibility spots. Resembling wanted posters, the flyers listed Morrisett's personal information: his home address, and the phone numbers of his office, home, and cell phone. The flyers urged students to 'Call Richard

Morrisett and tell him to get the hell out now!' They were signed with hammer and sickle symbols.

'Our goal is to make him feel unsafe on campus,' stated the Revolutionary Student Front in a social media post, according to campus police."

The University's response? They genuflected to the protestors. The school's administration not only accepted their call for his dismissal, they made him promise to leave Austin.

A month later, when Morrisett committed suicide, The Revolutionary Front was triumphant. On their website, they commented, "The world is better off, if only marginally, for having one less abusive, dangerous man breathing in it."

Let's go all the way back to Berkeley's famous Free Speech Movement in 1964. While many of its leaders, like Mario Savio and Bettina Aptheker, were in fact leftists with zero real interest in free speech (Mario Savio was a member of the Young People's Socialist League; Bettina Aptheker the daughter of Communist Party USA stalwart Herbert Aptheker; Jack Weinberg was later on the National Council of the Trotskyite International Socialists) the university's faculty gave them their full support. So, few Berkeley professors foresaw the dangers of the activism they advocated – and which was already evident in the violence then – that at an Academic Senate meeting in December, the faculty voted overwhelming support for the student radicals. Just two professors spoke out against them: Lewis Feuer and Nathan Glazer. Sociology professors and both former leftists, the pair also had in common, as Jewish-Americans, a keen understanding of how fascism had triumphed in Germany. As one historian has noted:

"Feuer offered an amendment that committed the university to nonintervention in matters of speech and advocacy only when they were 'directed to no immediate act of force and violence.' He observed to his colleagues that the failure of the German universities in the early 1930s to insist that students be disciplined for off-campus attacks on Jews, liberals, and socialists had enabled Nazi students to destroy German freedom and prepared the way for the rise of Hitler."

Feuer and Glazer saw what fascism really was. They knew how totalitarians gain power through violence and intimidation, and they understood the necessity of protecting civil society against their methods.

In Weimar Germany, faculty members of the college campuses were sympathetic to totalitarian movements, providing winking support for the activities of extremist groups. Civil order deteriorated as more and more young people came to believe that democracy had failed, and had to be replaced.

Surprisingly, the greatest contrast with how today's administrators differ from their predecessors is found at, of all places, Harvard.

On April 11, 1969 a group of Harvard students, members of the Students for a Democratic Society, stormed into the school's main administration building, threw out the staff and claimed it as revolutionary property. The students presumed that they would go unpunished. It was a reasonable assumption, since the university had taken no action in response to a series of lesser offenses, and as their counterparts at other elite schools had paid little or no price for their violence or destruction of property.

But Harvard surprised them. First, it called on units of the Boston Tactical Squad to remove them. Then it expelled them.

In the aftermath of the crackdown, a strange thing happened. Students at other schools took note, and the excessive violence and aggression of student radicals across the country began to ebb. It was a basic law of economics playing out: As the costs of disobedience rose, the supply of militants fell.

Alas, today's Antifa radicals have learned exactly the opposite lesson, that unchecked permissiveness breeds violence without limit. There are few imposing meaningful legal or scholastic costs on their extremism.

In fact, many faculty members on American campuses aren't just defenders of campus violence, some actually use their positions as tenured faculty members to act as Antifa organizers. Take, for instance, Purdue University Professor Bill Mullen and Stanford University Professor David Palumbo-Liu. Recently, the pair joined forces to create the "Campus Antifascist Network" (CAN), designed to assist students in setting up Antifa chapters on their own campuses. Among its backers are dozens of professors from major universities across the country. Entire academic departments have given CAN their official endorsement. Among the enthusiasts, as listed on its website, are the history faculty of Occidental College; the English Department at Ohio State; and the Department of Sociology at Trinity University in Hartford.

CAN's organizers make no secret of their own beliefs or the organization's goals. According to *The Stanford Review*, Palumbo-Liu, the Louise Hewlett Nixon Professor of English and Comparative Literature, placed photos of Antifa violence on his website, and has enthusiastically promoted a radical, anti-Israel website associated with Holocaust denial. In 2015, he congratulated several of his students for taking part in an anti-Israel protest that caused car crashes and blocked traffic on the San Mateo Bridge for an hour.

When a reporter pointed out to Palumbo-Liu that many of Antifa's targets are not actually fascists, his response was telling. He called such a contention "literally an academic argument in the worst sense of the word. We need to pay attention to what is happening, not the labels that we feel are most fitting."

When Dartmouth President Philip Hanlon released a statement saying that the school believed in free speech and opposed violence, CAN actually wrote Hanlon asking him to rescind his statement.

Nor do such professors merely talk the talk – a number have engaged in violence themselves. Michael Isaacson, of New York City's John Jay College of Criminal Justice (part of its mission is to train police) was in the nation's capital before Trump's inauguration, working with the Smash Racism DC/Disrupt J20 Antifa groups to assault Trump supporters at the inauguration. Among the tactics of choice was to punch them in the windpipe. Isaacson sent out notorious tweets declaring, "it's a pleasure to teach future dead cops," and "dead cops are good cops." (Odd footnote: the subject taught by this professor was… economics.)

Then there are the junior faculty, and the perpetual student types and assorted hangers-on who tend to be part of every large college community. Failed academics and failures at life, they are especially drawn to Antifa's mix of convoluted theoretical argument and decisive action.

The archetype might be Bay Area Antifa rioter Eric Clanton. During riots in Sacramento, Clanton used a metal bike lock to bash the skulls of unarmed Trump supporters. Clanton was fully clad in Antifa black bloc garb, but was later identified by his backpack by users of the internet message board 4chan. In a lengthy profile that appeared in *Rolling Stone* magazine, he is described as:

"[An] ethics professor who taught philosophy and critical thinking at Diablo Valley College in the East Bay suburb of Pleasant Hill…his work encompassed 'restorative justice from an anti-authoritarian perspective'…[on his OKCupid account he calls himself] a 'gender-nonconforming' sapiosexual interested in 'helping to precipitate the end of civil society.'"

Clanton may also have issues with drugs. When police first picked him up, at an anarchist "collective," they found, along with brass knuckles and knives, a Tupperware container filled with psilocybin.

A short man with a goofy mustache, Clanton says he was first drawn to Antifa during the Occupy Wall Street Movement, and soon began showing up at Black Lives Matter rallies. Meanwhile, his career as an academic has been in steady decline. While his arrest for the assaults with the bike lock was his first, he'd earlier had another criminal citation, after being let go from a position as an adjunct community college philosophy professor. He has no record of academic publication, and seems not to have been able to hold onto any job, including one teaching inmates at a local prison.

Clanton is far from the only irregularly employed academic to be identified as an active Antifa member. Another is Jeff Klinzman, formerly an adjunct professor of English at Kirkwood Community College in Cedar Rapids, Iowa. Klinzman's views may be encapsulated in a line from a "poem" he composed about Christian evangelicals: "Kill them all and bury them in the ground."

Tariq Khan is another. An anarchist and 40-something grad student, he was formerly a history instructor in the University of Illinois history department whose floundering academic career appears to have ended in November 2017 when he cold-cocked a peaceful Trump supporter. It seems Khan's fury was prompted by having been recorded participating in an anti-Trump rally. In addition to slugging the kid recording him, he was also moved to steal and destroy the offending phone.

A somewhat more successful member of the fraternity of college professors moonlighting for Antifa is George Ciccariello-Maher, formerly an associate professor at Drexel University in the field of Politics and Global Studies. He got the job despite having previously advocated the end of American police forces and calling for the killing of an allegedly racist South Carolina police officer, as well as having written, as a self-described "actual communist," in support of Venezuelan dictator Hugo Chavez. Ciccariello-Maher also "joked" on Twitter that "All I Want For Christmas Is A White Genocide." Arrested for his role in far-left riots in Cambridge and Oakland, Ciccariello-Maher is now unemployed.

Sam Lavigne, formerly a New York University adjunct faculty member, is the man behind Antifa's doxxing of nearly 1,600 ICE agents. Though he calls himself an "artist," he seems to have had little commercial success, and his LinkedIn profile does not list a current employer.

And the beat goes on. James Anderson, editor of the Antifa newsblog and website *ItsGoingDown* and a leader of Berkeley's Antifa chapter, is a Berkeley post-doc who's managed to secure low-level, low-salaried positions at the university. This has allowed him to pursue his real focus: recruiting and organizing mayhem for Antifa.

The postings on the Berkeley Antifa Community webpage reveal a vast assemblage of the overeducated and underemployed. College towns have always been beset by more than their fair share of those who graduated and never left, never growing up and made to believe by their surroundings that they never had to. However, those academic hangers-on of times past differ from today's many

Antifa supporters in one vital respect: Yes, they were always proudly liberal but until recently, that meant openness to new ideas and, even more, the readiness to unhesitatingly declare, along with the Voltairian adage, "I may not agree with what you say, but I will defend to the death your right to say it."

Today, with Antifa, it's more like: "If I don't agree with what you say, I'll beat you to death for saying it."

SIXTEEN

WOKE, INC. AND OTHER USEFUL IDIOTS

Vladimir Lenin may have been one of history's most vicious totalitarians, but it can never be said that he did not know his enemies. His classic formulation was: "The capitalists will sell us the rope with which we will hang them."

The truth of that prophecy has been borne out over and over again, with disastrous consequences to peoples and societies the world over who have been plagued with the disease of communism.

Yet given the attitude of America's corporate culture toward Antifa, those words – and warning – have rarely been more apt than in America today.

It's not as if Antifa's leaders, or pseudo-intellectuals like Bob Avakian, have made any secret of their deep hostility toward capitalism and capitalists – or of their intentions if things continue to move their way. Yet the would-be targets carry on, insulated and oblivious, unable to conceive that they could possibly mean what they say. All too often, these corporations are happy to use Antifa to achieve their own ends, such as shock troops against real populist movements in the West.

Even worse, many go out of their way to support Antifa, both in spirit and financially. In a time when CEOs of major corporations quake at the thought of taking on the social justice brigades, and virtue signaling passes for compassion, the payoffs that capitalists dole out to angry anti-capitalists and hate-for-profit centers are simply a routine business expense, a blood tax.

And that's when the corporatists are not already ideologically in bed with their would-be adversaries.

Back in the 1930s, when the American Communist Party was in fashion in Hollywood and among the literary set, there was a handful of super-rich who likewise supported the murderous Soviet regime; chief among them, Corliss Lamont, son of the chairman of J.P. Morgan Co. who, as the head of the National Council of American-Soviet Friendship, was Stalin's chief American apologist among the elites. He was aided by disgraced *New York Times* reporter Walter Duranty, who covered up the forced starvation of Ukraine by Stalin.

But within his circle Lamont was an outlier. Unlike the "intellectuals," American businessmen knew what would happen to them if Uncle Joe and his American cohorts ever assumed real power. As a class, they were foursquare against socialism wherever it sought to make inroads in American life.

That was then. In today's America, where, by the millions, miseducated millennials regard that failed philosophy as the solution to every social ill, to vocally *oppose* socialist thought in any of its many guises can literally be career-ending.

This is especially the case in the most dominant sector of all, social media. Consider the case of James Damore, a Google software engineer who was fired after writing an internal memo challenging the sacrosanct notion that there are no biological differences between the sexes, and instead arguing that these differences resulted in unequal distribution of men and women in the tech field. Google was quickly revealed to be an ideological gulag, where even the slightest deviation from radical leftist orthodoxy was subject to instant denunciation by both management and fellow employees; such a view was not just unworthy of consideration, it was intolerable. Damore was soon out of a job.

But it's the same across the social media landscape. To take a strong, principled, right-of center stand on Facebook challenging any of the left's pet victim groups or beliefs is to risk immediately being blocked, or "fact-checked" by the unseen, Orwellian powers-that-be, this despite the company's professed commitment to freedom of expression.

At the same time, Facebook leaves Antifa alone, even when it is in violation of its own guidelines, which clearly state that material advocating violence, personal intimidation or harassment is to be removed. Nonetheless, the popular Antifa cell Redneck Revolt regularly posts calls for its members to carry guns to protests. Portland's Rose City Antifa page took joyful credit for an attack on Journalist Andy Ngo. New Orleans' NOLA Antifa page likewise urges followers to provide named enemies with "concrete milkshakes." California's Orange County Anti-Fascism Anti-Capitalism Revolutionary Front calls for their followers to attack "fascists" with bricks, and the Hoosier Anti-Racist Movement (better known by its acronym HARM), encourages partisans to take part in a "Trans Day of Vengeance," its logo showing a hand with a knife. Needless to say, there are other examples aplenty. Facebook takes no action against these explicit calls to violence.

Obviously, with 2.7 billion regular users for its various forums and services worldwide, Facebook doesn't need Antifa's business. Antifa's footprint on Facebook, as of July 2019, consisted of 119 Antifa Facebook pages, with a total of 351,948 followers.

It's the same with Twitter. While the service routinely shuts down accounts of conservative groups that it claims engage in hate speech, Antifa's Twitter accounts, including those used to clearly promote hate and violence or to encourage doxxing, go unmolested. When the conservative Media Research Center demanded an explanation in one especially egregious case, Smash Racism D.C.'s doxxing of talk show host Gavin McInnes, the company characteristically issued a bland non-response: "We don't comment on individual accounts for privacy and security reasons."

Meaning: We do whatever we please, however we please.

Twitter also suspended the account of Eoin Lenihan, a writer who exposed the links between supposedly unbiased journalists and the Antifa members they use as friendly sources. Too, the company temporarily suspended Steven Crowder for mocking *Vox* writer Carlos Maza. Yet it left untouched Maza's own account, which he used to endorse assaults on conservatives.

For these reasons and more, anti-trust action must be taken against internet giants, and the FCC should regulate them as public utilities. Certainly, they should remove the outdated Section 230 immunity that shields internet giants from litigation by those who have been deplatformed and from defamed users and companies that are mistreated by these tech giants.

Other vast corporations, especially those similarly interested in the youth market, are even more overt in their public support for the radical left and its assorted causes. Nike proudly made divisive Black Lives Matter activist Colin Kaepernick its public face after his controversial campaign of kneeling during the National Anthem. The ad's message – "Believe in something. Even if it means sacrificing everything." – was intended to summon up the nobility of iconic figures like Martin Luther King and JFK. As Black Lives Matter co-founder DeRay McKesson approvingly noted, "I think it's important that Nike is standing behind him in this moment. It's important that we celebrate the people that sacrifice while the moment is still here and while the person is alive. And remember, Colin was saying basic things — Colin's saying that racism is alive and present, and that it's in the criminal justice system, in society, and in policing."

Of course, professional sports and its affiliate enterprises, like ESPN, have been especially notable in their pandering. The National Hockey League's Philadelphia Flyers covered a statue of the legendary singer Kate Smith, and the New York Yankees banned the playing of her iconic version of "God Bless America," when it came to light that she long ago recorded a song now deemed politically incorrect. Major League Soccer officially decreed that it would permit the flying of an Antifa flag at games. In the Pacific Northwest especially, radicals like to wave it in the stands.

At the same time, in the corporate sphere, the tolerance for individuals accused of insensitivity on issues of race or gender ranges from little to none. Perhaps the most telling case in this regard is that of Papa John's iconic founder John Schnatter, forced from his own company in 2018 for having used the "n-word" in a conference call discussing public relations, is an example of what *not* to do.

Arguably worse than the cringing fear that is the reflexive response of so many businessmen and public authority figures to leftist militancy is that often they also lend them financial support.

Few would be surprised to learn that the notorious Hungarian liberal billionaire George Soros, funder of all manner of radical projects, had backed RefuseFascism.org or the Alliance for Global Justice (AfGJ). He also helped fund the United For Equality and Affirmative Action Legal Defense Fund (UFEAALDF), which in turn wrote checks to the Antifa surrogate, By Any Mean Necessary (BAMN), which acts as legal counsel for Antifa, and functions as the group's public face. Liberal billionaire Tom Steyer lavishly donates to environmental extremists, and may have also backed Refuse Fascism, according to their statements caught on candid camera by Project Veritas. Hippie ice cream entrepreneurs Ben Cohen and Jerry Greenfield also back the Alliance for Global Justice.

What is stunning is that the Alliance for Global Justice also receives funding from such major corporations as Charles Schwab and the Bank of America. Apparently they do not know or care that their money is likely to end up in the hands of militant anti-government extremists.

Despite its benign sounding name, the Alliance for Global Justice was set up as a front group for Central American radicals in the 1980s, promoting the Sandanistas in Nicaragua and used as a conduit to fund the pro-Soviet Committee in Solidarity with the People of El Salvador (CISPES).

Meanwhile, to cite an even more appalling example, the Southern Poverty Law Center, which professes to be anti-hate by labeling mainstream conservative organizations and individuals hate groups, receives major funding from the likes of JPMorgan Chase, Apple, Charles Schwab, Verizon, Newman's Own, and Kraft Heinz.

Corporate America is hardly alone in its embrace of Antifa. A greater, and far more knowing sympathy, is found among such key rising figures in the Democrat Party as Minnesota's Keith Ellison, the first Muslim elected to Congress and the former Deputy Chair of the Democrat National Committee, now the Attorney General of Minnesota and fellow unregenerate leftist Representatives Alexandria Ocasio-Cortez, Rashida Tlaib, Ayanna Pressley and Ilhan Omar, collectively known as 'The Squad.' Ellison once posted a picture of himself proudly holding up Mark Bray's *Anti-Fascist Handbook*, writing beneath that it should "strike fear into the heart" of Donald Trump and his followers. The Squad members, for their part, have pointedly refused to criticize even Antifa's most heinous violence, its attacks on ICE offices, the mass shooting in Dayton, or radical violence in the Summer of Rage 2020.

Closet extremists are one thing, but Democrats across the board, including purportedly moderate ones, can be counted on to refuse to call out Antifa publicly – and in fact, usually come to its defense. While it is beyond inconceivable that any Republican-elected official of even modest stature would fail to denounce the Ku Klux Klan or neo-Nazis, a Democrat's most-likely-heard response to Antifa's extreme excesses is a mild expression of not condoning violence, but rarely the group itself. Democrat Leader Jerry Nadler went so far as to say once that, "Antifa is a myth."

The most powerful internet entity of all, Google, might have been even more obsessed with ridding America of Trump than his Democrat foes. In June 2019, a Project Veritas sting caught Jen Gennai, the company's director of responsible innovation, on video declaring outright war on Trump's re-election. In her words:

"We all got screwed over [by Trump's election] in 2016.

Again, it wasn't just us, it was the people got screwed over, the news media got screwed over, like, everybody got screwed over. So we're rapidly been like, it happened there and how do we prevent it from happening again. We're also training our algorithms, like, if 2016 happened again, would we have, would the outcome be different?

"…Elizabeth Warren is saying we should break up Google. And like, I love her but she's very misguided, like that will not make it better. It will make it worse because all these smaller companies who don't have the same resources that we do will be charged with preventing the next Trump situation. It's like a small company cannot do that."

Gennai went on to say that congressional hearings and investigations wouldn't prevent Google from going ahead with its plans.

And, as we've learned, she was speaking the truth.

But if history is any guide, they and theirs ignore the threat of Antifa at their peril. They don't know, but should, that the groups that ran riot at Trump's inauguration began planning their mayhem a month before the election – at the time they expected the winner to be Hillary Clinton. In fact, much as they despised Trump, they despise even more "neo-liberals" like Hillary – and Biden – who in their worldview would coopt and undermine the revolution.

Antifa is not waging war against any individual, but against democracy itself and especially capitalism.

There is another phrase that applies – "useful idiots." It, too, is often attributed to Lenin, though probably inaccurately. No matter. If he didn't say it, he certainly knew it when he saw it, and took full advantage.

SEVENTEEN

THE BOOGALOO BOYS

In the late 2010s and early 2020s, a new sort of anarchist group arose. Like every other movement in the information age, this group began as an open-source movement formed on social media rather than arising from a specific geographic locality. This group did not share the anarcho-communist tradition of Antifa, but followed a more anarcho-capitalist branch of the ideology. They called themselves the Boogaloos.

Born on anonymous websites frequented by disaffected youth and federal agents, the movement then moved to Facebook, which provided a solid platform for the Boogaloo movement to grow and coalesce in 2019-2020.

The Boogaloo anarchist movement is a multi-faceted group of pro-gun, pro-BLM, pro-LGBT, anti-government militia movements expressing themselves mostly by wearing Hawaiian shirts and carrying rifles at protests, but have committed some of the most heinous violence in recent history of any political group.

The Boogaloos speak of a violent uprising against the government, an event they prophetically call "Boogaloo," or even "the Big Luau." The movement takes its name from the 1984 movie *Breakin' 2: Electric Boogaloo*. Adherents wear surplus tactical gear along with Hawaiian shirts, and carry heavy assault rifles. The group is erroneously described by media as right-wing, even though members have called for the death of President Trump. Some members immortalize domestic terrorist hall of famer Timothy McVeigh.

Indeed, political views held by Boogaloo members are myriad and murky, even among chapters. Some have spoken at Black Lives Matter rallies. All members hold extreme pro-gun and antigovernment stances. Boogaloo boys have turned out at anti-lockdown protests and were named by former Attorney General William Barr, along with Antifa, as "outside agitators" during the George Floyd protests and riots. At times, groups of Boogaloo anarchists will align with Antifa for action during these events.

While the Boogaloo anarchists began forming on social media, the movement has been far too violent to be merely categorized as angry young men simply playing dress up. Major headline-stealing incidents aside, the Boogaloo boys have engaged in a low-intensity but constant irregular state of warfare against police and the United States government, regardless of the political landscape. They have plotted bombings, participated in violent protests, incited riots and committed both mass and small-scale shootings. Members of the Boogaloo movement also participated in the storming of the U.S. Capitol on January 6th, 2021, latching onto any movement or excuse to attack the federal government. In fact, in an interview with

Reuters, one Boogaloo follower claimed several groups of Boogaloos took part in storming the Capitol.

In perhaps their most violent act to date, United States Air Force sergeant Steven Carrillo and Robert Justus, both avowed Boogaloo boys, perpetrated a string of shootings and pipe bomb attacks in California in 2020, slaying two police officers and injuring three other individuals. The pair had met on Facebook, with Justus replying, "Let's boogie" to a Carrillo post about inciting violence against police officers. Carrillo was a highly trained airman and military police non-commissioned officer. Carrilllo trained in the Air Force Security Forces, the self described "Marine Corps" of the USAF. If the Air Force and Space Force were going to have a ground combat unit, the Security Forces would be it. Carrillo served in the Phoenix Ravens, a high-speed anti-terrorism squad. The unit has conducted operations all over the world, including guarding unsecured airfields overseas. Carrillo, tapping into the warrior esprit de corps of his new outfit, the Boogaloos, scrawled Boogaloo graffiti on the hood of his vehicle in his own blood before killing a sheriff's deputy and a federal security officer.

In one alleged plot, members of the Boogaloo anarchist movement plotted to kidnap Michigan Governor Gretchen Whitmer and overthrow the state government. A group of fourteen Boogaloo adherents, grouped under a splinter cell "Wolverine Watchmen" to evoke the superhero concepts of Marvel's Wolverine and DC Comics the Watchmen, were charged with both federal and state crimes of kidnapping, gang activity, firearms offenses and terrorism. The group was agitated by Governor Whitmer's pro-lockdown response to the coronavirus pandemic. The FBI's investigation revealed that the group had plotted the kidnapping for several months over various online group chats. After the bureau became aware of the plot in early 2020, it interviewed a Boogaloo member who agreed to become a confidential informant after hearing other members discuss killing police officers. The FBI subsequently infiltrated the plot and in October, arrested its ringleaders. During the arrest, ringleader Barry Croft was found to have included President Trump's name on a list of politicians he wanted to hang.

The Boogaloo ideology and tradecraft also advocates for lone wolf attacks. In 2020, the movement exploded. In October, Boogaloo member Ivan Harrison Hunter was apprehended in San Antonio, Texas. The self-described Boogaloo boy was charged with firing a loaded AK-47 assault rifle into a manned Minneapolis police building. Hunter had been in online contact with Carrillo, and other Boogaloo adherents who committed violent crimes.

Also in October of 2020, police in Dundalk, Maryland arrested Boogaloo boy Frank William Robertson Perry. In his home were a rifle, ammunition and a tactical ballistics vest. The FBI's Joint Terrorism Task Force stated that Perry was a Boogaloo member and parolee who had served time for burglary.

In Minneapolis, in September, FBI agents successfully posed online as members of Hamas, convincing Boogaloo boys Michael Solomon and Benjamin Ryan Teeter. The pair spoke of providing support and material to the Middle Eastern terrorist organization, destroying a courthouse, inciting a riot with attacks on police and white supremacists, and slaying police officers to bring about the Boogaloo, the cumulative civil war event that the group prophesizes. Solomon and Teeter expressed an interest in acting as freelance terrorists for hire to earn money for the movement. Two months prior to their arrest, the pair gave a confidential FBI informant five silencers, and expressed an interest in providing automatic weapons and more silencers to who they believed was Hamas. Both believed that the ordinance would be used to attack Israeli and American service members.

In August, Alan Viareno was charged with sending at least two dozen threatening anonymous letters to the Santa Clara County Health Inspector's office in Gilroy, California. Viarengo took issue with measures the office introduced to limit the spread of the coronavirus pandemic. The word "Boogaloo" was used in his correspondence. Upon his apprehension, police discovered over 100 weapons in addition to explosives and ammunition in Viarengo's home.

In Texas, the months of May and June saw three Boogaloo boys arrested for threatening law enforcement and the military. Wyatt Winn was apprehended by Ector County sheriff's office deputies for his part in engaging in an armed standoff with seven other perpetrators against police over local lockdown measures. Six of the eight were armed with assault rifles, for which they were charged with possession on a licensed property. Winn followed no less than two dozen Boogaloo-related pages on Facebook, posted pictures of himself in Hawaiian shirts, and shared memes referencing Duncan Lemp, a police shooting victim. In Lancaster, Texas a 29 -year-old bodybuilder named Phillip Russel Archibald was charged with conspiracy to distribute steroids. Arcihbald was a public member of the organization, following it on social media on multiple accounts, and had talked about using guerilla warfare against National Guardsmen patrolling the ubiquitous Black Lives Matter protests going on at the time. In Bartonville, just an hour drive away, Marine Corps veteran Daniel Austin Dunn was indicted for threatening law enforcement officers on Facebook and Twitter. Dunn, a firearms owner, spoke of Boogaloo in online posts, including the group's trademark flag.

Earlier in April, in Texarkana, Aaron Swenson of Arkansas was arrested after livestreaming himself on Facebook where he drove around hunting for police officers to ambush and execute. Svenson wrote on his Facebook, "I feel like hunting the hunters." The 36 year old was arrested wearing an armored vest and several loaded firearms in his vehicle. Swenson was charged with attempted capital murder of a police officer, attempted murder and terroristic threats. Swenson had liked several dozen Boogaloo pages on Facebook. He had also changed his profile picture to a photo of himself wearing a Hawaiian shirt and an armored vest, and tagged the photo with #HisName-WasDuncan in reference to Duncan Lemp.

Not all Boogaloo anarchists commit crimes that are large scale or violent. Kevin Ackley and Joshua Barnard, the former of whom wore Boogaloo clothing and the latter was a self-described follower, were both arrested for inciting a riot in Columbia, South Carolina in late May and June. Ackley had thrown a water bottle at police officers during a protest. Barnard was charged with breaking into a car, instigating a riot and numerous other offenses including stealing a police jacket. Barnard was rearrested on June 12th for sexual exploitation of a minor.

Trevan Young, an African American who had liked and shared Boogaloo content on Facebook, was arrested in Chattanooga in June. The charges were listed as possession of a broken-down assault rifle in his backpack as well as magazines for it, two of which were loaded and ready to go. Young was carrying a sign referencing the police shooting of African Americans Duncan Lemp and Breonna Taylor.

Three members of a Nevada based Boogaloo group, Andrew Lynam, William Loomis and Stephen Parshall, were brought up on conspiracy charges. The trio planned to blow up an energy substation and had possession of a Molotov cocktail at a Black Lives Matter protest. Police allege the three men planned to incite protestors to attack police officers. Parshall was furthermore charged in both state and Federal court with sexually abusing his teenage stepdaughter.

A Loveland, Colorado resident named Bradley Bun was arrested by federal agents and charged with possession of pipe bombs in May. Bunn openly told investigators after his arrest that he was "willing to take out a few law enforcement officers in order to wake people up to what's going on." Bunn's involvement in the Boogaloo movement is unconfirmed, but several Colorado groups made online comments after his arrest, suggesting they knew him and ran with the same crowds.

The Boogaloo anarchist movement represents an evolution of tactics as well as a direct visage into 21-century extremism. The movement began online, like so many others, but as its name inherently promotes violence, adherents of the group began committing violence almost immediately. This should not be taken to mean that anyone who posts a Boogaloo meme is a violent criminal. However, taken on its face, the movement itself is centered around the concept of a force of citizens rising up against the U.S. government – an actual insurrection. Curiously, the FBI has not sought to link the events on January 6th 2021 to the Boogaloo movement, even though members claim several of their groups took part, and it is an event specifically in line with the movement's ultimate goal.

But perhaps that's a story for another day.

EIGHTEEN

FROM CHAZ TO LINCOLN

Fast-forward to June 2020.

The smell was the first thing I noticed. As I turned the corner from Broadway and made my way up the small, grassy incline to where the reflecting pool was supposed to be, the acrid scent of body odor, smoke, and the lingering fumes of spray-paint hit me. Off in the distance, a booming, sub-bass beat reverberated off the townhomes and apartment buildings surrounding the long rectangle of Cal Anderson Park.

I walked up the path to check out the reflecting pool, but found it bone dry. The city had drained the water when the riots began. Now the pool's edges had become a concrete canvass for graffiti and street art. "ACAB" and "1312" were painted all around it. On one edge, someone had repeated the phrase "land back land back land back" over and over. On the cobblestone fountain, someone had drawn a face with the eyes X'd out and the words "Kill the Masters."

Welcome to the Occupied Zone.

I had just flown cross-country from Washington, D.C. and landed in Seattle, Washington, where a day before, a group of protesters, anarchists, and assorted dissidents had established what they called the Capital Hill Autonomous Zone within six blocks of the largest American city in the Pacific Northwest.

The CapHill neighborhood was known as an artsy, hipster part of town, and local protesters and anarchists frequently recruited from the area during marches to swell their numbers. Inside the zone, beyond the confines of the park, was the Seattle Police Department East District. For several days and nights before the occupation began, CapHill had been the site of hostile standoffs between black-clad protesters and the SPD riot squad.

Things came to a head when lines were drawn and the police force established a concrete barrier in the street for protection, as a black bloc employed low-level siege tactics to the precinct. Activists swarmed the streets, lobbing projectiles at officers, and brought gas masks and umbrellas to counter any tear gas volleys that might come from the SPD. And come they did. This went on night after night, until one day, in a move that neither side predicted, Mayor Jenny Durkan ordered the SPD to effectively abandon the precinct.

Viral videos quickly spread on social media around the country of officers and uniformed National Guardsmen carrying boxes and equipment out of the East Precinct. Many Americans were wondering what was going on in CapHill. But to the members of the black bloc, they knew exactly what it meant. The Eastern District was standing down, and the territory was theirs.

Almost immediately, the assorted groups moved into the space around the precinct, established a perimeter, and repositioned the barriers to the ends of every street that led to the precinct within the six blocks of CapHill. They put up new signs along the way. "Capital Hill Autonomous Zone," "Welcome to Free Capital Hill," and above the precinct they changed the words Seattle Police Department to Seattle People's Department - language evocative of the Bolsheviks and Chinese Communist Party.

By declaring this an autonomous zone, they made a statement that, effectively, the CapHill zone was outside the bounds of the United States government, and had now formed a new polity within the geography of the United States, but separate from the Republic, and not subject to its laws. Case in point, the lack of a police presence to enforce those laws. In a show of appeasement, Jenny Durkan, had allowed the territory to be taken under their control.

Following a public backlash to the declaration of an autonomous zone, the CHAZ would be renamed the Capital Hill Occupied Protest or CHOP. But the bell could not be unrung. It was an occupation. The zone was theirs.

I ended up spending 72 hours inside the autonomous zone, both day and night. What I saw was at some points not far-removed from festival concerts and street fairs I attended growing up in Philadelphia. But the cracks in the facade were always there at the edges, and at night, they'd exploded into tectonic fissures.

Days in the occupied zone were an amorphous festival of life, dissent, evangelizing, anger, chaos, and indeed, flashes of violence. I made sure to keep a COVID mask on at all times, and wore a hat, sometimes with sunglasses, sometimes not. I had spent hours watching live-stream videos from inside the zone before arriving to get a sense of how people dressed, acted, and moved within the space.

I learned to understand its rhythms and patterns of life before setting foot inside so I could more easily blend in with the crowd.

Early on, the occupiers had produced an annotated map of the six-block area, which I spent committing to memory during the cross-country flight from D.C., making special note of the barricaded checkpoints along the main thoroughfares, as well as key points of interest. I decided early on to utilize the park for entrance and exit as it was the least-watched, and booked accommodations a short walk away as a place to rest, edit video, and plan my next moves.

From my previous experience in the military, I knew to locate and include all the closest emergency facilities in my operational planning, and to lay out the best route to each on foot should the need arise for medical, fire, or law enforcement attention, even if 9-1-1 was not available.

Inside, I found a mixed coalition. There were protesters raging against what they viewed as an oppressive system, thrill-seekers, tourists and some families hoping to catch a glimpse of the scene; street artists tagging walls and roads with anti-police/anti-capitalist graffiti and BLM art; thugs eyeing up the crowd as they passed; and armed anarchists constantly on the lookout for what they viewed as mortal threats to their radical aims. Eyes constantly darted back-and-forth above masked faces from those in the crowd on the lookout for undercover officers and unwelcome guests. Music blared from various speakers, heavy-beats clashing with one another, while in other areas speakers testified their stories and called the crowds to share in their passion. Food was handed out freely from makeshift tents and co-ops (cops not allowed), some homemade, some delivered, all of it free for the taking.

Members of the John Brown Gun Club of Puget Sound, a local antifascist group linked to an ICE firebombing, could be seen in black, armed, walking throughout the zone on patrol, using shortwave radios on earpieces to communicate. The JBGCs also maintained the checkpoints, sometimes with rifles or handguns showing. Some drove patrol around the zone in one-manned vehicles with their plates removed, also communicating via shortwave. They appeared to have broken the zone up into sectors with various patrols on standing watch.

In addition to the JBGCs, there was a cadre of black-clad individuals with duct-taped red crosses who were moving throughout the zone. They called themselves medics and facilitators. Though the medic corps and JBGCs appeared to be working in concert, they did not seem to be members of each others' respective groups. In instances of participant blackouts, breakdowns, fighting, and injury, these medics would quickly rush to the area. However, the field medics did not seem to have put much thought into their efforts. Clearly they had not run emergency drills, had few supplies beyond basic first aid kits, and seemed more concerned with making sure I did not film what was going on than in rendering aid. Twice I saw participants who'd blacked out from substance abuse carried outside the barricades by the medics, since there was no way for real ambulances and EMTs to enter.

Within a few hours of arriving, I met up with a few local friends who came down to the event. These were folks who both looked the part and could handle themselves if need be, and we began walking the inner field of Cal Anderson Park. One of the first things we saw was a man who appeared to be homeless and on some cocktail of street drugs running around and wildly slashing the air with an actual machete. I pulled out my phone and began filming as he rushed off, moving past people sitting around chatting, unaware of the danger. He ran north into the tent city that had quickly sprung up around a small garden. A light rain was falling, and the machete man appeared to be swinging at the raindrops as he ran towards a tree at the edge of the area. Once he got there, he placed his machete on the ground, then picked up a discarded plastic bag and began waving it around. One of my friends picked up the machete. At that point, the medics arrived, and asked to be given the machete so they could "take care of it". Not wanting to break cover, we handed it over, and I inquired what they would do about the man who had been running about and nearly stabbing people. They assured me they would keep an eye on him, but that everyone was welcome within the space.

The second day I was there, I was walking around Pine Street near the stairs at the entrance to the baseball field with my brother Kevin, who had flown in the night before to watch my back in the occupied territory. Once I had told him I was going, he refused to let me go without him. He's that kind of brother. We came up on a Christian street preacher and two of his team members trying to spread the Gospel inside the zone. Earlier, we had watched a video of this peaceful preacher being attacked and put into a chokehold by individuals later identified as known antifascists who had travelled up to Seattle from Portland. The preacher was being held on the steps by a group of protesters, who had him on the ground, and he was unable to stand. When people asked why, they yelled back that the Capital Hill zone was not meant for Christian preachers, and he was not welcome there. For half an hour he remained stuck on the staircase as protesters held him down against his will, forcing him on the ground. Eventually, after much heated discussion with his two prayer team members, they dragged him to the barricade and threw him out. I caught up with him down the street and asked what he thought about the experience. He told me they had stolen his wallet and phone, beaten him, choked him, all for the transgression of speaking the Christian Gospel. He called the Seattle mayor and the President to put an end to the attacks on religion going on in the occupied zone, and pleaded for a restoration of the rule of law so that he could go on preaching peacefully without threat of violence. I didn't see him come back after he left that day.

All of what went on during the day paled in comparison with to the anarchy that arose at night. Each day, after spending hours walking the occupied zone and filming as much as we could, we headed back to our room to charge phones and batteries, check in with the world, upload videos, and plan out our next moves. After the sun set, we would make our way back through the now-darkened park and into the zone beyond to see what we would find after the news cameras and reporters had retreated to their luxury hotels, and the day-trippers and hipsters departed in search of craft beer and Netflix.

There were well-meaning people of good faith who took part in the Capital Hill demonstration; they wanted to peaceably assemble and petition their government for a redress of their grievances. But during our time undercover, we saw it all.

Before we arrived, we knew the nighttime already had a reputation, and a viral video showed the emergence of a sort of power structure in the zone. One especially notorious figure was Raz Simone. His exploits earned him the moniker Warlord Raz. In a video that aired one day before we got to the occupied zone, Raz was shown passing out assault rifles to a crowd from the trunk of his Tesla while he himself carried an AK-47 and a handgun in a thigh holster. The legality of this irresponsible weapons-handling is dubious at best, and I certainly hope the ATF is looking at that video, though as of this writing, they have not responded. In another video taken at night, Raz is seen squaring up with a street artist who was spray-painting a section of wall that had already been tagged. Raz, in no uncertain terms, tells him this is not allowed, and refers to himself and his entourage of personal security personnel as a policing force inside the zone. Needless to say, we knew the nighttime needed more coverage, as mainstream outlets typically dropped their coverage after sunset. One local media crew was actually assaulted on the first day of the CHAZ at night, but was sufficiently intimidated such that they did not release their footage until days later.

The first night we were there, thefts had already begun inside the tent city, with at least one MacBook Pro and a lot of cash reportedly stolen. The owner had left it inside thinking it would be safe. We saw protesters scaling buildings up a rusty ladder to spray paint on the roof. The next night, a fight broke out between groups of protesters as one graffiti artist scaled a fence to spray paint the boarded-up police precinct. Another protester screamed and attempted to stop him, and a fistfight erupted. They were pulled apart by some of the crowd and forced to leave the area. Later that night, we went into one of the only businesses nearby that remained open – a local tobacco shop that also sold personal defense items. The clerk there told us that they had been broken into, with thieves coming in through the skylight and stealing "a lot of merchandise," but that police had done nothing when they called. Their store was just around the corner from where the SPD East Precinct now stood abandoned. It seemed as though the business owners had decided to remain at the store overnight to protect their wares from further theft. I was reminded of my time living in China and seeing street vendors drag a full bed down to their dried fruit stands to sleep out of doors with their goods.

On night three, the dam broke. My brother and I had been doing interviews with a few people on 12th and Pine when a commotion broke out down the street from us. We heard someone on stage yell to go quickly and that someone was about to get shot. Immediately, we ended the interview as a crowd of hundreds began running from the stage up the hill of Pine Street toward us. We saw that a few others were running down 12th, so we took off in that direction. We came to an auto shop called Car Tender, which was a few blocks down, with a fenced-in auto lot. We picked up snippets about a break-in, an arson attempt, and a theft. People were saying that a thief had been caught inside by the owner, and he and his son and were being held at gunpoint. Before we could size up the situation, the mob arrived, whipped into a fury by the speaker on stage. They crashed against the gate, shaking it back and forth until it fell to the ground. The first line of the mob entered the auto yard as the owner and a few employees came out -- one armed with an AR-15, but not pointing it at anyone. What followed next was a tense standoff as the owner explained the thief had already been let go, and the police had not responded to his 9-1-1 call as he was too close to the occupied zone. Eventually, cooler heads prevailed and the mob backed down from what could have turned into a very ugly scene.

The owner spoke to a few members of the mob and some independent journalists who were covering the scene. He told them that between COVID and the occupation, he was losing his business, and that the Mayor and his local city council rep had done absolutely nothing to help him. As he spoke, an ambulance and fire truck drove past to pick up another blacked-out participant down the street. No police responded. The field medics and JBCGs arrived and again tried to get people to stop filming. At that point, Warlord Raz arrived with his retinue to talk with the business owner. Raz and the owner spoke about de-escalation, as well as community relations between the protesters and the local businesses. Then, the unexpected happened. The thief himself reappeared. The owner and his still-armed son looked over and pointed out that the thief, a skinny young man with a long ponytail, was wearing the owner's jacket. The thief took off running in the direction of the barricade, and the owner's son and Raz sped off in pursuit of him. My brother and I flipped our phones on record and took off with them to document the situation.

As we ran around participants and cars in the dark, the thief came closer to the barricade and the group maintaining a checkpoint there. Someone yelled out to stop the thief, and another person yelled, "He's got a knife!" Sure enough, the thief appeared to have a curved pocketknife in his hand, without the blade released. As I kept filming, keeping up with the mad dash, Raz drew his sidearm and racked a round into the chamber as he approached the young man, but onlookers yelled, "No, don't", and he put his handgun away for the time being. A crowd formed around the accused thief, and pushed him up against the hood of a car. Again, medics, JBGCs, and one of Raz's crew challenged me for filming and demanded I stop. I said I was fine, and continued documenting the exchange as it grew sharper.

No police were in sight as Hobbesian human nature played out before my camera lens. The crowd that had thrown the police out were now struck with a dilemma, how to deal with a criminal? They demanded that he open his schoolbag. He refused. They took it from him and began searching. The young man squirmed as they pushed him up against the hood of the car. The questioning continued, and Raz stood front and center, along with the owner's son. At one point, the tense exchange seemed to be dying down, but the crowd was not moving back an inch. They had no clue what to do with the criminal, as their entire protest demanded they could not turn him over to police. The owner's son said he simply wanted to recover what had been stolen, declaring that he would let him go, but the thief did not seem to have the items with him. Suddenly, a green-taped fist reached through the crowd as one individual rushed forward and began pummeling away at the thief. Apparently someone had grown impatient with doing things the easy way. A scuffle ensued, and in the confusion, the thief bolted and escaped into the park.

A few minutes after this, the crowd made its way back into the center of the zone, Raz at the center of it all. I went to sit with my brother and journalist Kalen D'Almeida from Scriberr News on a few "conversation couches" that had been set up nearby in the street. Then I took a quick video of the scene to show the aftermath, and the dynamics at play after the mainstream news crews had abandoned the zone. Kalen began filming as well. At that point I noticed Raz looking at his phone, angrily. He gazed over at us, sitting on the couches, then turned back towards the crowd. A minute later, one of his crew came marching toward us. It was the same thug with the green-taped hand. He strode up to Kalen and yelled at him to give him his phone. Kalen refused. Immediately, the green-taped fist came out again and punched Kalen in the head from the other side of the couch.

Kalen scrambled back, but the man with the green-taped hand lunged forward, and I realized he was holding onto Kalen's coat with his other hand. Kalen called for help, and I walked forward to get the man's attention, while calling for security. My brother ran over to the nearby crowd in the intersection, bringing them a few feet closer. All of this happened in less than ten seconds. As others from the group began getting involved, green-taped hand focused on yet another member of the crowd, and Kalen broke free from his grasp, running full out down the street.

I later interviewed Kalen for One America News, and he told me that when he arrived at the barricade, the so-called guards there actually tried to detain him, and followed him out beyond the confines of the occupied zone. They said they had been told he was stealing security plans and needed to be stopped. Kalen then saw a vehicle pulling out from the barricade area and coming after him. He realized there was an open construction site nearby, quickly found his way in, and hid out in a concrete pit while dialing 9-1-1. When the police arrived a few minutes later, Kalen emerged and saw the car was still waiting there, the driver clad in all black.

I left CHAZ shortly after 2 AM on June 15th. On the way out, I activated my Periscope app, and launched a live-stream on Twitter to my nearly one million followers. My brother and I took off our masks, and as we walked through the occupied parks, past the CHAZ farm and the tent city, we revealed we had been there all along undercover documenting what we could see on the ground for the past three days and three nights. On that live video, I implored Seattle Mayor Jenny Durkan and Washington Governor Jay Inslee to shut CHAZ down immediately, because the writing was on the wall. Someone was going to get seriously hurt. The irresponsible gun use, lawless environment, and mob justice from Warlord Raz and the Antifa JBGCs were a recipe for bloodshed. It was a disaster waiting to happen.

However, as I came to learn later, other media outlets, even Fox News, were reporting that CHAZ was not a violent place. They were committed to disseminating a narrative pushed by Mayor Durkan that the militant-occupied zone was merely a "Summer of Love". The national media turned into a supporting chorus, happily feeding this false narrative to the public. The media ate up the daytime images of peaceful protests, food donations, and information operations put forward by the CHAZ organizers and their online supporters and allies. This narrative selectively omitted the daylight attacks on dissenters, and dropped any coverage of the nighttime violence. This was an easy job for national outlets since their field reporters only showed up during the daytime, employing full lights and cameras from a fixed location and interviewing random passersby, then calling it a day. This enabling, surface-level reporting allowed CHAZ to continue far longer than it would have. If those outlets had instead done even rudimentary journalism – the work of blending in, spending considerable time inside the occupied zone, using unobtrusive cell phones to collect footage, and staying out until 2 and 3 a.m. – to see what happened when the crowds of gawkers headed home. Several young guerilla journalists from both local outlets and digital outlets, and even Twitch streamers, took on this task, and their reporting has held up much better than many of their on-air colleagues because they were able to show what happens when the big news cameras are turned off.

Less than a week after I left Seattle, the CHAZ shootings began. In all, there were five shootings on four separate evenings. These shootings left two black teenagers dead and three others wounded. In some of the shootings, ambulances were unable to enter the area and render aid due to the lack of a police escort, which is necessary in an active shooter situation. In at least one case, the so-called CHAZ medics attempted to treat one of the victims, who later died. That blood is on the hands of the ideologues and patsies who allowed this farce to drag on.

It has also been reported that armed barricade guards shot at two black teens who were driving into the CHAZ, killing a 16-year-old and wounding a 14-year-old. While the investigation is still ongoing, early reports are that it was members of the CHAZ security who opened fire and killed these homeless black teens as they were driving a stolen white SUV into CHAZ. A friend of theirs later told reporters that they were heading into CHAZ because they thought that they would be safe there. Instead, they were shot by armed anarchists, waging a war against phantom "white racists" who never materialized. As of the time of this writing, no arrests have been made in any of the shootings, including the ones that left dead bodies in the same area where protesters had painted Black Lives Matter on the road.

CHAZ is a warning to us all about several factors: the cowardice of politicians in the face of the mob, the level to which national news media outlets will fall for convenient propaganda narratives, and the need for agencies that enforce the rule of law in our republic. These systemic failures can only be solved if citizens tell their governments that enough is enough. That is what happened in CHAZ, when after the fifth shooting, Mayor Jenny Durkan finally allowed SPD to retake the area, clear out and arrest occupiers, and return to their abandoned precinct.

Mayor Durkan then promptly blamed the entire situation on someone else.

But the problem is not gone. In fact, only about a week after I returned from CHAZ to Washington, D.C., the spirit of anarcho-communist public vandalism reared its head once again: members of Antifa were attacking statues around the nation's capital. In one instance, they also decided to call for the tearing down of a statue of Abraham Lincoln — the president who ended slavery. As it happened, this statue was only a few minutes from the One America News studio, and so I went down with a camera crew and one other reporter to document the situation. When we arrived, we found that half the crowd amassed in the park was not in favor of destroying a statue of Abraham Lincoln, and that some individuals, like Don Folden, the founder of D.C. Black History Tours, actually appeared in favor of keeping the statue. Yet, as Don spoke, he was pushed back and silenced by masked marauders. I ventured closer to catch what was going on, but was suddenly recognized by the crowd, and within moments surrounded by a swarm of black-clad Antifa adherents. The apparent leader of the group squared off with me, hurling nonsensical insults and profanity in my direction. In response, I calmly replied, "I am not running away." At that point, he and his cohort attempted to push me down the steps onto the concrete walkway below the statue. As the crowd pushed in, I lost my footing, but regained it quickly, despite the assault. For the next few minutes they shoved, kicked, and threw things at me until a security crew from another news service was able to escort me out and D.C. police arrived.

Throughout the ordeal, I did not use force to defend myself other than to push away their attacks, and as a Catholic, I quietly repeated the prayer to St. Michael the Archangel.

The rise of anarchist violence in America is akin to a cultural revolution that has taken place in our society. Its parallel with so-called cancel culture is not happenstance, but by design. Whether individual actors realize it or not, they are agents of nihilistic forces that seek to undermine, subvert, and eventually usurp the institutions of the American republic. Their aim is not reform of the Western system, but a wholesale replacement through a new moral imperialism. Anyone who takes a stand for the republic is labeled a counterrevolutionary and targeted for isolation and shunning — this is the purpose of cancel culture. The only remedy is for patriots to understand these illiberal, Alinsky-derived tactics, see them for what they are, and reject the bad faith actors who pursue them. Americans everywhere must remain faithful to the republic, its virtues, and the preservation of the American experiment from those who would see it ended.

NINETEEN

DOMESTIC TERRORISTS

In December 2019, *FrontPageMag* ran a piece ominously headlined: "Antifa Home Invasions: Can It Happen Here?"

The story detailed how, a month earlier, in Germany's fastest growing city, Leipzig, two Antifa adherents broke into the apartment of a 24-year-old woman who worked at a real estate development company and beat her severely. Along the way, they made clear that the attack was intended as a message.

The company that the young woman worked for was constructing luxury apartment buildings, the kind that in Antifa's anti-capitalist worldview, house fascistic enemies of the people. Earlier, they had destroyed cranes and other equipment at work sites, causing 10 million Euros worth of damage. Now they were taking things to the next level and going after human beings.

Antifa has already been behind hundreds of assaults in North America. While most receive little media coverage, they have become a regular occurrence, particularly in urban centers.

Antifa grew even bolder in 2020, with the summer riots, and cities and governors seemingly unwilling to stop what became almost nightly anarchy and rioting.

What's more, it isn't only beliefs, but community traditions, that are subject to radical attack. In 2017, Antifa actually forced the cancellation of Portland, Oregon's annual Rose Festival Parade because a local Republican group was to participate. "Nazis will not march through Portland unopposed," declared an email from the Antifa's Direct Action Alliance, warning parade organizers that suspected Trump supporters would be dragged out of the parade and attacked *en route*.

In June 2020, as left-wing riots enflamed New York City, the city's top terrorism official told the public the truth about what was happening. According to NBC4 News, Deputy Commissioner for Intelligence and Counterterrorism, John Miller, said there is "a high level of confidence within the NYPD that these unnamed groups had organized scouts, medics, and supply routes of rocks, bottles and accelerants for breakaway groups to commit vandalism and violence. There are strong indicators they planned for violence in advance, using at times encrypted communications."

Miller continued, "One out of every seven arrests, of 686 so far since May 28, has been people from out of state. Those arrested came from Massachusetts, Connecticut, Pennsylvania, New Jersey, Iowa, Nevada, Virginia, Maryland, Texas and St. Paul, Minnesota.

"Before the protests began, organizers of certain anarchist groups set out to raise bail money and to recruit medics and medical teams with gear to deploy in anticipation of violent interactions with police.

"They prepared to commit property damage and directed people who were following them that this should be done selectively and only in wealthier areas or at high-end stores run by corporate entities." Miller stated that the anarchist cells employed coordinated distraction and diversion tactics. "Developed a complex network of bicycle scouts to move ahead of demonstrators in different directions of where police were, and where police were not, for purposes of being able to direct groups from the larger group to places where they could commit acts of vandalism including the torching of police vehicles and Molotov cocktails where they thought officers would not be."

Who are these people who travel around the country in order to riot? Let's look at one case.

Michael Forest Reinoehl was 48 years old and had decided that Trump supporters deserved to die. He worked as a contractor in construction and took odd jobs from friends to support himself. On social media, he posted about snowboarding and claimed he was an Army veteran, though that was later disproven. On social media, Reinoehl posted that he was "100% ANTIFA all the way."

Reinoehl was a key supporter of the Portland riots of 2020, and known as a fixture there. He had a criminal record for narcotics and gun violations and had been estranged from his family. He later described his views in an interview on *Vice*. "A lot of people don't understand what Antifa represents. And if you just look at the basic definition of it, it's just anti-fascist. And I am 100% anti-fascist."

On August 29, 2020, supporters of President Trump decided to hold a march through the city of Portland, which had been rocked by three months of nightly rioting by anarchists and mobs. After the march, one Trump supporter and his friend were walking through the city by themselves, several blocks away from the Justice Center. One, named Aaron Danielson, was wearing the hat of a local conservative group; his friend was named Chandler Pappas.

Surveillance footage released by Portland authorities shows that Reinoehl spotted Danielson walking behind him, and then moved to hide in the entryway of a parking garage alcove, to allow the Trump supporters to pass in front.

Now Reinoehl was behind Danielson and Pappas. Reinoehl waited, and watched as the two walked ahead.

A motorist later told police he saw a man in the vicinity yell out, "Hey, there's the guy!"

Reinoehl and an accomplice then confronted the Trump supporters.

One witness later told police he heard Reinoehl or the accomplice say, "We're going to kill you."

Threatened, Danielson picked up a can of bear spray he was carrying to defend himself, and on footage can be seen spraying it into the air.

Reinoehl had had enough.

He drew his .380 pistol and fired two rounds.

The first round struck the bear spray canister.

The second round struck Danielson, killing him. The round hit him in the upper right chest, and was found lodged in his back. He was pronounced dead 10 minutes after the shooting on Southwest Third Avenue in Portland, Oregon.

Reinoehl fled. His accomplices covered his tracks. He had just committed a political assassination.

In an interview from an undisclosed location, Reinoehl later spoke to *Vice News*. In it, he falsely claimed he was acting in self-defense and that Danielson was about to stab another protester with a knife. All evidence showed this was a lie, propaganda spread to cover up his cold-blooded murder for political purposes. *Vice* gladly promoted this disinformation, despite all evidence to the contrary.

Days later, a federal task force was waiting for Reinoehl. He had been tracked to Lacey, Washington, a sleepy suburb of Olympia. Reinoehl had fled across state lines after committing his assassination. Reportedly, he was staying in a safe house with other anarchist adherents.

The fugitive task force made up of U.S. Marshals and FBI agents was conducting surveillance of the apartment complex where Reinoehl was holed up, waiting for the appropriate moment to arrest him. That evening, as Reinoehl exited the building alone and walked to his car, two dark SUVs converged.

Reinoehl knew he had been caught, and multiple witnesses reported he drew a gun on the federal agents. Within minutes, the task force neutralized the threat, and Michael Forest Reinoehl went down in a hail of gunfire.

His .380 hand gun was recovered at the scene.

Reinoehl is not the first Antifa member to take a human life, but he may be the first to carry out an assassination of opportunity in the modern era. As earlier anarchists promoted, this was an act of propaganda of the deed.

Mary Grabar, author of a *FrontPageMag* piece, noted that in 2011 she saw Antifa in its nascent state at Atlanta's Occupy encampment while teaching at Emory University, "I've seen things progress at an alarming rate… Back then I saw George Soros-supported 'Cop Watch' punks in orange T-shirts putting their video cameras in the faces of police…Today we have masked protestors with weapons calling for the death of police and attacking reporters and attendees of public events, like campus speeches and political rallies… Today we have Dartmouth history professor/Antifa apologist Mark Bray, author of *Antifa: The Anti-Fascist Handbook*, openly advocating violence. Bray admits that the goal is to make such 'everyday fascists' fearful of leaving their homes, and to make their views 'recede into hiding.' Americans who refuse to yield will find it 'politically, socially, economically, and sometimes physically costly to articulate [their views]'… In 2011, I mocked the plastic drum-beating, kazoo-playing Occupy misfits marching down Peachtree Street, and wrote about student antics on college campuses. Today, 'tent cities occupy public spaces in Los Angeles and other major cities, and law-abiding Americans are finding themselves chased out of political rallies, restaurants, and stores, and finding no help from police who have been ordered to 'stand down.'"

Grabar, herself the daughter of Eastern European refugees from communism, knows far better than most how it happened. She is also the author of a recent biography of the communist historian Howard Zinn. In it, she recounts how Zinn's *A People's History of the United States* became the primary source for the teaching of American history in high schools, altering the story of America for a generation of young American minds, lying and distorting with abandon as he cast the founders and other once-sacrosanct figures as nothing but racist oppressors, and otherwise teaching the young to despise their country and celebrate victimhood. He even instructs that America's interest in fighting World War II was not to defeat fascism, but to spread its own version of it – imperialist capitalism.

President Trump announced a 1776 Commission to combat this false indoctrination project, as well as the lies of the *New York Times'* so-called 1619 Project. Time will tell whether the return to fact-based historical education will prevail in American schools. Certainly, one hopes that it does.

Yet the corruption of American education was itself only one step in the left's march to take over society's key institutions, anticipated by Antonio Gramcsi. Today, this radical political ideology holds sway over American academia, media outlets, Hollywood, sports, many religious institutions, and the corporate sector. If you think it doesn't, a trip to the HR Department will clear that up for you very quickly.

It is so-called conservative leaders who let it happen. In their obsession with free market economics and corporate bottom lines, they lost sight of what America had always been about. In short, they embraced free market corporatism so zealously that they gave up on having any cultural influence in America. And when corporations began to threaten freedom of speech online, conservative leaders didn't lift a finger to fight for this sacred right of the American people.

As Breitbart Media's late legendary founder Andrew Breitbart put it, "Politics is downstream from culture."

Ultimately, it is culture that matters most, for it is culture that shapes beliefs and ideals, determining how we see the world and act within it. When the right surrendered the culture, the left quickly moved into the vacuum, led by the Clintons and Obamas who embraced pop culture.

In places where the left holds absolute sway, those who have contrary views tend to keep as quiet as dissidents used to behind the Iron Curtain, lest they succumb to cancel culture for an errant comment in the workplace or social media post.

What is most needed is legislation formally listing Antifa as domestic terrorists. Fifteen states already have such statues on the books, and an all-important federal version was introduced, with presidential support, by Republicans Ted Cruz of Texas and Bill Cassidy of Louisiana in June 2019. In the outbreak of urban violence in 2020, President Trump vowed to label Antifa a domestic terrorist organization.

"Antifa is a group of hateful, intolerant radicals who pursue their unhinged agenda through aggressive violence," said Cruz. "Time and time again, their actions have demonstrated that their only purpose is to inflict harm on those who oppose their views. The hate and violence they spread must be stopped…"

Cassidy rightly termed Antifa "violent masked bullies, protected by liberal privilege" who profess to "fight fascism with actual fascism" and called for "courage, not cowardice" by elected officials "who allow violence against the innocent."

Among key features of the legislation is the prohibition of masks in public demonstrations, an idea that, though it would clearly be an invaluable tool in limiting assaults (and was used to break the KKK), is of course fiercely opposed by the American Civil Liberties Union. "It could be argued that the mask is an important symbolic part of a protester's message," an ACLU spokeswoman maintained. "There are many legitimate reasons people wear masks, including political and religious reasons." In the wake of the coronavirus pandemic, mask-wearing became mandated in many states in 2020.

Federal investigators must use the full resources of the national security apparatus, the FBI, and the Joint Terrorism Task Forces around the country to bring these anti-government extremists to justice. Anti-riot laws must be enforced at the federal level for those crossing state lines.

Where local district attorneys refuse to step in, federal prosecutors must uphold the rule of law. This is a non-partisan issue. Liberals, conservatives, and independents all deserve to live in peaceful cities and towns. Anarchy and mob violence are not political expression, they are crimes and must be dealt with as such.

There are still today's useful idiots, and if history is any guide, things will not end well for them. Because the ideas they are defending – the destruction of capitalism, the overthrow of our republic, and the brutal, even murderous methods intended to bring it about – are inimical to everything in the American spirit. And when they fail, as inevitably they will, their radical allies will take no responsibility, and turn on them. As in Russia and China, today's comrade is tomorrow's counter-revolutionary. Everyone thinks it can't happen here. Enlightened Frenchmen thought that in 1789, Russian moderates in 1917, Chinese nationalists in the 1930s.

There is no place for the Antifa movement in the United States of America. These roving bands of criminal militants are not a legitimate political organization, and the First Amendment does not cover their violence. That Antifa does not maintain a traditional organizational structure has no bearing on the fact that its adherents are criminal agitators, with multiple laws at the state and federal level that can and must be applied to them. Should America face destabilization from extremist anti-government groups, the examples of Weimar Germany and imperial Russia are readily available for us to see.

America has faced threats both internal and external before, and always triumphed. It is my hope that with a true understanding of what Antifa is, and is not, that the American people can make their voice clear on how their government must live up to its duty to enforce law and order, and provide a safe environment for our communities and families. From Seattle to South Dakota, from Portland to Pennsylvania, we are all American citizens first, and we deserve a government that serves justice under the precepts of our constitutional republic, not cowers in the face of a radical militancy.

TWENTY

OUTLOOK ASSESSMENT

There is no national consensus on the definition of domestic terrorism. However, many law enforcement and intelligence entities have employed the general definition of terrorism, most commonly applied to foreign terrorist organizations, to cover this deficiency. Domestic terrorism is acts of violence or threats of violence to achieve political or social ends by U.S.-based groups and individuals. Often, the word "extremist" is used interchangeably with domestic terrorism by government agencies, and this is due to prosecutorial discretion and to avoid specific legal implications of the terrorism label. Extremism means individuals or groups who justify the use of violence to achieve their political goals. This violence may be against persons, property, or both. Mainstream political groups and individuals across the political spectrum from left to right do not condone violence, and seek to achieve social ends through the political process. Those who condone, promote, and conduct violent means are extremists.

In studying the antifascist movement, it is notable for its mixture of ideological and tactical connections with the anarchist terrorism of the 19th-century, and inspiration from Weimar German communists in the 1930s. Antifascism found a resurgence in Cold War Germany, then spread to Western Europe, and ultimately North America. This extremist movement's growth has been fueled first by the increase in globalization in the 1990s, financial capitalism in the 2000s, and later by the spread of international populism in the late 2010s. From the perspective of an Antifa adherent, this all represents violations of their preferred social order. Simultaneously, social media platforms have permitted the vast spread of antifascist ideology, recruitment, organization, and crowdfunding across state and international borders in ways never before possible.

I assess with high confidence that the Antifa movement will continue its growth and expand as a threat to American citizens in the near-term as their extremist ideology is permitted to spread on mainstream digital platforms and law enforcement and elected officials fail to appropriately address the rise of the movement across international borders. Additionally, Antifa adherents will become increasingly violent as their radicalization is given tactical endorsement by mainstream organization, companies, and media outlets that promote, defend, and cover up the movement's activities. Their perceived past successes and also failures will serve the dual purpose of swelling their ranks and radicalizing their adherents. It goes without saying they will continue their focus on soft targets, like political opponents, businesses, churches, rallies, and, when emboldened, even police stations and federal law enforcement. I predict Antifa will eventually come into conflict with U.S. military forces should their extremist movement be permitted to grow. Tactically, Antifa will continue its use of improvised explosive devices such as firebombs and Molotov cocktails, pipe bombs, firearms, and vehicle attacks. Use of roadside or vehicle-born IEDs targeting police forces would be foreseeable as the Antifa evolve into a low-level insurgency. The use of digital media will continue to be employed by Antifa cells with ever-advancing techniques for spreading disinformation across social media, propaganda, doxxing political opponents and journalists, posting manifestos, organizing, livestreaming, and, importantly, crowdfunding their operations.

The information contained in this book and its appendices serve only as an introductory summary of the scope and breadth of this network, which operates cells in numerous regions across Western Europe and North America, and is growing increasingly tactical. Still, due to the mainstream whitewashing of Antifa, there remains a widely-held perception that Antifa is a benign actor, or perhaps even a benevolent force in society. This is wrong, and a dangerous error. Anti-government and anti-social extremist movements are never benign, regardless of where they lie on the political spectrum. Should you encounter someone who fails to heed this basic principle, by all means give them a copy of this book.

The Antifa movement today exists as much as a symptom of the decline and breakdown of social cohesion in the West as it is a catalyst for it. Just as the original Antifa worked to accelerate the demise of the Weimar Republic in the 1930s through destabilization, so too does this movement play a role in accelerating the demise of the American republic, as is their stated aim. Already toward the end of 2020, we have seen chaos and anarchy run rampant in the streets of major North American cities, and political leaders unwilling or unable to fulfill their basic duties of the social compact by providing law, order, and safety to basic citizens. Armed militia threatened a 12-block neighborhood of Capital Hill in Seattle, and the mayor's decision was to abandon the precinct of its police force, allowing the militia to take *de facto* control of the area, and lawlessness and anarchy to take hold. In Kenosha, Wisconsin, roving bands of rioters and looters attacked downtown businesses, and the governor was reluctant to call in the needed number of National Guard to stem the violence. This vacuum of political leadership creates social and physical space for Antifa anarchists to fill with their unique blend of anger and nihilism.

The Antifa movement justifies its use of violence as a form of self-defense against police violence. Its members view police responses as state-sanctioned illegitimate violence and their own brutality and aggression as a form of self-defense against a society they define as fascist. Antifa defines capitalism, the two-party system, organized religion, financial institutions, and even basic law itself as fascism. Many media outlets and even some national security officials misunderstand this aspect of the Antifa movement, due to ignorance of Antifa's goals. The common refrain from those who have not studied this movement is essentially that if Antifa means anti-fascism then it must simply mean that it is against everyone who is fascist or racist. Those who fall for this ruse reveal their lack of familiarity with the subject matter. The use of the label "antifascist" is a term of art for communists to unite the various strands of anti-establishment leftism, and has been in use since the days of the Weimar Republic, and later when East Germany was ruled by communism. As previously stated, the official title of the Berlin Wall was the "Antifascist Rampart."

The goals of law enforcement and national security officials must be to detect, disrupt, and deter Antifa extremist activity, using existing legal statutes and capabilities provided to government. Federal and state governments have ample security capabilities to bring to bear against threat actors such as intelligence collection, communications intercepts, and financial asset tracking and seizure. Violent anti-government extremism's criminal nature affords the use of such capabilities to ensure law and order across jurisdictions.

The goals of political parties, media outlets, journalists, and individual citizens must be to understand the threat of Antifa and their affinity groups. Politicians and media should refrain from over-stating as well as understating the role of anti-government extremist groups, and adhere to fact-based narratives when dealing with them. Mainstream actors must refrain from knowingly engaging in misinformation, and must deal with the truth as it is.

In these pages, we have seen that when anarchy, lawlessness, and nihilistic insurrectionist groups are allowed to spread, they destabilize societies, erode confidence in the political system, and undermine governments. Anarcho-communists are not interested in a conversation or a debate. Their stated goal is social destruction and violent insurrection of the systems of liberal democracy and the constitutional republic. As they have told us again and again, they will seek their ends by any means necessary, and they have shown how serious they are by their deadly actions. It is time for the world to start listening.

ACKOWLEDGEMENTS

This book would not have been possible without the support of the following incredible people:

My loving wife Tanya and our two boys. My brother Kevin who had my back in CHAZ and multiple Antifa situations. My parents and family for always being there for me no matter what and the entire team at Calamo Press. The research efforts of Noah Sell, Johnny Steak, and Rafello J. Carone. Niko House, David Reaboi, Lee Smith, Raheem Kassam, Libby Emmons, Gabriel Nadales and the entire documentary crew that worked on Antifa: Rise of the Black Flags. The Herring Family and the amazing team at One America News Network for giving a platform to this important work.

APPENDIX

APPENDIX ONE: ANARCHIST FEDERATION (HTTP://AFED.ORG.UK/ABOUT/ABOUT-THE-AF/) STATEMENT OF PURPOSE:

"As anarchist communists we fight for a world without leaders, where power is shared equally amongst communities, and people are free to reach their full potential."

WHO WE ARE:

"As anarchists we are members of the working class who are conscious of the class struggle and who strive for full freedom and equality. This form of society will only work through the voluntary practice of self-organisation and mutual aid which we try to undertake in the here and now. Being an anarchist means not only throwing off the chains of hierarchy and coercion and striving for personal freedom but also taking responsibility for our actions where they affect others, making ourselves accountable to those we chose to work with, and practising solidarity with other people in struggle.

"We believe that in order to get from our current society to a world free of exploitation and oppression there is a need for revolutionary organisations. This is the basis of the Anarchist Federation. We are committed to building an effective organisation which has a collective identity and works towards the common goal of anarchist communism. We believe that such a collective identity must be based on free association and respect for the autonomy of the individual.

We value the diversity of our members as we continue to develop our ideas in the light of new developments in the world and from our experiences of struggle.

WHAT WE WANT

"The AF works for the creation of an international libertarian communist movement. We believe this movement cannot be created without building a specific anarchist communist organisation. We believe that for social revolution to be successful it will require the activity of this revolutionary organisation as a part of the working class, while rejecting any idea that it acts as a self-appointed leader.

WHAT WE DO

"While being a member of the AF should not take over our entire lives, and personal circumstances make different levels of activity possible for different people, we are not a passive fan club for anarchy. It is hoped that all members will contribute in some way both to the development of our ideas and to our activities, both locally and throughout the federation, as and when they are able.

"The AF has a number of vital roles to perform in order to reach our goal. We must:

"Support resistance against capitalism, state, and other oppression where it exists, and attempt to spark it where it does not.

"Produce information and analysis against capitalist society and argue the case for anarchist communism.

"Be the memory of the working class by making the lessons of past gains and defeats widely known.

"Be a forum for debate and discussion between all elements of the revolutionary working class.

"Work to understand the developments in our society and deliver a coherent communist response to them.

"Seek to win the leadership of ideas within the working class.

"Intervene and co-ordinate our actions in the workplace and the community.

"Work to build a global anarchist movement as part of the International of Anarchist Federations.

HOW WE ORGANISE

"For an anarchist organisation to remain non-hierarchical and non-authoritarian it is essential that roles and responsibilities are distributed evenly. For federation-wide officer roles, we operate a formal structure of delegation and direct democracy with recallable delegates, meaning that if someone is not fulfilling responsibilities they can have those tasks passed on to someone else in a non-judgemental and supportive way for the good of the organisation. Many roles are informal and temporary, however, and it is hoped that members will also fulfill these as best they can and in an accountable way. One of the key ways to support the organisation is to anticipate something that needs doing and take some responsibility for seeing that it is addressed.

"The organisation is based on the following fundamental criteria:

FEDERALISM

"The AF is a decentralised organisation made up of individual members who form into groups based on location. We have no leaders or central decision-making body and the direction of the organisation is decided upon by its members. Members come together regularly to develop theory, strategy and tactics through debate and discussion, aiming for participation of all members in decision-making such that effective consensus can be reached. Most decisions are made at Federal Delegate Meetings. Those who cannot attend these meetings can mandate any other member to act as their delegate to bring their positions to these meetings to ensure that their opinion is included.

POLITICAL UNITY

"The AF is based on a common set of aims and principles, with its structure detailed in the membership handbook. Before joining, a potential member must agree with the outlined aims and principles of the organisation. In addition, we may adopt policies and analyses that are the result of discussion and elaboration by all the members. As these will be developed collectively, it is expected that they will reflect the views of the whole organisation.

"Members may propose changes to these structures, but it must be the result of a genuine change of view emerging from new ideas and experiences since their joining the organisation. When an individual joins, it is expected that they join as a result of genuine agreement with the political and organisational principles of the AF. As membership is sponsored by a group or regional secretary it is their responsibility to ensure that new members fully understand these documents.

TACTICAL UNIT

"The AF seeks to act in a co-ordinated way, developing strategies and tactics through discussion and debate which members are expected to implement where appropriate.

COLLECTIVE RESPONSIBILITY
AND SOLIDARITY

"Members must not act so as to undermine the federation but instead must seek to support the federation in practice and show solidarity for other members.

FREE ASSOCIATION AND AUTONOMY

"The individual does not subsume their identity into the collective. A member is one who has chosen to associate with others and retains their autonomy. If a member or group does not agree with policies, strategies or tactics adopted by the federation once they have become members, then they do not have to implement these decisions and may express their disagreement."

APPENDIX TWO:
SUMMER OF RAGE 2020 TIMELINE:

March 2020

- Mid-to-late-March - Nationwide lockdowns begin due to a global pandemic caused by a novel coronavirus originating from Wuhan, China. Schools shut down, all public events cancelled, workers deemed non-essential and laid off by the millions in one fell swoop, all in an effort to "flatten the curve" of medical staff and ICU capacity. NYC particularly hard hit. Government and public health officials offer unclear information, polarizing debates break out immediately. Citizens first told lockdown will only be 15 days, then this is extended to 30 days, then extended without end. Uncertainty sets in while rent and bills pile up, yet people unable to work. Government increases unemployment payments. Run on supermarkets, rationing, mail delayed, tensions mount.

April 2020

- Rallies begin popping up to oppose the lockdowns. Several include armed protesters. Over 30 states hold one form of anti-lockdown rally or another.

- Social media cancel culture picks up steam. "Twitter do your thing" left-wing online mobs get dozens of children and adults doxxed and have their lives ruined for their social media posts deemed politically incorrect both recent and from years prior.

May 2020

- 5th: Video of the shooting of Ahmaud Arbery is released and increases tensions nationwide. Gregory and Travis McMichael are arrested and charged after pressure forces DA's hand. The shooting causes the Black Lives Matter organization to take center stage in the national media again. The McMichaels fit the perfect description of a "white, backwards, redneck, conservative, gun-toting, racist."

- 25th: George Floyd dies of a drug-induced heart attack in police custody, according to coroner's report. Video of officer Derrick Chauvin kneeling on Floyd's neck goes viral, officially sparking the summer of rage.

- 26th: In the morning, the Minneapolis PD holds a press conference about the incident which downplays the events. Chauvin and the three on-looking officers are placed on paid leave pending an investigation

  □ Minneapolis Mayor Jacob Frey, and Police Chief Medaria Arradondo hold a press conference in which they express solidarity with the black community and those outraged across the country. Frey says, "The simple truth is that he should be with us this morning" and Arradondo, "Being black in America should not be a death sentence" officially solidifying the "racist cop" narrative. Frey also tweets his official statement.

  □ Protests begin midday. A shrine is erected on the spot of Floyd's arrest. Hundreds gather at the spot and chant "I can't breathe."

  □ Mid-afternoon, Chief Arradondo announces firing of the four officers. Floyd's family calls for murder charges and the Minnesota BCA and the FBI open investigations.

  □ Around 6 p.m., protestors march across town to the 3rd police precinct, where the officers worked. The protest devolves into a riot as they clash with police protecting the precinct. The rioting and violence become so much that the MPD has to defend the precinct with tear gas and rubber bullets. Anti-police City Councilman Jeremiah Ellison urges Mayor Frey to leave the rioters alone.

▫ Protestors show up outside the house of ex-officer Derrick Chauvin.

• 27th: Protests continue throughout the day at many locations across the city.

▫ Protestors gather again at the third precinct which is once again defended by officers with tear gas and rubber bullets. The protestors have expanded to include not only the people from the local predominantly black neighborhood but also many white outsiders fitted with masks, helmets, milk for tear gas, etc.; presumably these are Antifa.

▫ The Autozone near the precinct has its windows smashed by a masked man in attire similar to the Antifa black bloc with a hammer and umbrella, the first signs of vandalizing private property. This man is latter claimed by the media and MPD to be a "white supremacist" attempting to incite the protestors to violence. The identity of the "Umbrella Man" has never been revealed and as such this claim cannot be verified.

▫ In the evening, the Target near the precinct is heavily vandalized and looted. This is caught on film by multiple different people, becoming the first major looting of the riots. A disabled white woman blocks the entrance to the Target with her mobility scooter and is beaten and sprayed with a fire extinguisher. She defends herself against the mob with a swiss army knife to little avail.

▫ The Autozone is set on fire, the first building to be torched.

▫ Riots continue through the night with businesses in the area being looted and many burned. One pawn shop owner defends his shop and is shot and killed a looter. The Minneapolis Fire Department is delayed in reaching fires and a police escort is required to reach the few buildings they could.

• 28th: The damage done is caught on camera the next morning and the city looks like a bombed-out warzone.

▫ Mayor Frey declares a state of emergency and asks Governor Tim Walz for the Minnesota National Guard.

▫ Protests resume in Minneapolis during the day and crowds gather in multiple locations across the city.

▫ In Columbus, Ohio, protests turn into riots as activists clash with police and vandalize state capital buildings.

▫ By nightfall, Minneapolis riots resume and the police once again has to defend the Third Precinct. Crowds march on the Frist Precinct and to the downtown shopping district. The Max It Pawn shop near the Third Precinct is looted and burned. A charred body is found two months later within the wreckage, bringing the riot death toll to two.

▫ Violence at the Third Precinct escalates and Mayor Frey gives the order to abandon the precinct. The officers in the precinct are forced to break through the mob's barricade and flee as bottles, bricks, and other objects are hurled at them. The precinct is subsequently burned.

▫ An MSNBC reporter, broadcasting live from the riots, covers for the rioters claiming "This is mostly a protest. It is not, generally speaking, unruly." – as a building burns behind him.

▫ In neighboring St. Paul, 170 businesses are damaged and looted in the riots overnight.

▫ Riots begin in Phoenix. Rioters clash with police and attack government buildings.

▫ Riots begin in Denver. Rioters clash with police and multiple gunshots are heard but no one is shot. Three police officers are injured.

▫ Riots begin in Indianapolis. Rioters clash with police and vandalize buildings.

• 29th: Governor Walz imposes an 8:00 p.m. curfew on the Twin Cities.

▫ Chauvin is charged with third-degree murder and second-degree manslaughter.

- President Trump tweets "When the looting starts, the shooting starts." and is subsequently censored by Twitter, claiming he was inciting violence.

- A CNN reporting crew in Minneapolis is arrested during protests. They are released an hour later.

- Riots continue in Minneapolis through the night. Rioters gather near the fifth precinct. More looting and burning occur. St. Mary's Catholic Basilica is vandalized and lit on fire, although the damage was not extensive.

- Riots continue in Columbus as rioters injure police and loot and damage over 100 buildings.

- Riots erupt in D.C. and the White House goes on lockdown as Secret Service battles rioters. Multiple agents are injured by rioters.

- Riots and looting break out in New York City. Demonstrators clash with police throwing bottles, bricks, etc. One young woman is arrested and charged with attempted murder for throwing a Molotov cocktail at a police van.

- Riots and looting breakout in downtown Los Angeles and scuffle with police, injuring officers.

- Riots start in Portland Oregon. Mayor Ted Wheeler declares a state of emergency. The County Justice Center is set on fire and two officers are injured.

- Riots begin in Richmond, VA. Rioters clash with police.

- Riots begin in Seattle.

- □ Riots continue in Phoenix with multiple government buildings being damaged.

- □ Protests in Atlanta turn violent. Rioters clash with police and damage the CNN center, light the College Football Hall of Fame on Fire, and loot nearby businesses. Governor Brian Kemp declared a state of emergency and deploys the Georgia National Guard. One rioter is shot.

- □ Riots begin in Chicago. Rioters clash with police and demonstrate in front of Trump International Hotel.

- □ During protests in Detroit, shots are fired at a car, killing the driver.

- □ Riots begin in Salt Lake City. A man defending himself with a bow and arrow is beaten by the mob. Governor Herbert activates the Utah National Guard.

- □ An officer is shot during riots in Milwaukee.

- □ Riots kick off in Dallas. St. Jude's Cathlic Chapel is vandalized.

- 30th: Riots subside in Minneapolis but demonstrators continue to gather at the George Floyd memorial and in front of government buildings.

- □ President Trump tweets responding to the previous nights riots claiming they were "professionally organized" and praised the Secret Service's work in defense.

- Rioters gather outside the Oakland California police headquarters, setting off fireworks and throwing projectiles. Nearby businesses are looted and damaged. Two federal officers are shot and one dies, raising the death toll to 3. DHS Acting Deputy Secretary Ken Cuccinelli calls it "an act of domestic terrorism."

- Minnesota politicians claim 80% of those arrested are from out of state and 40 people were tied to white supremacist organizations. This information has not been confirmed.

- Protestors gather outside the Ohio Statehouse in Columbus and soon turn to rioting. Governor Dewine deploys the Ohio National Guard to the city. Mayor Ginther announces 10 p.m. curfew.

- Riots continue in D.C. in front of the White House and elsewhere. The Lincoln Memorial and WWII Memorials are defaced.

- In San Francisco, looting and vandalism take place and Mayor London Breed issues a curfew.

- Rioting continues in New York City. St. Patrick's Cathedral is vandalized.

- Rioting and looting continue in New York City, 33 NYPD officers are injured.

- Los Angeles Mayor Eric Garcetti authorizes the deployment of the California National Guard. Our Lady of Mt. Lebanon-St. Peter Maronite Catholic Cathedral is vandalized.

- In Albany, New York, rioters burn and loot banks and businesses and attack the south police precinct.

- A 10:30 pm curfew is imposed in Buffalo, NY in response to rioters.

- Protests turn violent in Rochester, NY and a 9 pm curfew is imposed. Rochester officials later claim the riots were fueled by "outsiders" and anarchists and that the riots were "very organized."

- Looters take to Beverly Hills and an 8pm curfew is put in place.

- Rioters violently clash with police and loot La Mesa, CA

- Riots continue in Portland. Rioters clash with police and the Portland Law and Justice Center is set on fire.

- Riots continue in Richmond. Multiple Confederate monuments on Monument Avenue are vandalized. The Memorial to the Women of the Confederacy museum is set on fire.

- Riots and looting continue in Seattle. Rioters loot two AR-15's from a police car. They are disarmed by a security guard.

- In Denver, three police officers are hit by a speeding car leaving all three with serious injuries. The suspect is later arrested. The Cathedral Basilica of the Immaculate Conception is vandalized.

- In Chicago, riots continue. Six people are shot and one dies. A dozen officers are injured. Mayor Lori Lightfoot imposes a 9 pm curfew. The drawbridges are raised to prevent travel.

- Riots continue in Indianapolis. Government buildings are damaged and multiple officers are injured. A molotov cocktail is thrown at a vehicle injuring one. Multiple people are shot and 3 die.

- Riots in Louisville lead Governor Andy Beshear to call in the Kentucky National Guard. LPD and the National Guard are fired on from a crowd. Officers return fire and kill one.

- In St. Louis, riots breakout and demonstrators block I-64 and I-70. One protestor is killed by being run over and dragged by a FedEx semi-truck.

- In Salem, Oregon, police report "explosive devices" thrown during protests at Oregon State Capitol.

- Riots escalate in Pittsburgh. Two local newscasters are beaten by a mob for filming the riots.

- Riots begin in Philadelphia. Stores are looted and a statue of Mayor Frank Rizzo is vandalized and unsuccessful attempts are made to tear it down. 13 officers are injured while clashing with rioters. One officer is hit by a car and hospitalized.

- In Charleston, South Carolina, two men wearing MAGA hats are beaten by a mob.

- □ A man is brutally beaten attempting to defend his store during riots in Dallas.

- □ Protesters topple a statue of Edward W. Carmack in Nashville.

- 31st: Protests continue in Minneapolis. 5,000 to 6,000 protestors block the I-35 freeway. A truck driver, unaware of the protests, speeds into the crowd. He is then pulled from his cab and beaten.

  - □ President Trump announces he will designate Antifa as a domestic terror organization.

  - □ Long Beach, California is looted.

  - □ New York Deputy Commissioner John Miller claims groups "used encrypted messaging apps ahead of the protests to raise bail money and recruit medics in anticipation of violent interactions with the police. The groups also developed supply routes to transport gasoline, rocks and bottles during the protests. One out of every seven people arrested lived outside of New York, including from as far away as Texas and Minnesota."

  - □ Rioting and looting occur across D.C. and at the White House. Historic St. John's Episcopal Church across from the White House is set ablaze.

  - □ Businesses are looted and burned in Santa Monica, California.

- Rioting and looting continue in New York City, most heavily in Soho and Union Square. 12 officers are injured.

- Mayor Wheeler declares an 8 p.m. curfew in Portland.

- Riots and looting begin in Spokane, Washington and a curfew is enacted.

- Rioting and looting in Birmingham, Alabama leads to a state of emergency being enacted.

- Activists burn the American Flag outside the Fort Lauderdale Police Headquarters.

- The Illinois National Guard is deployed to Chicago. Rioting and looting become widespread. By the end of the night, 82 people are shot and 19 killed, making it the deadliest weekend of the year.

- In Davenport, Iowa three people are shot and two die. One officer is shot in a drive-by.

- Riots in Boston lead the city to deploy the Massachusetts National Guard. Clashes with police leave seven officers injured.

- In Klamath Falls, Oregon, it is reported that multiple busses of Antifa with bricks and weapons are en route to the local protest. The busses never arrive.

- Rioting and looting continue in Philadelphia and the Pennsylvania National Guard is deployed.

- □ The United Daughters of the Confederacy in Alexandria Virginia remove the Appomattox statue.

June 2020:

- 1st-7th: - Clashes begin in Seattle's Capitol Hill Neighborhood between anarchists and Seattle PD of the East Precinct.

- 1st: Mayor Bowser of D.C. imposes a 7 p.m. curfew.

  - □ President Trump addresses the nation and threatened to invoke the insurrection act to quell the riots.

  - □ Secret Service clears a path through rioters outside the White House for President Trump to walk to St. John's Church and take a photograph holding up a Bible.

  - □ William McKinley Monument in Columbus is vandalized. McKinley was assassinated by an anarcho-socialist.

  - □ The City of Columbus removes a statue of Christopher Columbus at City Hall.

  - □ Protesters topple statue of Robert E. Lee in Montgomery, Alabama.

  - □ The City of Columbus declares racism a public health crisis.

  - □ Rioting and looting continue in New York City, mainly centered in Manhattan and the Bronx. The iconic Macy's is looted. Mayor Bill de Blasio declares an 11 p.m. curfew.

- □ The Florida National Guard is deployed in Fort Lauderdale.

- □ Police in Davenport, Iowa are ambushed. Two officers are shot and a third returned fire. Two people are shot and killed.

- □ In St. Louis, four police officers are shot during riots. David Dorn, a black former St. Louis police captain is shot and killed defending a pawn shop.

- □ In Philadelphia, riots continue and a group of 50 to 70 armed Italians protect their neighborhood from the mob.

- □ Birmingham officials remove a statue of Confederate Charles Linn.

- 2nd: "Blackout Tuesday" occurs on Tuesday as people post black squares in solidarity with BLM.

- □ Protests continue in D.C.

- □ President Trump visits the St. John Paul II National Shrine.

- □ The City of Birmingham removes the Confederate Soldiers and Sailors monument.

- □ Attorney General Barr deploys federal agents to Miami.

- □ Bust of General Lee is removed in Fort Myers, Florida.

- □ Four officers are shot during riots in St. Louis.

- □ In Philadelphia, rioting and looting continue. One person is shot by a gun store owner while attempting to loot it. Another rioter is killed by his own explosive device.

- 3rd: In Minnesota, Chauvin's murder charge is upgraded to second degree murder and the three other officers are charged with aiding and abetting second degree murder.

  - □ Attorney General William Barr deploys federal agents of various agencies to D.C. to quell riots and protect monuments.

  - □ San Diego County requests the California National Guard.

  - □ La Mesa, California requests the California National Guard.

  - □ In Brooklyn, two officers are shot and one stabbed in the neck defending against looters.

  - □ New York Mayor de Blasio defunds the NYPD, lowering their budget from $6 billion to $5 billion.

  - □ Philadelphia officials remove the statue of fmr Mayor Frank Rizzo.

- 4th: The Floyd family holds a George Floyd memorial service which is attended by many prominent political figures.

  - □ A statue of Jesus is decapitated at St. John the Evangelist Catholic Church in Wasco, California.

- Bronx Commissioner Dermont Shea claims the demonstration the previous day was "led by 'outside agitators.' Interlopers had come to the neighborhood with guns and gasoline," he claimed, "advertising that they were going to burn things down, that they were going to injure cops, that they were going to cause mayhem."

- Dallas city officials remove the *One Riot, One Ranger* statue.

• 5th: Activists paint "Black Lives Matter" on 16th street NW in D.C. and rename Lafayette square "Black Lives Matter Plaza."

- City officials remove a statue of Confederate Admiral Raphael Semmes in Mobile, Alabama.

• 6th: In a confrontation with protestors outside his home, Mayor Frey denies that he is willing to abolish the Minneapolis PD. He is then booed back into his house.

- Activists paint "Defund the Police" on 16th street NW in D.C.

- A statue of Confederate General Wickham is toppled by protesters in Richmond.

• 7th: In Dearborn, Michigan a statue of Mayor Orville Hubbard is removed.

• 8th: The Seattle East Precinct is abandoned and the "Capitol Hill Autonomous Zone" aka CHAZ is declared in the surrounding six blocks.

- □ Confederate Soldiers and Sailors Monument is removed by city officials in Indianapolis.

- □ A statue of Confederate John B. Castleman is removed by the City of Louisville, Kentucky.

- 9th: Statues of Christopher Columbus and Jefferson Davis are toppled in Richmond.

  - □ The City of Jacksonville removes the Jacksonville Confederate Monument.

- 10th: An American Indian Movement group tears down a statue of Christopher Columbus at the state capitol in St. Paul, Minnesota.

  - □ Los Angeles officials announce that homicides have increased 250% from May 31st to June 6th.

  - □ Protestors attempt and fail to set up an autonomous zone in Portland.

  - □ Protesters topple the Jefferson Davis Memorial in Richmond.

  - □ Protestors behead and topple the Confederate monument in Portsmouth, Virginia.

- 11th: In St. Louis, Catholics begin to gather for a rosary protest in response to calls to remove the statue of St. Louis IX. They will continue gathering daily for weeks.

  - □ County officials remove the Gadsden Confederate Memorial in Quincy, Florida.

- City officials remove Confederate Cow Cavalry Monument in Plant City, Florida.

- Protesters in Boston decapitate the statue of Christopher Columbus.

- City officials in Camden, New Jersey remove a statue of Christopher Columbus.

- Richmond officials remove the Richmond Police Memorial.

• 12th: Atlanta police shoot and kill Rayshard Brooks outside a Wendy's after he steals the officer's taser and fires at them. Riots ensue.

- The Minneapolis city council unanimously votes to disband the MPD, however they are unable to do so thanks to the city charter.

- Protestors declare an autonomous zone in Nashville, Tennessee.

- Protestors paint "Defund the Police" on the street in Baltimore.

- City officials remove the Delaware Law Enforcement Memorial in Dover, Delaware.

- City officials remove the Equestrian Statue of Caesar Rodney in Wilmington, Delaware.

- Protestors declare the "Nashville Autonomous Zone" on capitol grounds in Nashville, Tennessee. It is dismantled by state authorities hours later.

- A statue of Confederate Sam Davis is removed in Nashville.

- City officials in Wilmington, Delaware remove a statue of Christopher Columbus.

- City officials in Columbia, South Carolina remove a statue of Christopher Columbus.

• 13th: Rioters in Atlanta burn down the Wendy's where Rayshard Brooks was killed.

- Protesters topple a bust of John McDonogh in New Orleans.

- County officials remove Confederate Monument in Fort Worth, Texas.

- Kentucky officials remove a statue of Jefferson Davis in Frankfort.

- Cherokee Nation officials remove a statue of Confederate Cherokee Stand Watie and the Confederate Soldier Fountain in Tahlequah, Oklahoma.

- Protesters topple *The Pioneer* and *The Pioneer Mother* statues in Eugene, Oregon.

• 14th: A statue of President Thomas Jefferson is toppled in Portland. A statue of York, the only black person on the Lewis and Clark voyage, is vandalized and removed at The University of Portland.

• 15th: City officials remove Confederate Soldiers' Memorial Bridge sign and statue in Clarksville, Tennessee.

- □ County officials remove the Equestrian Statue of Juan de Oñate in Alcalde, New Mexico.

- □ A bust of Christopher Columbus is removed by Detroit city officials.

- 16th: A statue of Christopher Columbus is removed by city officials in St. Louis.

- □ City officials remove the Norfolk Confederate Monument in Virginia.

- □ City officials remove the Statue of Juan de Oñate in Albuquerque, New Mexico.

- □ The statue of John Sutter is removed in Sacramento, California.

- 17th: The Confederate Howitzer monument it toppled in Richmond.

- □ The Fulton County DA announces 11 charges against the officer who killed Rayshard Brooks prompting Atlanta police officers to not answer calls for the next three days in protest of the DA's decision.

- □ Spirit of the Confederacy monument removed by city officials in Houston, Texas.

- □ City officials remove Jefferson Davis Memorial Boulder in Brownsville, Texas.

- □ Grave marker of 17 unidentified Confederate soldiers vandalized by rioters in Silver Spring, Maryland.

- County officials remove the Marker of Jefferson Davis Highway in Bakersfield, California.

- 18th: Activists paint "Black Lives Matter" on P street in Fresno, California. Mayor Lee Braund declares June 18th "Black Lives Matter Day."

  - San Francisco officials remove a statue of Christopher Columbus in Pioneer Park.

  - Georgia officials remove Dekalb County Confederate Monument.

  - A statue of President George Washington is toppled in Portland.

  - San Diego Parks and Rec officials remove Robert E. Lee Highway marker.

  - Little Rock officials remove Memorial to Company A, Capitol Guards.

  - The University of Portland removes the Captain William Clark Monument.

- 19th: Juneteenth

  - Rioters tear down a statue of Albert Pike in Judiciary Square D.C.

  - Rioters in Golden Gate Park, San Francisco tear down and vandalize statues of St. Junipero Serra, Francis Scott Key, Ulysses S. Grant, Miguel Cervantes, Don Quixote, and Sancho Panza. Archbishop Cordileone condemned the act as "an act of sacrilege [and] an act of the Evil One."

- Nancy Pelosi removes four paintings of Confederates from the Capitol Building.

- The City of Columbus removed the statue of Christopher Columbus at Columbus State Community College.

- Franklin County, Ohio declares the replacement of Columbus Day with Juneteenth as a paid holiday.

- Protesters topple North Carolina State Confederate Monument in Raleigh.

- City officials removes a statue of Christopher Columbus in Houston, Texas.

- 20th: Two shootings take place in Capitol Hill, Seattle at CHAZ, where first responders are unable to respond due to lack of police protection. A 19-year old black teenager Horace Lorenzo Anderson Jr is killed, 33-year old DeJuan Young is shot but survives and blames the 'KKK' with no evidence.

  - A monument to the Revolutionary War First Virginia Regiment is torn down in Richmond.

  - United Daughters of the Confederacy remove Confederate Monument in Pine Bluff, Arkansas.

  - Protesters topple a statue of St. Junipero Serra in Los Angeles.

- 21st: 3rd shooting in CHAZ, a 17-year-old male who survives and refuses to speak to police.

  ▫ Black NASCAR driver Bubba Wallace's crew finds a "noose" hanging in his Talladega garage, prompting an investigation and national outcry.

  ▫ Demonstrators remove the Confederate Soldiers and Sailors Monument, Confederate Women's Monument, and Henry Lawson Wyatt Monument in Raleigh, North Carolina.

  ▫ The United Daughters of the Confederacy remove the Loudoun County Confederate monument in Leesburg, Virginia.

- 22nd: The FBI concludes that Bubba Wallace did not find a noose but rather a garage rope-pull and the hate crime was a hoax.

  ▫ County officials remove Confederate Soldiers Monument in Greenville, North Carolina.

  ▫ Prominent Black Lives Matter activist Shaun King tweets "I think the statues of the white European they claim is Jesus should also come down… All murals and stained glass windows of white Jesus, and his European mother, and their white friends should also come down."

- 23rd: Fourth shooting in CHAZ, victim is a man in his 30s who refuses to assist police investigation.

- Rioters try but fail to tear down a statue of President Andrew Jackson in Lafayette Square, D.C.

- Huntsville, Alabama police chief Mark McMurray claims Antifa orchestrated the violent protests in his city. "Everything about antifa was here on the backside of the event, not the front side."

- The remaining Confederate monuments in Raleigh, North Carolina are removed by city officials.

- Italians in Philadelphia brawl with rioters as they defend a statue of Christopher Columbus.

- City officials remove the John C. Calhoun Monument in Charleston, South Carolina.

- Protesters topple a statue of Hans Christian Hegs in Madison, Wisconsin.

- 24th: City officials remove Confederate War Memorial in Dallas.

  - County Officials remove the Warrenton County Confederate Soldiers Monument in North Carolina.

  - County Officials remove "The Granville Gray" monument in Oxford, North Carolina.

  - City Officials remove the Judah Benjamin marker in Charlotte, North Carolina.

  - City officials remove statue of Christopher Columbus in New Haven, Connecticut.

- □ Protesters topple the *Forward* statue in Madison, Wisconsin.

- 25th: County officials in Denton, Texas remove the Denton Confederate Soldier Monument.

  - □ Protesters topple a Civil War Monument in Denver.

  - □ City officials remove a statue of Christopher Columbus in Norwalk, Connecticut.

- 26th: President Trump signs executive order to protect monuments and prosecute vandals.

  - □ The United Daughters of the Confederacy remove Confederate Memorial in Minden, Louisiana.

  - □ Protesters topple a statue of Christopher Columbus in Denver.

  - □ City officials remove the statue of Kit Carson in Denver.

- 27th: Archbishop Cordileone holds exorcism in Golden Gate Park at the site of the statue of St. Junipero Serra which was toppled.

  - □ Two are shot and one killed at a Breanna Taylor protest in Louisville. The suspect is injured by bystanders and arrested.

  - □ In St. Louis, after Catholic rosary protestors were slandered as white supremacists by activist Umar Lee, they were assaulted and harassed by counter protesters while praying. Two suspects are arrested.

- □ The United Daughters of the Confederacy remove Monument to the Confederate Dead in Fayetteville, North Carolina.

- 28th: Protesters in St. Louis break into a gated community where they are met by Mark and Patricia McCloskey and their firearms.

- 29th: Two black teenagers are shot in CHAZ, with multiple reports stating antifascist security opened fire on them when their SUV was driving towards the CHAZ barricade. 16-year old Antonio Mays Jr. dies, and video is posted to social media of anarchists removing evidence from the scene.

  - □ City officials remove "To our Confederate dead" monument in Louisburg, North Carolina.

  - □ City officials remove "Our Confederate Soldiers" monument in Beaumont, Texas.

  - □ Charleston, West Virginia officials remove Confederate Kanawha Riflemen memorial.

  - □ Protestors behead and topple the Confederate Soldier statue in Frederick, Maryland.

  - □ City officials remove a statue of Christopher Columbus in Hartford, Connecticut.

- 30th: Mississippi State legislature votes to remove the Confederate flag from the state flag.

  - □ County officials remove a Confederate monument in Rocky Mount, North Carolina.

- ▢ County officials remove the Rockdale County Confederate Monument in Conyers, Georgia.

July 2020:

- 1st: Richmond officials remove monument to Confederate General Stonewall Jackson.

  - ▢ County officials remove Lenoir County Confederate Monument in North Carolina.

  - ▢ City officials remove a statue of Christopher Columbus in Columbus, Ohio.

  - ▢ A statue of Christopher Columbus is removed by city officials in San Antonio.

- 2nd: Federal agents are deployed to Portland as a part of President Trump's Operation Legend and begin rounding up rioters.

  - ▢ Richmond officials remove the monument to Confederate Matthew Fontaine Murray.

  - ▢ A statue of the Blessed Virgin Mary is decapitated at St. Ann's Church in Crown Point, Indiana.

- 3rd: Protesters topple a statue of Confederate Benjamin Welch Owens in Lothian, Maryland.

- 4th: Protestors gather on Interstate 5 in Seattle. A car drove and struck two protestors, killing one.

  - ▢ The San Jose Mission in Fremont, California is vandalized.

- □ Protesters decapitate a statue of Christopher Columbus in Waterbury, Connecticut.

- □ Protesters topple a statue of Christopher Columbus in Baltimore.

- □ Protesters topple a statue of St. Junipero Serra in Sacramento.

- □ Heavily armed black protestors march through Stone Mountain Georgia to protest the monument, the largest Confederate monument in the world.

- □ A 500-foot "Black Lives Matter" mural is painted on the street in Boston.

- □ Seattle protesters topple the United Confederate Veterans Memorial.

- 5th: City officials remove a statue of Confederate Judah P. Benjamin in Sarasota, Florida.

  - □ Protesters topple a statue of Frederick Douglas in Rochester, New York.

- 6th: City officials remove a statue of Christopher Columbus in Bridgeport, Connecticut.

- 7th: Richmond officials remove monument to Confederate General J.E.B. Stuart.

  - □ City officials remove Confederate *Gloria Victis* monument in Salisbury, North Carolina.

  - □ Protesters topple the Greensboro Confederate Statue in North Carolina.

- □ The California State Legislature removes *Columbus' Last Appeal to Queen Isabella* in Sacramento.

- 8th: County officials remove the Anson County Courthouse Confederate monument in Wadesboro, North Carolina.

  - □ City officials remove the Confederate Soldiers and Sailors monument in Richmond.

  - □ City officials remove a statue of Christopher Columbus in Trenton, New Jersey.

- 9th: New York City officials paint "Black Lives Matter" on the street in front of Trump Tower.

  - □ City officials remove the Confederate Fitzhugh Lee Cross and the Joseph Bryan statue in Richmond.

- 10th: County officials remove the Robert E. Lee Dixie Highway, Colonel John Connally Marker in Asheville, North Carolina.

  - □ City officials remove a statue of Christopher Columbus in Buffalo, New York.

  - □ Protesters topple a Bust of Confederate Charles Didier Dreux in New Orleans.

  - □ City officials remove Confederate David O. Dodd Memorial and Historic Marker in Little Rock, Arkansas.

  - □ County officials remove the 1929 Confederate Reunion Marker in Charlotte, North Carolina.

- 11th: Protesters damage the Sampson County Confederate Monument in Clinton, North Carolina.

- A statue of the Blessed Virgin Mary is vandalized in Queens, New York.

- A statue of the Blessed Virgin Mary is lit on fire at St. Peter's Catholic Church in Boston.

- In Ocala, a man drives his car into the Queen of Peace Catholic Church and sets the church on fire with people inside.

- The San Gabriel Mission in Los Angeles burns, the investigation into the cause is not yet complete.

- 13th: City officials remove a statue of Thomas Ruffin in Raleigh, North Carolina.

- 14th: County officials remove monument to the 60th Regiment NC Volunteers and the Battle of Chickamauga in Ashville, North Carolina.

- 15th: A statue of Jesus is decapitated and toppled at a Catholic Church in Miami.

  - A statue of the Blessed Virgin Mary is decapitated and toppled in Chattanooga.

- 16th: Monument to the Union 77th New York Volunteer Infantry is destroyed by protesters in Saratoga Springs, New York.

- 17th: Uprisings in Portland hit 50 consecutive days

  - St. Joseph's Catholic Church in New Haven, Connecticut is vandalized.

- ◻ Protests surrounding a Christopher Columbus statue in Chicago result in multiple injuries.

- 18th: City officials remove the Farmville Confederate statue in Farmville, Virginia.

- 22nd: Portland Mayor Ted Wheeler attempts to address protestors and is booed and told to resign. He is subsequently tear gassed by the Feds.

- 23rd: The United Daughters of the Confederacy remove the Memorial to Arizona Confederate troops in Phoenix.

  - ◻ The United Daughters of the Confederacy remove the Jefferson Davis Memorial Highway marker in Gold Canyon, Arizona.

  - ◻ Protesters topple the Robert E. Lee memorial in Roanoke, Virginia.

- 24th: Mayor Lightfoot of Chicago removes a statue of Christopher Columbus.

- 25th: A Black Trump-supporting journalist is stabbed in downtown Portland for filming riots.

  - ◻ A protestor shoots another protestor in Aurora, Colorado.

  - ◻ In Austin, Texas, a protestor was shot and killed after aiming his rifle at a driver.

  - ◻ City officials remove the Virginia Beach Confederate Monument.

- 26th: City officials remove the statue of St. Junipero Serra in Ventura, California.

- 29th: County officials remove the Henry County Confederate Monument in McDonough, Georgia.

- 30th: City officials remove a statue of Christopher Columbus in Chicago.

August 2020:

- 1st: Anarchists burn Bibles and American Flags in Portland

- 9th: In Chicago, a police shootout results in the death of a black man. In response the community migrates downtown and loots Chicago's Magnificent Mile. Mayor Lightfoot later claims "the core of what happened — that's organized criminal activity… It was a planned attack."

  - President Trump is temporarily escorted out of a press conference by Secret Service after a man attacks Secret Service agents on Pennsylvania Ave. and is shot and killed.

- 10th: Confederate monument is removed by city officials in Athens, Georgia.

APPENDIX THREE:
LIST OF ANTIFA GROUPS

ANTI-RACIST ACTION NETWORK

Anti-Racist Action was the joining of several anti-fascist groups in the Minneapolis, Minnesota area. Skinheads may be known solely as a racist group today, but their origins are a great deal more complex: a working class of youths in England rebelling against upper class elitism. A group of anti-racist skinheads, the Minneapolis Baldies, helped to found the Anti-Racist Action Network with left wing anarchist punk rockers, a go-to ally when leftist extremists unite. The group was formed in retaliation to the presence of racist skinheads in major cities across America.

Anti-Racist Action has been active throughout the years, perhaps most famously at events where they counter-protested a white nationalist. This was the case in 2002 in Washington, D.C.; 2005 in Toledo; 2010 in Chicago; 2011 in Pemberton, New Jersey and again in Chicago in 2012. Anti-Racist Action Network is decentralized, but its spiritual headquarters is in Portland, Oregon.

TORCH NETWORK

Anti-Racist Action also gave birth to an organization now calling itself either Torch Network or Torch Antifa. While it attempts to cloak itself in an aura of authenticity, with call backs to both Anti-Racist Action and so called "mainstream" Antifa (a misnomer), Torch Network is a self proclaimed internet-age antifascist group. They align themselves by their Points of Unity:

1. We disrupt fascist and far-right organizing and activity.

2. We don't rely on the cops or courts to do our work for us. This doesn't mean we never go to court, but the cops uphold white supremacy and the *status quo*. They attack us and everyone who resists oppression. We must rely on ourselves to protect ourselves and stop the fascists.

3. We oppose all forms of oppression and exploitation. We intend to do the hard work necessary to build a broad, strong movement of oppressed people centered on the working class against racism, sexism, nativism, anti-Semitism, Islamophobia, homophobia, transphobia, and discrimination against the disabled, the oldest, the youngest, and the most oppressed people. We support abortion rights and reproductive freedom. We want a classless, free society. We intend to win!

4. We hold ourselves accountable personally and collectively to live up to our ideals and values.

5. We not only support each other within the network, but we also support people outside the network who we believe have similar aims or principles. An attack on one is an attack on all.

Torch is a splinter cell group in that it is a rebranding of Anti-Racist Action, which is still very much a major player among anti-fascist groups. Torch is the militant brainchild of Antifa royalty, the Tinley Park Five, a group of close-knit Anti-Racist Action members from Indiana. In May of 2012 Jason Sutherlin, his half brothers Dylan and Cody, their cousin John Tucker and a then 22-year-old antifascist activist named Alex Stuck, attacked a group of white nationalists at a restaurant in Tinley Park, Illinois.

REFUSE FASCISM/ALLIANCE
FOR GLOBAL JUSTICE

There are many links between anarchist leftist extremist groups and international communism. One such is finance. Refuse Fascism is a leftist group based out of New York City, the activist wing of the Revolutionary Communist Party, an organization that advocates for revolution and world communism. In February 2017, it was discovered that the Alliance for Global Justice had given the extremist group $50,000. The organization also solicits donations on its website.

Refuse Fascism specializes in non-violent, but raucous, protests that have shut down speeches by the likes of Ben Shapiro and Milos Yiannopoulos. This group is particularly opposed to Donald Trump. It was formed in the wake of his election and organized marches on his New York properties.

ROSE CITY ANTIFA

Rose City Antifa hails from the antifascist heartland of Portland, Oregon. Founded in 2007, it is believed to be the oldest active Antifa group in the United States. Together with their counterpart on the far right, Patriot Prayer, Rose City Antifa has been the public face of the movement, active in Portland and beyond since 2016. Rose City Antifa (RCA) is considered the "blueprint" for Antifa in the United States.

RCA's playbook is deep. They have been known to doxx suspected Alt Right and Neo-Nazi figures, as well as take part in vigorous direct action. They were involved in a high profile attack on right wing journalist Andy Ngo in June of 2020, one that they were sued for to the tune of nearly a million dollars.

NYC ANTIFA

New York City is home to another Antifa group. NYC Antifa has been accused of planning organized political violence, complete with members working as military style scouts and medics and employing top level civilian encrypted communications by New York Deputy Commissioner for Intelligence and Counterterrorism John Miller. Antifa members, he stated, had battle plans that included planned routes, supplies of rocks and accelerants for improvised weapons.

New York being the megalopolis it is, a fifth of Antifa members arrested in 2020 come from other states. According to a recent NBC article, Miller said the agitators "developed a complex network of bicycle scouts to move ahead of demonstrators in different directions of where police were and where police were not for purposes of being able to direct groups from the larger group to places where they could commit acts of vandalism including the torching of police vehicles and Molotov cocktails where they thought officers would not be."

D.C. ANTIFA (SMASH RACISM DC)

America's capital is also a hotbed of quasi-legal antifascist action. Prominent groups in Washington D.C. include Smash Racism DC, a crew that has grabbed headlines by confronting conservative politicians in public.

In September 2018, Smash Racism stormed a trendy D.C. restaurant, Fiola, to harass one of the many politicians on both sides of the aisle who dines there, Ted Cruz. A month later they appeared at the home of Fox News host Tucker Carlson, complete with bullhorn, shouting, "Tucker Carlson, we will fight, we know where you sleep at night!"

"This is a message to Ted Cruz, Bret Kavanaugh, Donald Trump, and the rest of the racist, sexist, transphobic, and homophobic right-wing scum," wrote Smash Racism DC in its statement regarding the Ted Cruz incident. "You are not safe. We will find you. We will expose you. We will take from you the peace you have taken from so many others."

BY ANY MEANS NECESSARY (BERKELEY)/YVETTE FELARCA

By Any Means Necessary is the truncated name for "the Coalition to Defend Affirmative Action, Integration & Immigrant Rights, and Fight for Equality By Any Means Necessary". They are a militant leftist group based in California, with a particular presence on the University of California, Berkeley campus.

The group's most noteworthy leader is a middle school teacher and activist named Yvette Felarca. In June 2016, BAMN counterprotested a large demonstration by Neo-Nazi groups the Traditionalist Worker Party, the Golden State Skinheads and the National Socialist Movement, which is the largest far right white hate group in the United States. Felarca was caught on tape attacking a Neo Nazi who was holding a broom. She admitted during her trial that the broom wielding man had not attacked her, but she had experienced prior attacks from such implements. The film shows Felarca striking the man until police intervened. Felarca was given 90 hours of community service and permitted to keep her teaching position.

In February 2019, By Any Means Necessary was under active investigation by the FBI as a domestic terrorist group. Their activities also include guarding migrant caravans arriving at the Mexican-United States border. Their armed presence in Tijuana, Baja California has been judged as too extreme by less hardcore members of the group.

LONDON ANTIFA

Antifa's activity in London was in response to a far right political group, the British National Party (BNP). In 2004, the BNP, itself an offshoot of the vaguely named fascist group Nationalist Front, reached its greatest success in the U.K. in the mid 2000s. Not to be outmatched, far left groups copied mainstream Antifa cells on mainland Europe, and Antifa in London was born.

Deploying eerily similar tactics to football hooligans, Antifa in London disrupted far right summits, stockpiled bricks, disguised themselves as civilians and engaged in direct action. They were similarly successful at pressuring high value far right political figures to retire.

Antifascist fervor spread over the whole of England, perhaps even beyond its original founders' expectations; so much so that U.K. police cracked down hard on the group in 2009. By the end of that year it had dispersed, only to reform in the wake of Trumpism as the far right English Defense League, and in the Boris Johnson administration as the Anti-Fascist Network.

PARIS / MUNICH

In the fall of 2018, the world watched as brawls erupted in the streets of Paris. Right-wing groups, aligned with fringe members of local football supporter clubs, battled the "Yellow Vests" movement. The latter group consisted of middle and lower class Parisians who united to protest taxation rates that benefited the wealthy and rising fuel prices. French law requires that all drivers have a high visibility yellow vest in their car in case of emergencies, which was used as a rallying symbol for the new movement. It is doubtful that government authorities intended this outcome.

The Yellow Vests blocked roads and gas stations, causing the city to have what some judged to be the worst Parisian riots in half a century. Far right groups such as Action Francaise and Zouaves Paris continually clashed with Yellow Vest and Antifa squads throughout the country nearly continuously ever since.

PNW YOUTH LIBERATION FRONT

The Pacific Northwest has long been a political extremism hot zone, from the true constitution militia groups of the late part of the last century to Antifa of today. The PNW Youth Liberation Front describes itself on Twitter as a "decentralized network of autonomous youth collectives dedicated to direct action towards total liberation." The PNW Youth Liberation Front is highly active on social media.

The group claims that it does not coordinate with Antifa groups, especially Rose City Antifa, with whom it shares a home base. According to Radical-Guide.com, the PNW Youth Liberation Front has the following goals:

•We want all youth and students to rise up, be heard, and question our government and demand change.

•We want a completely reformed school system based of ALL of the students NEEDS, youth internationally deserve a real education system that educates and prepares students, instead of spewing out state propaganda.

•We want to end the war on the working class by ending brutal gentrification practices and other anti-working class policy.

•We want to end the militarization of local police depart-ments by putting an end to the use of flashbangs, teargas and other extremely militarized weapons and stopping "preemptive protest crackdowns".

•We want the ruling class and government officials to be taxed heavily and for that money to go towards local school districts, prioritizing working class areas.

•We want to put an end to all I.C.E and D.H.S opera-tions nationally, we refuse to allow literal fascist systems terrorize our community's.

REDNECK REVOLT

Kansas based Redneck Revolt, also known as the John Brown Gun Club, is a direct action anttfascist extremist organization founded in 2009 to counter the Tea Party Movement. Founding members have been known to engage in weapons training with Second Amendment advocates, and run anti-racist information stalls at gun shows.

After a lull in activity, the group was revived in 2016 in the wake of Trumpism in America. Rough estimates show that there are at least 45 chapters in 30 states. They frequent events traditionally attended by white supremacists (as well as civilians): NASCAR races, country music concerts, and rodeos. Their message is uniquely directed at rural whites.

SOCIALIST RIFLE ASSOCIATION

The Socialist Rifle Organization (SRA) was initially founded as a joke and meme page on Facebook, but in yet another case of life imitating art became a reality soon after. Also, Kansas-based SRA was organized as a non-profit civic organization in 2018.

The SRA aims to provide an alternative for LGBT left-leaning gun owners, the majority of whom are white hetereonormative conservatives, and to provide a platform for such people to engage in dialogue about self defense and gun politics. The group describes itself as "working class, progressive, anarchist, socialist, communist, eco-warrior, animal liberator, anti-fascist, anti-racist, anti-capitalist, PoC, and LGBTQ-plus."

KNIGHTS FOR SOCIALISM

The Knights for Socialism is a splinter group of the Young Democratic Socialists of Orlando at the University of Central Florida. In 2017, the group was investigated for holding a so-called "fight club" on that institution's campus. The Knights held the event to teach self-defense against supporters of President Donald Trump, barring entry to anyone who self identified as a Republican. Their social media also equates Republicans with terrorists and uses the now ubiquitous Antifa catchphrase, "All cops are bastards."

The organization has held a "BASH THE FASH" event to combat anyone they see as antifascist, a label they apply liberally. Prominent member Dylan Tyer has been accused of harassing right-wing UCF students, but was not formally charged. The Knights do not directly associate with any formal Antifa groups, nor do they carry the label themselves, but they employ much of the same imagery and ideology.

APPENDIX FOUR – SIEGE OF MINNEAPOLIS

THE SIEGE OF THE THIRD PRECINCT IN MINNEAPOLIS

An Account and Analysis – Crimethinc.org

https://crimethinc.com/2020/06/10/the-siege-of-the-third-precinct-in-minneapolis-an-account-and-analysis

In this anonymous submission, participants in the uprising in Minneapolis explore how a combination of different tactics compelled the police to abandon the Third Precinct.

The following analysis is motivated by a discussion that took place in front of the Third Precinct as fires billowed from its windows on day three of the George Floyd Rebellion in Minneapolis:

We joined a group of people whose fire-lit faces beamed in with joy and awe from across the street. People of various ethnicities sat side by side talking about the tactical value of lasers, the "share everything" ethos, interracial unity in fighting the police, and the trap of "innocence." There were no disagreements; we all saw the same things that helped us win. Thousands of people shared the experience of these battles. We hope that they will carry the memory of how to fight. But the time of combat and the celebration of victory is incommensurable with the habits, spaces, and attachments of everyday life and its reproduction. It is frightening how distant the event already feels from us. Our purpose here is to preserve the strategy that proved victorious against the Minneapolis Third Precinct.

Our analysis focuses on the tactics and composition of the crowd that besieged the Third Precinct on Day Two of the uprising. The siege lasted roughly from 4 p.m. well into the early hours of the morning of May 28. We believe that the tactical retreat of the police from the Third Precinct on day three was won by the siege of day two, which exhausted the Precinct's personnel and supplies. We were not present for the fighting that preceded the retreat on day three, as we showed up just as the police were leaving. We were across the city in an area where youth were fighting the cops in tit-for-tat battles while trying to loot a strip mall — hence our focus on day two here.

CONTEXT

The last popular revolt against the Minneapolis Police Department took place in response to the police murder of Jamar Clark on Nov. 15, 2015. It spurred two weeks of unrest that lasted until Dec. 2. Crowds repeatedly engaged the police in ballistic confrontations; however, the response to the shooting coalesced around an occupation of the nearby Fourth Precinct. Organizations like the NAACP and the newly formed Black Lives Matter asserted their control over the crowds that gathered; they were often at odds with young unaffiliated rebels who preferred to fight the police directly. Much of our analysis below focuses on how young Black and brown rebels from poor and working-class neighborhoods seized the opportunity to reverse this relationship. We argue that this was a necessary condition for the uprising.

George Floyd was murdered by the police at 38th Street and Chicago Avenue between 8:20 and 8:32 p.m. on Monday, May 25. Demonstrations against the killing began the next day at the site of his murder, where a vigil took place. Some attendees began a march to the Third Precinct at Lake Street and 26th, where rebels attacked police vehicles in the parking lot.

These two locations became consistent gathering points. Many community groups, organizations, liberals, progressives, and leftists assembled at the vigil site, while those who wanted to fight generally gathered near the Precinct. This put over two miles between two very different crowds, a spatial division that was reflected in other areas of the city as well. Looters clashed with police in scattered commercial zones outside of the sphere of influence of the organizations while many of the leftist marches excluded fighting elements with the familiar tactic of peace policing in the name of identity-based risk aversion.

THE "SUBJECT" OF THE GEORGE FLOYD UPRISING

The subject of our analysis is not a race, a class, an organization, or even a movement, but a crowd. We focus on a crowd for three reasons. First, with the exception of the street medics, the power and success of those who fought the Third Precinct did not depend on their experience in "organizing" or in organizations. Rather, it resulted from unaffiliated individuals and groups courageously stepping into roles that complemented each other and seizing opportunities as they arose.

While the initial gathering was occasioned by a rally hosted by a Black-led organization, all of the actions that materially defeated the Third Precinct were undertaken after the rally had ended, carried out by people who were not affiliated with it. There was practically no one there from the usual gamut of self-appointed community and religious leaders, which meant that the crowd was able to transform the situation freely. Organizations rely on stability and predictability to execute strategies that require great quantities of time to formulate. Consequently, organization leaders can be threatened by sudden changes in the social conditions, which can make their organizations irrelevant. Organizations — even self-proclaimed "revolutionary" organizations — have an interest in suppressing spontaneous revolt in order to recruit from those who are discontent and enraged. Whether it is an elected official, a religious leader, a "community organizer", or a leftist representative, their message to unruly crowds is always the same: wait.

The agency that took down the Third Precinct was a crowd and not an organization because its goals, means, and internal makeup were not regulated by centralized authority. This proved beneficial, as the crowd consequently had recourse to more practical options and was freer to create unforeseen internal relationships in order to adapt to the conflict at hand. We expand on this below in the section titled "The Pattern of Battle and 'Composition.'"

The agency in the streets on May 27 was located in a crowd because its constituents had few stakes in the existing order that is managed by the police. Crucially, a gang truce had been called after the first day of unrest, neutralizing territorial barriers to participation. The crowd mostly originated from working-class and poor Black and brown neighborhoods. This was especially true of those who threw things at the police and vandalized and looted stores. Those who do not identify as "owners" of the world that oppresses them are more likely to fight and steal from it when the opportunity arises. The crowd had no interest in justifying itself to onlookers and it was scarcely interested in "signifying" anything to anyone outside of itself. There were no signs or speeches, only chants that served the tactical purposes of "hyping up" ("Fuck 12!") and interrupting police violence with strategically deployed "innocence" ("Hands up! Don't shoot!").

ROLES

We saw people playing the following roles:

MEDICAL SUPPORT

This included street medics and medics performing triage and urgent care at a converted community center two blocks away from the precinct. Under different circumstances, this could be performed at any nearby sympathetic commercial, religious, or not-for profit establishment. Alternatively, a crowd or a medic group could occupy such a space for the duration of a protest. Those who were organized as street medics did not interfere with the tactical choices of the crowd. Instead, they consistently treated anyone who needed their help.

SCANNER MONITORS AND TELEGRAM APP CHANNEL OPERATORS

This is common practice in many US cities by now, but police scanner monitors with an ear for strategically important information played a critical role in setting up information flows from the police to the crowd. It is almost certain that on the whole, much of the crowd was not practicing the greatest security to access the Telegram channel. We advise rebels to set up the Telegram app on burner phones in order to stay informed while preventing police stingrays (false cell phone towers) from gleaning their personal information.

PEACEFUL PROTESTORS

The non-violent tactics of peaceful protesters served two familiar aims and one unusual one:

They created a spectacle of legitimacy, which was intensified as police violence escalated.

They created a front line that blocked police attempts to advance when they deployed outside of the Precinct.

In addition, in an unexpected turn of affairs, the peaceful protestors shielded those who employed projectiles.

Whenever the police threatened tear gas or rubber bullets, non-violent protesters lined up at the front with their hands up in the air, chanting "Hands up, don't shoot!" Sometimes they kneeled, but typically only during relative lulls in the action. When the cops deployed outside the Precincts, their police lines frequently found themselves facing a line of "non-violent" protestors. This had the effect of temporarily stabilizing the space of conflict and gave other crowd members a stationary target. While some peaceful protestors angrily commanded people to stop throwing things, they were few and grew quiet as the day wore on. This was most likely because the police were targeting people who threw things with rubber bullets early on in the conflict, which enraged the crowd. It's worth noting that the reverse has often been the case — we are used to seeing more confrontational tactics used to shield those practicing non-violence (e.g., at Standing Rock and Charlottesville). The reversal of this relationship in Minneapolis afforded greater autonomy to those employing confrontational tactics.

BALLISTICS SQUADS

Ballistics squads threw water bottles, rocks, and a few Molotov cocktails at police, and shot fireworks. Those using ballistics didn't always work in groups, but doing so protected them from being targeted by non-violent protestors who wanted to dictate the tactics of the crowd. The ballistics squads served three aims:

They drew police violence away from the peaceful elements of the crowd during moments of escalation.

They patiently depleted the police crowd control munitions.

They threatened the physical safety of the police, making it more costly for them to advance.

The first day of the uprising, there were attacks on multiple parked police SUVs at the Third Precinct. This sensibility resumed quickly on day two, beginning with the throwing of water bottles at police officers positioned on the roof of the Third Precinct and alongside the building. After the police responded with tear gas and rubber bullets, the ballistics squads also began to employ rocks. Elements within the crowd dismantled bus bench embankments made of stone and smashed them up to supply additional projectiles. Nightfall saw the use of fireworks by a few people, which quickly generalized in days three and four. "Boogaloos" (Second Amendment accelerationists) had already briefly employed fireworks on day one, but from what we saw they mostly sat it out on the sidelines thereafter. Finally, it is worth noting that the Minneapolis police used "green tips," rubber bullets with exploding green ink tips to mark lawbreakers for later arrest. Once it became clear that the police department had limited capacity to make good on its threat and, moreover, that the crowd could win, those who had been marked had every incentive to fight like hell to defy the police.

LASER POINTERS

In the grammar of the Hong Kong movement, those who operate laser pointers are referred to as "light mages." As was the case in Hong Kong, Chile, and elsewhere in 2019, some people came prepared with laser pointers to attack the optical capacity of the police. Laser pointers involve a special risk/reward ratio, as it is very easy to track people using laser pointers, even when they are operating within a dense and active crowd at night. Laser pointer users are particularly vulnerable if they attempt to target individual police officers or (especially) police helicopters while operating in small crowds; this is still the case even if the entire neighborhood is undergoing mass looting (the daytime use of high-powered lasers with scopes remains untested, to our knowledge). The upside of laser pointers is immense: they momentarily compromise the eyesight of the police on the ground and they can disable police surveillance drones by interfering with their infrared sensors and obstacle-detection cameras. In the latter case, a persistently lasered drone may descend to the earth where the crowd can destroy it. This occurred repeatedly on days two and three. If a crowd is particularly dense and visually difficult to discern, lasers can be used to chase away police helicopters. This was successfully demonstrated on day three following the retreat of the police from the Third Precinct, as well as on day four in the vicinity of the Fifth Precinct battle.

BARRICADERS

Barricaders built barricades out of nearby materials, including an impressive barricade that blocked the police on 26th Avenue just north of Lake Street. In the latter case, the barricade was assembled out of a train of shopping carts and a cart-return station pulled from a nearby parking lot, dumpsters, police barricades, and plywood and fencing materials from a condominium construction site. At the Third Precinct, the barricade provided useful cover for laser pointer attacks and rock-throwers, while also serving as a natural gathering point for the crowd to regroup. At the Fifth Precinct, when the police pressed on foot toward the crowd, dozens of individuals filled the street with a multi-rowed barricade. On the one hand, this had the advantage of preventing the police from advancing further and making arrests, while allowing the crowd to regroup out of reach of the rubber bullets. However, it quickly became clear that the barricades were discouraging the crowd from retaking the street, and it had to be partially dismantled in order to facilitate a second press toward the police lines. It can be difficult to coordinate defense and attack within a single gesture.

SOUND SYSTEMS

Car sound systems and engines provided a sonic environment that enlivened the crowd. The anthem of days two and three was Lil' Boosie's "Fuck The Police." Yet one innovation we had never seen before was the use of car engines to add to the soundscape and "rev up" the crowd. This began with a pick-up truck with a modified exhaust system, which was parked behind the crowd facing away from it. When tensions ran high with the police and it appeared that the conflict would resume, the driver would red line his engine and make it roar thunderously over the crowd. Other similarly modified cars joined in, as well as a few motorcyclists.

LOOTERS

Looting served three critical aims.

First, it liberated supplies to heal and nourish the crowd. On the first day, rebels attempted to seize the liquor store directly across from the Third Precinct. Their success was brief, as the cops managed to re-secure it. Early in the standoff on day two, a handful of people signaled their determination by climbing on top of the store to mock the police from the roof. The crowd cheered at this humiliation, which implicitly set the objective for the rest of the day: to demonstrate the powerlessness of the police, demoralize them, and exhaust their capacities.

An hour or so later, looting began at the liquor store and at an Aldi a block away. While a majority of those present participated in the looting, it was clear that some took it upon themselves to be strategic about it. Looters at the Aldi liberated immense quantities of bottled water, sports drinks, milk, protein bars, and other snacks and assembled huge quantities of these items on street corners throughout the vicinity. In addition to the liquor store and the Aldi, the Third Precinct was conveniently situated adjacent to a Target, a Cub Foods, a shoe store, a dollar store, an Autozone, a Wendy's, and various other businesses. Once the looting began, it immediately became a part of the logistics of the crowd's siege on the Precinct.

Second, looting boosted the crowd's morale by creating solidarity and joy through a shared act of collective transgression. The act of gift giving and the spirit of generosity was made accessible to all, providing a positive counterpoint to the head-to-head conflicts with the police.

Third, and most importantly, looting contributed to keeping the situation ungovernable. As looting spread throughout the city, police forces everywhere were spread thin. Their attempts to secure key targets only gave looters free rein over other areas in the city. Like a fist squeezing water, the police found themselves frustrated by an opponent that expanded exponentially.

FIRES

The decision to burn looted businesses can be seen as tactically intelligent. It contributed to depleting police resources, since the firefighters forced to continually extinguish structure fires all over town required heavy police escorts. This severely impacted their ability to intervene in situations of ongoing looting, the vast majority of which they never responded to (the malls and the Super Target store on University Avenue being exceptions). This has played out differently in other cities, where police opted not to escort firefighters. Perhaps this explains why demonstrators fired in the air around firefighting vehicles during the Watts rebellion.

In the case of the Third Precinct, the burning of the Autozone had two immediate consequences: first, it forced the police to move out into the street and establish a perimeter around the building for firefighters. While this diminished the clash at the site of the precinct, it also pushed the crowd down Lake Street, which subsequently induced widespread looting and contributed to the diffusion of the riot across the whole neighborhood. By interrupting the magnetic force of the Precinct, the police response to the fire indirectly contributed to expanding the riot across the city.

THE PATTERN OF THE BATTLE
AND "COMPOSITION"

We call the battles of the second and third days at the Precinct a siege because the police were defeated by attrition. The pattern of the battle was characterized by steady intensification punctuated by qualitative leaps due to the violence of the police and the spread of the conflict into looting and attacks on corporate-owned buildings. The combination of the roles listed above helped to create a situation that was unpoliceable, yet which the police were stubbornly determined to contain. The repression required for every containment effort intensified the revolt and pushed it further out into the surrounding area. By day three, all of the corporate infrastructure surrounding the Third Precinct had been destroyed and the police had nothing but a "kingdom of ashes" to show for their efforts. Only their Precinct remained, a lonely target with depleted supplies. The rebels who showed up on day three found an enemy teetering on the brink. All it needed was a final push.

Day two of the uprising began with a rally: attendees were on the streets, while the police were stationed on top of their building with an arsenal of crowd control weaponry. The pattern of struggle began during the rally, when the crowd tried to climb over the fences that protected the Precinct in order to vandalize it. The police fired rubber bullets in response as rally speakers called for calm. After some time passed and more speeches were made, people tried again. When the volley of rubber bullets came, the crowd responded with rocks and water bottles. This set off a dynamic of escalation that accelerated quickly once the rally ended. Some called for non-violence and sought to interfere with those who were throwing things, but most people didn't bother arguing with them. They were largely ignored or else the reply was always the same: "That non-violence shit don't work!" In fact, neither side of this argument was exactly correct: as the course of the battle was to demonstrate, both sides needed each other to accomplish the historic feat of reducing the Third Precinct to ashes.

It's important to note that the dynamic we saw on day two did not involve using non-violence and waiting for repression to escalate the situation. Instead, a number of individuals stuck their necks out very far to invite police violence and escalation. Once the crowd and the police were locked into an escalating pattern of conflict, the objective of the police was to expand their territorial control radiating outward from the Precinct. When the police decided to advance, they began by throwing concussion grenades at the crowd as a whole and firing rubber bullets at those throwing projectiles, setting up barricades, and firing tear gas.

The intelligence of the crowd proved itself as participants quickly learned five lessons in the course of this struggle.

First, it is important to remain calm in the face of concussion grenades, as they are not physically harmful if you are more than five feet away from them. This lesson extends to a more general insight about crisis governance: don't panic, as the police will always use panic against us. One must react quickly while staying as calm as possible.

Second, the practice of flushing tear-gassed eyes spread rapidly from street medics throughout the rest of the crowd. Employing stores of looted bottled water, many people in the crowd were able to learn and quickly execute eye-flushing. People throwing rocks one minute could be seen treating the eyes of others in the next. This basic medic knowledge helped to build the crowd's confidence, allowing them to resist the temptation to panic and stampede, so that they could return to the space of engagement.

Third, perhaps the crowd's most important tactical discovery was that when one is forced to retreat from tear gas, one must refill the space one has abandoned as quickly as possible. Each time the crowd at the Third Precinct returned, it came back angrier and more determined either to stop the police advance or to make them pay as dearly as possible for every step they took.

Fourth, borrowing from the language of Hong Kong, we saw the crowd practice the maxim "Be water." Not only did the crowd quickly flow back into spaces from which they had to retreat, but when forced outward, the crowd didn't behave the way that the cops did by fixating on territorial control. When they could, the crowd flowed back into the spaces from which they had been forced to retreat due to tear gas. But when necessary, the crowd flowed away from police advances like a torrential destructive force. Each police advance resulted in more businesses being smashed, looted, and burned. This meant that the police were losers regardless of whether they chose to remain besieged or push back the crowd.

Finally, the fall of the Third Precinct demonstrates the power of ungovernability as a strategic aim and means of crowd activity. The more that a crowd can do, the harder it will be to police. Crowds can maximize their agency by increasing the number of roles that people can play and by maximizing the complementary relationships between them.

Non-violence practitioners can use their legitimacy to temporarily conceal or shield ballistics squads. Ballistics squads can draw police fire away from those practicing non-violence. Looters can help feed and heal the crowd while simultaneously disorienting the police. In turn, those going head to head with the police can generate opportunities for looting. Light mages can provide ballistics crews with temporary opacity by blinding the police and disabling surveillance drones and cameras. Non-violence practitioners can buy time for barricaders, whose works can later alleviate the need for non-violence to secure the front line.

Here we see that an internally diverse and complex crowd is more powerful than a crowd that is homogenous. We use the term composition to name this phenomenon of maximizing complementary practical diversity. It is distinct from organization because the roles are elective, individuals can shift between them as needed or desired, and there are no leaders to assign or coordinate them. Crowds that form and fight through composition are more effective against the police not only because they tend to be more difficult to control, but also because the intelligence that animates them responds to and evolves alongside the really existing situation on the ground, rather than according to preexisting conceptions of what a battle "ought" to look like. Not only are "compositional" crowds more likely to engage the police in battles of attrition, but they are more likely to have the fluidity that is necessary to win.

As a final remark on this, we may contrast composition with the idea of "diversity of tactics" used by the alter-globalization movement. "Diversity of tactics" was the idea that different groups at an action should use different tactical means in different times or spaces in order to work toward a shared goal. In other words, "You do you and I'll do me," but without any regard for how what I'm doing complements what you're doing and vice-versa. Diversity of tactics is activist code for "tolerance." The crowd that formed on May 27 against the Third Precinct did not "practice the diversity of tactics," but came together by connecting different tactics and roles to each other in a shared space-time that enabled participants to deploy each tactic as the situation required.

THE AMBIGUITY OF VIOLENCE AND NON-VIOLENCE ON THE FRONT LINES

We are used to seeing more confrontational tactics used to shield those practicing non-violence, as in Standing Rock and Charlottesville or in the figure of the "front-liner" in Hong Kong. However, the reversal of this relationship divided the functions of the "militant front-liner" (à la Hong Kong) across two separate roles: shielding the crowd and counter-offense. This never rose to the level of an explicit strategy in the streets; there were no calls to "shield the throwers." In the U.S. context, where non-violence and its attendant innocence narratives are deeply entrenched in struggles against state racism, it is unclear if this strategy could function explicitly without ballistics crews first taking risks to invite bloodshed upon themselves. In other words, it appears likely that the joining of ballistics tactics and non-violence in Minneapolis was made possible by a tacitly shared perception of the importance of self-sacrifice in confronting the state that forced all sides to push through their fear.

Yet this shared perception of risk only goes so far. While peaceful protesters probably viewed each other's gestures as moral symbols against police violence, ballistics squads undoubtedly viewed those gestures differently, namely, as shields, or as materially strategic opportunities. Here again, we may highlight the power of the way that composition plays out in real situations, by pointing out how it allows the possibility that totally different understandings of the same tactic can coexist side by side. We combine without becoming the same, we move together without understanding one another, and yet it works.

There are potential limits to dividing front-liner functions across these roles. First, it doesn't challenge the valorization of suffering in the politics of non-violence. Second, it leaves the value of ballistic confrontation ambiguous by preventing it from coalescing in a stable role at the front of the crowd. It is undeniable that the Third Precinct would not have been taken without ballistic tactics. However, because the front line was identified with non-violence, the spatial and symbolic importance of ballistics was implicitly secondary. This leaves us to wonder whether this has made it easier for counter-insurgency to take root in the movement through "community policing" and its corollary, the self-policing of demonstrations and movements within the bounds of non-violence.

FACT-CHECKING: A CRITICAL NECESSITY FOR THE MOVEMENT

We believe that the biggest danger facing the current movement was already present at the battle of the Third Precinct—namely, the danger of rumors and paranoia. We maintain that the practice of "fact checking" is crucial for the current movement to minimize confusion about the terrain and internal distrust about its own composition.

We heard a litany of rumors throughout day two. We were told repeatedly that riot police reinforcements were on their way to kettle us. We were warned by fleeing crowd members that the National Guard was "20 minutes away." A white lady pulled up alongside us in her van and screamed "THE GAS LINES IN THE BURNING AUTOZONE ARE GONNA BLOWWW!!!" All of these rumors proved to be false. As expressions of panicked anxiety, they always produced the same effect: to make the crowd second-guess their power. It was almost as if certain members of the crowd experienced a form of vertigo in the face of the power that they nonetheless helped to forge.

It is necessary to interrupt the rumors by asking questions of those repeating them. There are simple questions that we can ask to halt the spread of fear and rumors that have the effect of weakening the crowd. "How do you know this?" "Who told you this?" "What is the source of your information?" "Is this a confirmed fact?" "The evidence seems inconclusive; what assumptions are you using to make a judgment?"

Along with rumors, there is also the problem of attributing disproportionate importance to certain features of the conflict. Going into day two, one of the dominant storylines was the threat of "Boogaloo boys," who had showed up the previous day. This surprised us because we didn't encounter them on day one. We saw half a dozen of them on day two, but they had relegated themselves to the sidelines of an event that outstripped them. Despite their proclaimed sympathy with George Floyd, a couple of them later stood guard in front of a business to defend it from looters. This demonstrated not only the limit of their claimed solidarity, but also of their strategic sensibility.

Finally, we awoke on day three to so-called reports that either police provocateurs or outside agitators were responsible for the previous day's destruction. Target, Cub Foods, Autozone, Wendy's, and a half-constructed condominium high rise had all gone up in flames by the end of the night. We cannot discount the possibility that any number of hostile forces sought to smear the crowd by escalating the destruction of property. If that is true, however, it cannot be denied that their plan backfired spectacularly.

In general, the crowd looked upon these sublime fires with awe and approval. Even on the second night, when the condominium development became fully engulfed, the crowd sat across from it on 26th Avenue and rested as if gathered around a bonfire. Each structure fire contributed to the material abolition of the existing state of things and the reduction to ash became the crowd's seal of victory. Instead of believing the rumors about provocateurs or agitators, we find it more plausible that people who have been oppressed for centuries, who are poor, and who are staring down the barrel of a Second Great Depression would rather set the world on fire than suffer the sight of its order. We interpret the structure fires as signifying that the crowd knew that the structures of the police, white supremacy, and class are based in material forces and buildings.

For this reason, we maintain that we should assess the threat posed by possible provocateurs, infiltrators, and agitators on the basis of whether their actions directly enhance or diminish the power of the crowd. We have learned that dozens of structure fires are not enough to diminish "public support" for the movement — though no one could have imagined this beforehand. However, those who filmed crowd members destroying property or breaking the law — regardless of whether they intended to inform law enforcement agencies — posed a material threat to the crowd, because in addition to bolstering confusion and fear, they empowered the state with access to information.

POSTSCRIPT: VISIONS OF THE COMMUNE

Ever since Guy Debord's 1965 text "The Decline and Fall of the Spectacle-Commodity Economy," there has been a rich tradition of memorializing the emergence of communal social life in riots. Riots abolish capitalist social relations, which allows for new relations between people and the things that make up their world. Here is our evidence:

When the liquor store was opened, dozens came out with cases of beer, which were set on the ground with swagger for everyone to share. The crowd's beer of choice was Corona.

We saw a man walk calmly out of the store with both arms full of whiskey. He gave one to each person he passed as he walked off to rejoin the fight. Some of the emptied liquor bottles on the street were later thrown at the police.

With buildings aflame all around us, a man walked by and said to no one in particular, "That tobacco shop used to have a great deal on loosies… oh well. Fuck 'em."

We saw a woman walking a grocery cart full of Pampers and steaks back to her house. A group that was taking a snack and water break on the corner clapped in applause as she rolled by.

After a group opened the Autozone, people sat inside smoking cigarettes as they watched the battle between cops and rebels from behind the front window. One could see them pointing back and forth between the police and elements in the crowd as they spoke and nodding in response to each other. Were they seeing the same things we were seeing?

We shopped for shoes in the ransacked storeroom of a looted Foot Locker. The floor was covered wall-to-wall with half-destroyed shoeboxes, tissue paper, and shoes. People called out for sizes and types as they rummaged. We spent 15 minutes just to find a matching pair until we heard the din of battle and dipped.

On day three, the floors of the grocery stores that had been partially burned out were covered in inches of sprinkler water and a foul mix of food that had been thrown from the shelves. Still, people in rain boots could be found inside combing over the remaining goods like they were shopping for deals. Gleaners helped each other step over dangerous objects and, again, shared their loot outside.

As the police made their retreat, a young Somali woman dressed in traditional garb celebrated by digging up a landscaping brick and unceremoniously heaving it through a bus stop shelter window. Her friends — also traditionally dressed — raised their fists and danced.

A masked shirtless man skipped past the burning Precinct and pumped his fists, shouting, "COVID IS OVER!" while 20 feet away, some teenage girls took a group selfie. Instead of saying "Cheese!" they said "Death to the pigs!" Lasers flashed across the smoke-filled sky at a police helicopter overhead.

We passed a liquor store that was being looted as we walked away from the best party on Earth. A mother and her two young teenagers rolled up in their car and asked if there was any good booze left. "Hell yea! Get some!" The daughter grinned and said, "Come on! I'll help you Mommy!" They donned their COVID masks and marched off.

A day later, before the assault on the Fifth Precinct, there was mass looting in the Midtown neighborhood. A young kid who couldn't be more than seven or eight years old walked up to us with a whiskey bottle sporting a rag coming out the top. "Y'all got a light?" We laughed and asked, "What do you wanna hit?" He pointed to a friendly grocery store and we asked if he could find "an enemy target." He immediately turned to the U.S. Bank across the street.

Editor's note: The partially constructed 189-unit housing complex referenced here ("Midtown Corner") was not, in fact, condominiums. Midtown Corner was a mixed-used development, with retail space on the first floor and a full 189 units of affordable housing.

APPENDIX FIVE – DANIEL ALAN BAKER

Daniel Alan Baker is a former member of the US Army who was removed for going AWOL before his unit was deployed overseas. He is an anarchist extremist with radical left-wing views. Following his discharge, Baker then traveled to Syria to train and fight with the YPG as a sniper.

Upon his return to the United States, Baker traveled to CHAZ to take part in the armed uprising against the US government, and claims he served as an armed militant there. Social media postings attributed to Baker link him to one of the CHAZ shootings which led to the death of a black teenager who was driving a Jeep.

He was arrested for planning an attack on the Florida capital in 2021.

The following is an excerpt from the federal charging document for Daniel Alan Baker:

> On October 8, 2020, the FBI was notified that BAKER was threatening the use of violence in the United States and was using social media to recruit and train like-minded individuals in furtherance of his Anti-Government or Anti-Authority Violent Extremism Ideology.
>
> In 2017, BAKER joined the People's Protection Units ("YPG"), a group fighting in Syria against ISIS and the Turkish Government. The YPG is a sub -affiliate of Kurdistan's Working Party (PKK) which has been designated a Foreign Terrorist Organization by the US Government.

BAKER endorses himself on his social media as a trained sniper for the YPG.

As documented in a VICE documentary, BAKER can be seen fighting ISIS or Turkish militant, as shown in a YouTube video. Through documented interviews with FBI Special Agents, BAKER admitted to training members who attended the YPG International Academy on military tactics and defensive tactics. Multiple overseas sources reported BAKER stated he intended to return to the United States with the intention to lure Turkish pilots training on United States military bass off the installation, after which he would kill or mutilate them in furtherance of helping the YPG fight the Turkish government. BAKER returned to the United States in April 2019 from the Middle East.

BAKER has traveled across the United States to participate in protests that have resulted in violence to include joining the CHAZ/CHOP movement in Seattle, Washington during the summer of 2020…BAKER is quoted as saying, "I told them, if they really wanted a revolution, we needed to get AK's and start making bombs."

In 2021, BAKER changed his Facebook cover picture to several soldiers posing behind YPG and Antifa (Antifascist Action) flags holding AK-47 style rifles.

BIBLIOGRAPHY

ONE: THE RISE

Davidson, Jordan, *The Federalist*, "Death Toll Rises To An Estimated 30 Victims Since 'Mostly Peaceful Protests' Began," August 19, 2020. https://thefederalist.com/2020/08/19/death-toll-rises-to-an-estimated-30-victims-since-mostly-peaceful-protests-began/

Bowden, Emily, *New York Post*, "More than 700 officers injured in George Floyd protests across US," June 8, 2020,

https://nypost.com/2020/06/08/more-than-700-officers-injured-in-george-floyd-protests-across-us/

Newhauser, David, "EXCLUSIVE: Dayton Shooter Was in a "Pornogrind" Band That Released Songs About Raping and Killing Women," Vice News, April 5, 2019. https://www.vice.com/en_us/article/j5yekp/exclusive-dayton-shooter-was-in-a-pornogrind-band-that-released-songs-about-raping-and-killing-women

Lawrence, Elizabeth, "Ex-girlfriend of Dayton shooter says she saw red flags and a dark side while they dated," *USA Today*, August 6, 2019. https://www.usatoday.com/story/news/nation/2019/08/06/dayton-shooting-ex-girlfriend-connor-betts-saw-red-flags/1930622001/

Ngo, Andy, "Dayton shooter Connor Betts may be antifa's first mass killer," *The New York Post*, August 6, 2019. https://nypost.com/2019/08/06/dayton-shooter-may-be-antifas-first-mass-killer/

https://pressfreedomtracker.us/all-incidents/?tags=45

Hunter, Shayne as told to Corinne Barraclough, "I established a terror movement in Australia, and I quit," News.com.au, October 25, 2017. https://www.news.com.au/lifestyle/real-life/true-stories/i-established-a-terror-movement-in-australia-and-i-quit/news-story/0e09cb729235d4316809b02bf9e54559

TWO: TRUE BELIEVERS

Burke, Dave, "92% of left-wing activists live with their parents and one in three is unemployed, study of Berlin protesters finds," *The Daily Mail* (quoting Bild), February 7, 2017. https://www.dailymail. co.uk/news/article-4200272/92-Berlin-left-wing-activists-live-parents.html

Hoffer, Eric, *The True Believer: Thoughts on the Nature of Mass Movements*, Harper & Brothers, New York, 1951, p. 109.

THREE: THE MANIFESTO

BieryGolick, Keith and Knight, Cameron, "Dayton shooting: What we know about the gunman's politics," USA Today, August 7, 2019. https://www.usatoday.com/story/news/2019/08/07/dayton-shooting-what-do-we-know-connor-betts-politics/1943289001/

Bovard, James, "Camera-Shy Antifa Hits Washington D.C.," *The American Conservative*, July 8, 2019. https://www.theamericanconservative.com/articles/camera-shy-antifa-hits-washington-d-c/

Associated Press, "The Latest: Friend Says Man Wanted To Provoke Deadly Fight," July 14, 2019, USNews.com. https://www.usnews.com/news/politics/articles/2019-07-13/the-latest-authorities-id-man-at-immigration-confrontation

Illing, Sean, "They have no allegiance to liberal democracy": an expert on antifa explains the group," August 13, 2018, Vox.com. https://www.vox.com/2017/8/25/16189064/antifa-charlottesville-dc-unite-the-right-mark-bray

https://theanarchistlibrary.org/library/anti-racist-action-the-green-mountain-anarchist-collective-black-bloc-tactics-communique

https://pressfreedomtracker.us/all-incidents/?tags=45

FOUR: WHITEWASHING ANTIFA

Wang, Amy B., "Trump breaks silence on Charlottesville: 'No place for this kind of violence in America'," *The Washington Post*, August 12, 2017. https://www.washingtonpost.com/news/the-fix/wp/2017/08/12/trump-responds-to-charlottesville-protests/

Merica, Dan, "Trump condemns 'hatred, bigotry and violence on many sides' in Charlottesville," CNN.com, August 13, 2017. https://www.cnn.com/2017/08/12/politics/trump-statement-alt-right-protests/index.html

Concha, Joe, "CNN's Cuomo Defends Antifa: Those who oppose hate 'are on the side of right,'" August 14, 2018. https://thehill.com/homenews/media/401699-cnns-cuomo-defends-antifa-those-who-oppose-hate-are-on-the-side-of-right

Schwartz, Ian, "Don Lemon Defends Antifa: 'No Organization Is Perfect,'" RealClearPolitics, August 28, 2018. https://www.realclear-politics.com/video/2018/08/28/don_lemon_defends_antifa_no_organization_is_perfect.html

Ernst, Douglas, "Antifa Activists are 'preserving the fabric of America' says Georgetown professor," August 17, 2017. https://www.washingtontimes.com/news/2017/aug/17/michael-eric-dyson-blasts-trump-says-antifa-preser/

Ngo, Andy, "Liberals Cheer As Antifa Violence Escalates," *The New York Post*, July 17, 2019. https://nypost.com/2019/07/17/liberals-cheer-as-antifa-violence-escalates/

Clancy, Liam, "CNN Host Defends Antifa As 'The Side of Angels,'" The Daily Caller, September 14, 2017. https://dailycaller.com/2017/09/14/msnbc-host-defends-antifa-as-the-side-of-angels/

Hunton & Williams, "Final Report: INDEPENDENT REVIEW OF THE 2017 PROTEST EVENTS IN CHARLOTTESVILLE, VIRGINIA," p. 24. https://www.charlottesville.org/home/showdocument?id=59691

FIVE: THE DELORABALL

Heine, Debra, "O'Keefe Catches Antifa 'Fight Instructors' Teaching How To Inflict Pain On Their Targets," PJMedia, August 1, 2018. https://pjmedia.com/video/okeefe-catches-antifa-fight-instructors-teaching-activists-how-to-inflict-pain-on-their-targets/

SIX: THE BLACK BLOC

"Blocs, Black and Otherwise," CrimethInc. https://crimethinc.com/2003/11/20/blocs-black-and-otherwise

Douglas-Bowers, Devon, "Unmasking The Black Bloc: Who They Are, What They Do, How They Work," Occupy, December 18, 2014. https://archive.is/UgmwK

Highleyman, Liz, "The Black Bloc: Behind the Mask," Salon, September 2001. http://www.black-rose.com/articles-liz/blackbloc.html

"Black Bloc Confidential," CrimethInc, February 21, 2012. https://crimethinc.com/2012/02/21/black-bloc-confidential
Dupuis-Deri, Francis, "The Black Blocs Ten Years after Seattle: Anarchism, Direct Action, and Deliberative Practices," , Journal for the Study of Radicalism, Vol. 4, No. 2 (FALL 2010), pp. 45-82.

SEVEN: LEON CZOLGOSZ: MODEL ANARCHIST

Zalman, Amy, "History of Terrorism: Anarchism and Anarchist Terrorism," ThoughtCo, May 21, 2018. https://www.thoughtco.com/anarchism-and-anarchist-terrorism-3209262

Sparrow, Jeff, "In the end, we forget the anarchists, bombers and 'lone wolves'. But the hysteria they provoke stays with us," The Guardian, January 1, 2015. https://www.theguardian.com/commentisfree/2015/jan/02/in-the-end-we-forget-the-anarchists-bombers-and-lone-wolves-but-the-hysteria-they-provoke-stays-with-us

EIGHT: WEIMAR ANTIFA

Lemmons, Russel, *Hitler's Rival: Ernst Thälmann in Myth and Memory*, University of Kentucky Press, Lexington, KY, 2013. Thälmann, Ernst, *Thälmann, Ernst: Selection of speeches and writings*, Vol. 3, Stuttgart 1977, pp. 361 – 387

NINE: THE STATE RELIGION

Frank, Helmut (16–20 April 2003), „Ich liebte ebte diesen naiven Christen", *Sonntagsblatt* (in German), Bayern, DE, archived from the original on 18 July 2011.

Davis, Belinda; Mausbach, Wilfried; Klimke, Martin (eds.), *Changing the World, Changing Oneself: Political Protest and Collective Identities in West Germany and the U.S. in the 1960s and 1970s.*

Malycha, Andreas (2000). Die SED: Geschichte ihrer Stalinisierung 1946–1953 [The SED: The History of its Stalinization]. Schöningh. Jesse, Eckhard (2015). *Extremismus und Demokratie, Parteien und Wahlen: Historisch-politische Streifzüge.* Böhlau Verlag. pp. 94–95.

Richter, Michael (2006). „Die doppelte Diktatur: Erfahrungen mit Diktatur in der DDR und Auswirkungen auf das Verhältnis zur Diktatur heute". In Besier, Gerhard; Stoklosa, Katarzyna (eds.). Lasten diktatorischer Vergangenheit – Herausforderungen demokratischer Gegenwart. LIT Verlag. pp. 195–208.

Herf, Jeffrey (2016). *Undeclared Wars with Israel: East Germany and the West German Far Left, 1967–1989.* Cambridge University Press. Kailitz, Steffen (2013). *Politischer Extremismus in der Bundesrepublik Deutschland: Eine Einführung* [Political Extremism in the Federal Republic of Germany: An Introduction] (in German). Springer. p. 126.

Ogman, Robert (2013). *Against The Nation.* New Compass Press. Mirja Keller, et al.: *Antifa*, Stuttgart 2013, S. 59 Ulrich Schneider: *Antifaschismus.* Köln 2014, S. 79f.

TEN: RED ULRIKE

Dutschke-Klotz, Gretchen (1996). *Rudi Dutschke*. Köln: Kiepen-heuer und Witsch. pp. 38, 53, 172, 227, 459.

ELEVEN: CHILDREN OF MAO

Kan, Karoline, "My Uncle Was a Red Guard in China's Cultural Revolution. He Isn't Sorry," Foreign Policy, May 16, 2016. https://foreignpolicy.com/2016/05/16/my-uncle-was-a-red-guard-in-chinas-cultural-revolution-he-isnt-sorry/

Mai, Jun, "Former Red Guards remember a time when killing was normal," South China Morning Post, June 8, 2016. https://www.scmp.com/news/china/policies-politics/article/1969051/former-red-guards-remember-time-when-killing-was-normal

Xiangzhen, Yu, "Confessions of a Red Guard, 50 years after China's Cultural Revolution," CNN, May 15, 2016. https://www.cnn.com/2016/05/15/asia/china-cultural-revolution-red-guard-confession/index.html

Agence France-Presse, "How political hatred during Cultural Revolution led to murder and cannibalism in a small town in China," South China Morning Post, May 11, 2016. https://www.scmp.com/news/china/policies-politics/article/1943581/how-political-hatred-during-cultural-revolution-led

Gross, Terry, "Newly Released Documents Detail Traumas Of China's Cultural Revolution," NPR, May 5, 2016. https://www.npr.org/2016/05/05/476873854/newly-released-documents-detail-traumas-of-chinas-cultural-revolution

Kristof, Nicholas, "A Tale of Red Guards and Cannibals," NY Times, January 6, 1993. https://www.nytimes.com/1993/01/06/world/a-tale-of-red-guards-and-cannibals.html

TWELVE: THE SIXTIES

Allyn, Bobby, "1969: A Year of Bombings," *The New York Times*, August 27, 2009. https://cityroom.blogs.nytimes.com/2009/08/27/1969-a-year-of-bombings/

Stern, Sol, "The Bomber As School Reformer," *City Journal*, October 6, 2008. https://www.city-journal.org/html/bomber-school-reformer-10465.html

Investors Business Daily, "Terrorist Ayers Confesses Sharing Obama's 'Dreams'", November 26, 2013. https://www.investors.com/politics/policy-analysis/bill-ayers-claims-authorship-of-obama-dreams-memoir/

THIRTEEN: GUIDING LIGHTS

Day, Annie, "Interview with Annie Day on The Bob Avakian Institute: Making the New Synthesis of Communism Known, Engaged, and Debated Everywhere," Revcom.us, October 31, 2016. https://revcom.us/a/463/interview-with-annie-day-the-bob-avakian-institute-en.html

Dix, Carl and Taylor, Sunsara, "An Invitation…To Meet The Revolution," Revcom.us, April 25, 2016. https://revcom.us/a/423/announcing-campus-tour-carl-dix-and-sunsara-taylor-en.html

Dix, Carl, *Revolution* newspaper, August 12, 2017. https://revcom.us/a/503/statement-from-carl-dix-from-charlottesville-en.htmldix

Avakian, Bob, "Why We Need An Actual Revolution and How We Can Make An Actual Revolution," The Bob Avakian Institute. http://thebobavakianinstitute.org/text-why-we-need-an-actual-revolution/

Mull, Teresa, "Militant public school teacher took students to Antifa protests, lied about absences, records show," TheBlaze, October 5, 2017. https://www.theblaze.com/news/2017/10/05/militant-public-school-teacher-took-students-to-antifa-protests-lied-about-absences-records-show

Avakian, Bob, *From Ike to Mao and Beyond: My Journey from Mainstream America to Revolutionary Communist*, Insight Press, USA, 2006, p. 393.

Weaver, Corinne, "Facebook Tolerates 119 Violent Antifa Pages, Despite New Rules," Newsbusters, July 3, 2019. https://www.newsbusters.org/blogs/techwatch/corinne-weaver/2019/07/03/facebook-tolerates-119-violent-antifa-pages-despite-new
Hasson, Peter, "Documents Tie Berkeley Riot Organizers To Pro-Pedophilia Group, NAMBLA," The Daily Caller, April 28, 2017.

FOURTEEN: THE ROJAVA REVOLUTION

Harp, Seth, "The Anarchists vs. The Islamic State," *Rolling Stone*, February 14, 2017. American Anarchists Join YPG in Syria Fighting ISIS, Islamic State - Rolling Stone
www.internationalistocmmune.com

FIFTEEN: CAMPUS GROUND ZERO

Lindsay, Tom, "35 Universities Adopt 'The Chicago Statement' On Free Speech -- 1606 To Go," Forbes.com, February 28, 2018 https://www.forbes.com/sites/tomlindsay/2018/02/28/35-universities-adopt-the-chicago-statement-on-free-speech-1590-to-go/#5661c527771b

Schlichter, Kurt, "A Safe Space Society Is A Totalitarian Nightmare," Townhall, December 9, 2019. https://townhall.com/columnists/kurtschlichter/2019/12/09/a-safe-space-society-is-a-totalitarian-nightmare-n2557640

Mac Donald, Heather, "The Cost of America's Cultural Revolution," *City Journal*, December 9, 2019. https://www.city-journal.org/social-justice-ideology

Lederman, Doug and Jaschik, Scott, "Amid Violence, Yiannopolous Speech At Berkeley Cancelled," *InsideHigherEd*, February 2, 2017.

https://www.insidehighered.com/news/2017/02/02/violent-protests-visiting-mob-lead-berkeley-cancel-speech-milo-yiannopoulos

Beinart, Peter, "A violent attack on free speech at Middlebury," *The Atlantic*, March 6, 2017. https://www.theatlantic.com/politics/archive/2017/03/middlebury-free-speech-violence/518667/

Kabbany, Jennifer, "'War on Cops' author Heather Mac Donald shouted down at UCLA by hysterical Black Lives Matter protest," The College Fix, April 6, 2017. https://www.thecollegefix.com/war-cops-author-heather-mac-donald-shouted-ucla-hysterical-black-lives-matter-protest/

Mac Donald, Heather, "Get Up, Stand Up," April 9, 2017, *City Journal*. https://www.city-journal.org/html/get-up-stand-up-15109.html

Weiss, Bari, "When The Left Turns On Its Own," *The New York Times*, June 1, 2017. https://www.nytimes.com/2017/06/01/opinion/when-the-left-turns-on-its-own.html

Richards, Connor, "Richards: What I Saw At The Ben Shapiro Speech," October 2, 2017. https://dailyutahchronicle.com/2017/10/02/what-i-saw-at-the-ben-shapiro-protest/

Zanotti, Emily, "YIKES: Ontario woman arrested with deadly weapon while protesting Jordan Peterson," DailyWire.com, March 8, 2018. https://www.dailywire.com/news/yikes-ontario-woman-arrested-deadly-weapon-while-emily-zanotti

National Post, "Activist accused of pouring bottle of urine on Rebel reporter during 'anti-fascist' rally in Vancouver," PostMedia News, March 7, 2016. https://nationalpost.com/news/canada/activist-pours-bottle-of-urine-on-rebel-reporter-during-anti-fascist-in-vancouver See also Houser, Adam, "Antifa 'marks' and attacks CFACT students but fails to stop Lauren Southern talk at University of Minnesota," CFACT, October 26, 2017. https://www.cfactcampus.org/antifa-marks-and-attacks-cfact-students-but-fails-to-stop-lauren-southern-talk-at-u-of-minnesota/

Airaksanen, Toni and Gockowski, Anthony, "VIDEO: Antifa, students shut down College Republicans Event," Campus Reform, October 10, 2017. https://www.campusreform.org/?ID=9944

O'Reilly, Andrew, "Antifa protests mean high security costs for Berkeley Free Speech Week, but who's paying the bill?," Fox News, September 15, 2017. https://www.foxnews.com/us/antifa-protests-mean-high-security-costs-for-berkeley-free-speech-week-but-whos-paying-the-bill

Brown, Spencer, "'We Don't Give A Fuck What You're Fine With': Antifa Attempts To Shut Down YAF Chapter Meeting," April 20, 2018. https://www.yaf.org/news/we-dont-give-a-fck-what-youre-fine-with-antifa-attempt-to-shut-down-yaf-chapter-meeting/

North, Anna, "A professor teaches about feminism and consent. Now he's been accused of abuse." April 17, 2018, Vox.com. vox.com/2018/4/17/17215554/metoo-movement-robert-reece-ut-austin-sexual-misconduct

Paulin, David, "A suicide at the University of Texas Reveals Dark Side of #MeToo Movement," *American Thinker*, November 18, 2018. https://www.americanthinker.com/articles/2018/11/a suicide at the university of texas reveals dark side of metoo movement.html

Burner, David, *Making Peace With The 60s*, Princeton University Press, Princeton, NJ, 1996, p. 145.

Rice-Cameron, John and Mitchell, Anna, "Antifa Thugs Find a Champion and Leader in Stanford Professor," January 18, 2017, *The Stanford Review*. https://stanfordreview.org/antifa-thugs-find-a-champion-and-leader-in-stanford-professor-3/

Gluckman, Neil, "Faculty Members Organize to Fight 'Fascist' Interlopers on Campuses," The Chronicle of Higher Education, August 31, 2017. https://www.chronicle.com/article/Faculty-Members-Organize-to/241081

LET Staff, "Professor, Antifa activist who said 'it's a privilege to teach future dead cops' gets fired," October 13, 2019, Law Enforcement Today. https://www.lawenforcementtoday.com/professor-antifa-activist-who-said-its-a-privilege-to-teach-future-dead-cops-gets-fired/

Feuer, Alan, "Antifa on Trial: How a College Professor Joined the Left's Radical Ranks," May 15, 2018, *Rolling Stone*. https://www.rollingstone.com/culture/culture-features/antifa-on-trial-how-a-college-professor-joined-the-lefts-radical-ranks-630213/

Rosas, Julio, "'Kill them all': Iowa professor resigns after his comments about evangelicals revealed," August 27, 2019, The Washington Examiner. https://www.washingtonexaminer.com/news/kill-them-all-iowa-professor-resigns-after-his-comments-about-evangelicals-revealed

Perisic, Kyle, "3 Student Journalists Sue University for Covering Up Teacher's Role in Anti-Trump Campus Rally," The Daily Signal, April 3, 2018. https://www.dailysignal.com/2018/04/13/3-student-journalists-sue-university-for-covering-up-teachers-role-in-anti-trump-rally/

Butterworth, Courtney, "The Drexel professor who tweeted, 'All I want for Christmas is white genocide' resigned," *The Daily Pennsylvanian*, January 10, 2018. https://www.thedp.com/article/2018/01/drexel-professor-controversial-christmas-tweet-resignation-philadelphia-upenn

SIXTEEN: CORPORATISTS AND OTHER USEFUL IDIOTS

Staff Report, "Insider Blows Whistle & Exec Reveals Google Plan to Prevent "Trump situation" in 2020 on Hidden Cam," Project Veritas, June 24, 2019. https://www.projectveritas.com/2019/06/24/insider-blows-whistle-exec-reveals-google-plan-to-prevent-trump-situation-in-2020-on-hidden-cam/

Weaver, Corinne, "Twitter Bans Doxxing, But Why Are Antifa Accounts Still Active?" Newsbusters, October 4, 2018. https://www.newsbusters.org/blogs/techwatch/corinne-weaver/2018/10/04/twitter-bans-doxxing-why-are-antifa-accounts-still-active

Cheong, Ian Miles, "Twitter Bans Analyst Who Revealed AntiFa Connections With Journalists," Human Events, May 29, 2019. https://humanevents.com/2019/05/29/twitter-bans-analyst-who-revealed-journalists-antifa-connections/

Seattle Times Sports Staff, "MLS lifts ban on Iron Front flag after working with Sounders supporters groups and others," Seattle Times, September 24, 2019. https://www.seattletimes.com/sports/sounders/mls-lifts-ban-on-iron-front-flag-after-working-with-sounders-supporters-groups-and-others/

Editorial, "Violent protests send the wrong message," Standard Democrat, February 8, 2017. https://standard-democrat.com/story/2505436.html

Schachtel, Jordan, "Antifa book endorsed by Keith Ellison promotes VIOLENCE against political opponents," January 4, 2018. https://www.conservativereview.com/news/antifa-book-endorsed-keith-ellison-promotes-violence-political-opponents/

Haverluck, Michael F., "MEDIA: AOC & her Squad refuse to condemn Antifa terror attack on ICE," One News Now, July 17, 2019. https://onenewsnow.com/media/2019/07/17/aoc-her-squad-refuse-to-condemn-antifa-terror-attack-on-ice

SEVENTEEN: THE BOOGALOO BOYS

ADL Blog, "The Boogaloo: Extremists' New Slang Term for A Coming Civil War," Anti-Defamation League, November 26, 2019. https://www.adl.org/blog/the-boogaloo-extremists-new-slang-term-for-a-coming-civil-war

Devine, Curt, Griffin Drew, Kuznia, Robert, "Gun-toting members of the Boogaloo movement are showing up at protests," CNN, June 4, 2020. https://www.cnn.com/2020/06/03/us/boogaloo-extremist-protests-invs/index.html

Staff Report, "The 'Boogaloo' Started as a Racist Meme," Southern Poverty Law Center, June 5, 2020. https://www.splcenter.org/hatewatch/2020/06/05/boogaloo-started-racist-mem

Phillips, Kristine, "Attorney General Barr creates task force to investigate anti-government extremists," USA Today, June 27, 2020. https://www.usatoday.com/story/news/politics/2020/06/26/william-barr-says-boogaloo-group-antifa-tied-violence-protests/3268527001

Cooke, Kristina, Harte, Julia, Hesson, Ted, Parker, Ned, "U.S. Capitol siege emboldens motley crew of extremists," Reuters, January 8, 2021. https://www.reuters.com/article/usa-election-extremists/u-s-capitol-siege-emboldens-motley-crew-of-extremists-idUSL1N2JJ0A0

Greenspan, Rachel, Goggin, Benjamin, "Who are the Boogaloo Bois? A man who shot up a Minneapolis police precinct was associated with the extremist movement, according to unsealed documents," Insider, October 26, 2020. https://www.insider.com/boogaloo-bois-protest-far-right-minneapolis-extremist-guns-hawaiian-shirts-2020-5

Gartrell, Nate, Kelliher, Fiona, "Authorities charge alleged Santa Cruz deputy killer with assassinating federal cop in Oakland, link attacks to Boogaloo movement," The Mercury News, June 16, 2020. https://www.mercurynews.com/2020/06/16/santa-cruz-deputys-alleged-killer-charged-with-assassinating-federal-cop-in-oakland-ambush/

Burke, Melissa, Snell, Robert, "Plans to kidnap Whitmer, overthrow government spoiled, officials say," The Detroit News, October 8, 2020. https://www.detroitnews.com/story/news/local/michigan/2020/10/08/feds-thwart-militia-plot-kidnap-michigan-gov-gretchen-whitmer/5922301002/